A LAP AROUND AMERICA

SHAWN INMON

Carlsbad, CA 92011
U.S.A.

A Lap Around America
By Shawn Inmon

A laundry room, somewhere in Louisiana

I opened the door and got a blast of heat in the face. It was sweltering outside, but add in the washers and dryers running in an enclosed room, and you end up with a near-sauna. I got to work separating clothes, getting the machines started, and mostly doing a lot of sweating. I decided to risk someone stealing our clothes and head back to our air-conditioned room. I reached for the door, and it didn't open. I twisted, I turned, I pushed, I pulled. It wouldn't budge. I felt the walls closing in. The room felt even hotter, and more oppressive.

Saying a silent prayer of thanks that I had brought my cellphone with me, I called Dawn and asked if she would run down with her room key and open the door from the outside. A minute later, she was there and inserted her card. It didn't budge.

I envisioned a small article in the Lafayette Advertiser tomorrow: *Travel writer saunas himself to death.*

Dawn made an "I'll be right back" motion and disappeared. I hoped that she had gone to get help, but as the will to live slowly faded from me, I realized she had probably gone back to Galveston to see if Bruce, the eight foot tall shark with the great abs, was single.

Bruce

After about six hours, or five minutes, depending on how you measure time, she brought the desk person with her. A lovely woman with a sadistic sense of humor, she couldn't contain her laughter upon seeing me, now weighing sixteen pounds less than I had at check-in.

She managed to stop laughing long enough to put a firm shoulder into the door, popping it open. It wasn't locked, it was just stuck. Dawn and the desk clerk were having a wonderful time, laughing so hard tears were running down their legs. I was just trying to determine if I'd actually suffered heatstroke or not.

I took a moment to wonder, *How did I get here?*

Have you ever wanted to quit your job and drive off into the sunset with the person you love the most?

Yeah. Me, too. We all have those little bursts of "I should just up and quit!"

In August 2016, I did it. So did my wife, Dawn. (Spoiler alert: she's the person I love the most, which is a good thing, right?)

We both quit jobs we liked. For me, it was a job that had paid very well for more than twenty years. We packed up our house, got into our car and drove around America. Beyond deciding to drive the country in a counter-clockwise direction, we didn't plan anything out. We just drove.

It was scary, of course. Who quits a good job these days?

Our Lap Around America began in August, but the adventure really started months earlier.

It was the last day of March, and I was six miles above the earth, somewhere over Oregon, on a half-empty flight with a row all to myself. My Kindle, loaded with a movie and more than a thousand books to read, remained tucked into my laptop bag. I spent the flight staring out at the clouds.

I had just spent three days at a writers' conference in Austin, Texas, called the Smarter Artist Summit. Yeah, with that title, I was a little surprised they let me in as well. Those three days were spent hanging out with kindred spirits—people who got my most obscure pop culture references.

I didn't completely escape the responsibilities of my real job during the conference. I was the Designated Broker for a real estate firm in the small town of Enumclaw, Washington. A few of my agents had called, looking for help on difficult files and transactions, but I didn't mind. I had also heard from the firm's owner a few times, wondering why we didn't have more agents, why our revenue was behind the previous year. Wondering, wondering.

I loved my job. I'd been selling real estate since 1993,

managing this office since 2002. I really did love my agents. I even loved the challenges of the job, and representing clients.

At the Smarter Artist Summit, I had talked with a lot of successful authors. In some ways, I was one of them. I had four well-received books out, with a fifth due to be published in the next few months. In the arena of indie publishing, though, putting four books out in four years puts you in the "tortoise" category. Almost all the authors I had met who were writing full time published more than that every year. I knew the only way I could increase my output that much was to say goodbye to real estate. That was crazy, though, right?

Real estate had provided a very good living for more than two decades. I had survived the Great Recession and come out healthy on the other side. It would be crazy to give that up now.

Right?

But then, there's that pull: That need to create. To make something where nothing existed before. My hands are inept. I can't sculpt, paint, build, or craft. I can't even pound a nail straight most of the time. But give me a keyboard and I can create a world. Better still, I love doing so.

These thoughts were still dancing around my head an hour later when we touched down at SeaTac. Dawn would be waiting for me there, with our two chocolate Labs, Hershey and Sadie. We were going straight from the airport to Long Beach, Washington, to spend a couple of nights.

As soon as I took my phone out of airplane mode, more than a dozen messages popped up. That wasn't good. It was highly unlikely that a dozen people had called me to just to say, "Welcome home."

I began sorting through my voicemails; just another office crisis. A check hadn't been deposited correctly. A commission check had bounced. Three calls were from my boss, increasingly urgent.

I called Barb, my office manager, and by the time I got to

the luggage area to claim my bag, we had the check problem solved.

The last message from my boss asked me to call him as soon as I touched down, so I did. I went into his voicemail, explained the problem and told him everything was handled. As my suitcase appeared, a text popped up. Not from my boss, but from his friend.

D wanted me to tell you that he's getting into vacation mode. That's why he didn't pick up.

I stared at the message in disbelief. He had called, texted, and messaged me the whole time I was on vacation. He had left me three messages, asking to be called back. When I did, he not only didn't pick up but asked someone else to call me to tell me he didn't want to be bothered.

I grabbed my suitcase off the conveyor and turned to find Dawn. Life always gets better when she is near, but I was still steaming.

"I think I want to quit my job."

"Oh, yeah?"

The perfect response. Very Dawn. Not saying, "Yeah, let's quit the job that supports us!" but not killing the idea, either.

"Let's go. Got the dogs?"

"Of course."

Ten minutes later, we were in our Subaru Outback, Hershey and Sadie wagging their approval of the situation, and everything seemed better.

Still.

D wanted me to tell you that he's getting into vacation mode. That's why he didn't pick up.

That night, sitting on the couch in our little condo at The Breakers in Long Beach, I said, "Do you think we could live in a place this small?"

Since our home in Orting was about 2,400 square feet, and the condo we were sitting in was just 500 square feet, it was a valid question. Dawn looked around at the small kitchen and living room, tiny bathroom and bedroom, and said, "I'm not sure. Maybe. Why, are we thinking about that?"

I was. I was thinking about chucking it all and moving into a tiny place at the beach.

By nature, I am a slow-to-react kind of guy. I'm pretty good to have around in an emergency if you need a cool head to analyze the situation. Less so if you need someone to act first and ask questions later.

We pondered our options for months after that return flight from Austin. I knew I could continue doing what I was doing. That was certainly the safest option. Or I could step down as Designated Broker but continue to sell real estate. That's where most of my income came from, anyway. Or, I could make the big jump—quit altogether, move somewhere cheaper than the Seattle area, and survive on what I could make as a writer.

We were only renting a house at the time, so we didn't have to worry about selling, but our lease gave us a drop-dead decision date. It expired in July, and we were renting from a large corporation that didn't let you slide on renewing. By June, we would need to either extend for another year or move out.

By May, we had decided. We would follow my favorite aphorism: *Jump, and a net will appear.*

We knew where we wanted to go—Long Beach, where we'd first hatched the idea. As a tourist area, it was an expensive place to stay short term, but long-term rents were about half what we were paying farther north. I've been going to Long Beach on vacation almost since I was born. After several hundred visits to the Long Beach Peninsula, though, I knew what year-round living there would entail.

Quiet in the off-season. Good. Storms, mostly wind and rain, with some freezing temperatures from October to May. That's good or bad, depending on how you look at it. For a writer wanting to spend endless hours hunched over a keyboard, looking out at howling winds and sideways rain is fine. For my housebound bride, we weren't so sure.

So, we made the decision to rent for a year before we bought a home, to make sure we would both love it there after surviving a full year of unpredictable weather. The primary problem was, there were next to no rentals available.

I crawled every website, constantly harassing—umm, I mean, staying in touch with—a real estate agent in each office on the peninsula. Nothing. As May turned to June and we had to give notice on our lease, I grew increasingly concerned. Dawn, who is a little less devil-may-care than I, was several notches past that. She was slipping into panic mode.

What do we do if we quit our jobs, give our notice, and have no place to go?

That's when the idea hit me: Why not take the time we would be homeless to drive all the way around America?

Of course, it didn't work out quite that way. Like the couple who adopt a baby and then immediately become pregnant, a week before we were to leave, we got a lead on a house. We had planned to put everything we owned into storage, so we didn't have to pay rent on the road, but I knew Dawn. She is a nester. She would feel much more comfortable while we were gone if she knew where we would be laying our heads when we returned.

So, we looked at the little house in Seaview, right next to Long Beach. Of course, it was perfect. I don't mean perfect in an "OMG, this house is *gorgeous*" sort of way. No, it was perfect *for us*. The outside was covered in weathered shingles that screamed, "We're living at the beach!" Inside, it was a funky little beach house. Nice kitchen and living room, with one tiny bedroom on the main floor and two more up a twisty little staircase. (We didn't dare to stop and think how we'd get any mattress bigger than a twin up the stairs.) There was even a nice little alcove with a window that would be a perfect writing den for me.

Thus, just a week before we were supposed to leave on our

trip, our agenda changed to a complete house move. Luckily, we were almost all packed, but everything else—renting a truck, loading it, driving and unloading it, then cleaning our big house to turn it back over—was draining. I desperately looked forward to our trip just so I could quit lifting boxes. I immediately missed my job in the real estate office, where no one ever asked me to move a box.

Once we got everything offloaded into our new house, we turned right around to make the three-hour drive back to our old house. On the way, we stopped for gas. I slid my debit card and put my wallet on the roof of the car. Please don't ask why I did that. There is no good answer. You can probably can guess the rest of that little story.

I didn't realize I had lost my wallet until the next day, a Saturday. So, we were leaving on Monday to set off on an eight-week trek, and I didn't have my driver's license, debit card, or any credit cards. I stayed behind and continued to clean, while Dawn made the seven-hour round trip to that gas station, hoping to find my lost wallet lying on the side of the road.

No luck. No wallet.

I am an idiot.

We decided to stay one extra day to give me time to at least get a replacement driver's license and ATM card. It didn't seem like a great idea to risk getting pulled over in some little town in Alabama or Michigan with no driver's license.

"Really, officer, it's a funny story…"

So, Monday was spent scurrying around from the bank to the Department of Licensing, sometimes referred to as hell. After a long wait, I got a little paper license just before the DOL closed at 5 p.m.

We went to the first of many, many crappy little motels we would stay in over the next two months, and collapsed.

Day One

Because I am not content to do anything the easy way, I came up with a series of rules for our trip:

✓ 1. Stay off freeways whenever possible. This is a trip through small-town America.

2. Stay in mom-and-pop motels wherever possible. We want to avoid corporate America.

3. No eating in chain restaurants. We want to sample the real cuisine wherever we go.

There were a few cities we wanted to hit, so we knew we couldn't avoid freeways altogether, but we intended to spend most of our time on small back roads, driving at 45 mph wherever possible.

Dawn Adele was up early, showered, packed, and ready to roll by 8:30. Since Dawn strongly falls into the "night person" camp, I knew that meant she really was excited. Part of it was the allure of adventures to come, of course, but I suspect much of it was the joy of having the drudgery—packing, moving, cleaning—behind us, and only the open road in front of us.

We drove to our hometown Safeway to pick up some last-minute reinforcements for our cooler. Sitting in the parking lot, with everything we were going to need for a two-month journey tucked into our trunk or nestled on our backseat, we paused and looked at each other.

We had talked about it, planned it, argued about it, and waited for it to arrive for so long, it was surreal that the moment, the trip, was finally upon us. We took our first picture of the trip—a shot of our odometer, reading 12,313 miles—and turned right, onto Highway 410, heading east toward Greenwater, Crystal Mountain, Eastern Washington, and beyond.

I'm happy you are coming along on the trip with us. If you're wondering who we are, and why you want to travel all the way around the United States with us, here's the condensed version of our story.

I grew up in a small town called Mossyrock, Washington. Dawn's parents moved her there from Southern California in 1975, much to her chagrin. Dawn is almost four years younger than me, so when she first arrived, that age difference meant that she and I were friends, nothing more.

My senior year (Dawn's freshman year), we became more than friends. We fell in love. Things happened, yada, yada, yada, and Dawn's parents decreed that we wouldn't see each other for three years. Those years stretched from three into thirty. Then lightning struck, we found each other again, and we got married October 16, 2010.

(Shameless plug: if you'd like to know all the good stuff that I skipped over in the yada, yada, yada, you can buy my books *Feels Like the First Time* and *Both Sides Now*. End shameless plug.)

Six years later, Dawn and I were still finding happiness with each other and living our happily-ever-after. It's a bit of an odd experience, having chronicled your most intimate thoughts and experiences and shared them with the world. For example, Dawn was once in having a mammogram. She had assumed the position when the X-ray tech looked at her chart, recognized her name, and told her she had read all about what she and I had gone through. From her vulnerable position, I think Dawn just wanted to focus on the mammogram.

All of us have a specific worldview that informs how we see things and everything we think and believe. Ours is that we are Westerners. We've both lived in Washington state most of our lives. We think it is pretty close to perfect, but we're willing to keep an open mind.

Dawn and I were the sentient members of our traveling party, but we were relying on one mechanical member—our 2016 Hyundai Sonata. It had been Dawn's Christmas present eight months earlier, and we were about to give her a real shakedown cruise. For purposes of the trip, we named her the Silver Bullet. Mostly because of her color and the fact that we love Bob Seger, not because we were sponsored by Coors Brewing, although I think they totally missed a bet there.

Washington State is divided by the Cascade Mountains. The parts east and west of that range couldn't be more different. The western half of the state, where I was born, is green, with plentiful lakes and rivers, and trees as far as the eye can see. Western Washington is also where the businesses and most of the people are—Boeing, Microsoft, Starbucks all have headquarters there. Politically, this side of the state leans far left.

In Eastern Washington, the prevailing color palette is brown, with a little beige and tan thrown in for good measure. Summers and winters can both be harsh. The primary businesses are farming—growing hops and wheat, and raising cattle. The political bent is decidedly conservative. However, since the bulk of the state's population is in the west, the state always skews blue on national issues. It's got to be frustrating to be a conservative in Eastern Washington, as the immense population of the west always drags politics in a different direction.

As we drove along Highway 410, slowly gaining elevation, I thought of the road ahead.

"Better drink these trees in. I don't know many other parts of the country that are going to have greenery like this. Upstate New York and the rest of the northeast, maybe." At that moment, upstate New York seemed very far away. A dream for another day.

"I miss them already, and they're not even gone yet," Dawn said.

Dawn loves three things above all others: animals, greenery, and ocean water. It was our goal to get her plenty of all three on this trip.

We entered the Mount Baker–Snoqualmie National Forest. Hills rose above us on both sides of the highway, densely packed with fir trees, undergrowth, pines, and the occasional glimpse of the gurgling White River.

Dawn looked at me. "How far from Enumclaw are we?"

"Mmm … maybe an hour?"

"How often do we come up here?"

"Almost never."

"What is wrong with us?"

"That's probably a question for clinical psychologists to answer, really."

She gave me her patented Dawn look, the first of many thousands I would no doubt receive on this trip.

"Seriously. I can't believe we have lived this close to this much beauty and never come here."

I think we are probably too typical when it comes to this. Life gets busy. You work all week, then when the weekend finally arrives, you're worn out, and a quiet day at home seems pretty good. Or, the chores that you put off all week are piled up waiting for you. Or, there's that new Jerry Lewis movie waiting for you down at the multiplex. (Really? Jerry isn't making movies anymore? I knew there was a void in my life.)

Whatever it is, you get to Sunday evening in an eye blink, and you've got to start thinking about what you're going to wear to work tomorrow. All of that doesn't leave a lot of time for gorgeous drives through national forests, even if there's one only an hour away.

That's a big part of what made us do the irresponsible thing and say, "Chuck it all," to our reliable jobs. My vision is already failing, and I have a difficult time driving at night. I had this terrible feeling that, if we worked another ten years to get everything "just right," we might never make this trip at all.

In fact, after I'd announced the trip on my author's page on Facebook, I was overwhelmed with messages from people saying, "My husband and I always dreamed of a trip like this, but …" There were a lot of causes that came after that "but," and we knew the best way to avoid them was to just go.

We stopped at a small picnic area alongside Highway 410 surrounded by tree-covered hills, a gorgeous meadow, and a pristine little lake. We had decided to eat at least one "picnic" per day, for two reasons. One, two meals per day at a restaurant would balloon our calorie count, and two, we wanted to try to keep costs down.

I thought it was boring just packing our food into a normal bag, so I immediately dubbed it The Magical Mystery Bag. Eating out of The Magical Mystery Bag seemed infinitely more exciting than just grabbing some trail mix and a PB&J sandwich.

We dined on french bread, cheddar cheese, and, yes, some trail mix. That seemed like part of our adventure, at least on Day One. Who knew what it would feel like on Day Forty-something?

Our first picnic spot

After lunch we hiked out to the little lake, reasoning that this adventure was absolutely about the journey, not caring a whit about the destination. We watched little polliwogs swim, soaked up the sun, and eventually made our way back to the Silver Bullet.

We drove eastward alongside the river, as it gurgled, sang, and beckoned to us. We gave in at last, pulled over, and walked down to listen to its song. We each found a flat rock, took off our sandals, and put our feet in the icy cold water. I was sure every day wouldn't be as relaxed as this first, but it was a good way to start.

For the most part, the goal was to keep schedules and appointments to a minimum. But I wanted to make sure that we would have a nice place to stay the first night, so I had made a reservation at the Weinhard Hotel in Dayton, Washington. The Weinhard looked old and funky.

Since those same adjectives can be applied to me, it looked perfect.

We had many miles to go before we slept at the Weinhard, though. When we dropped down into the beige eternity that is the state's eastern side, we skirted around Yakima, the Paris of Eastern Washington. (Not really. Spokane is probably the Paris of Eastern Washington. Do you ever wonder if Paris gets ticked off about being compared to all these backwater towns?)

Brown fields blended into brown hills that faded into a sky that, I noted gratefully, was still blue. Do you remember that movie *Pleasantville*, where much of the story takes place in a black-and-white world? Eastern Washington isn't quite that bad, but it does pull most of its color from the sepia part of the color wheel.

After we had driven through so many miles of brown haze and I had lost sense of any other color, a river appeared on our left.

"There's the mighty Columbia," I said to Dawn.

From our vantage point at that moment, looking down from on high, it didn't look so mighty.

"That stream?"

"Just remember you called it that." I knew we would see the

12

true power of that little stream before too long.

As I would do for the rest of the trip, I searched every available resource to see what lay ahead that we might want to see. Under my feet, I had tomes on all the national parks, a Reader's Digest book called *Off The Beaten Track*, and most important, Mama Google on my trusty Android Galaxy phone.

I came across something called the Gingko Petrified Forest.

"Okay," I said to Dawn, "There's a petrified forest up ahead, but it will take us about fifty miles out of our way. Whaddya think?"

"What's a petrified forest, really?"

I wanted to say it was like something you'd see in a Disney movie, with hundreds of once-lush trees and bushes all turned to stone. Instead, I said: "No idea, really."

"Good! Let's go, then."

I need to point out that this was still Day One of our trip. If it had been Day Fifty, I think we might have stuck to our route. Instead, we took a detour along the Columbia and finally found the Gingko Petrified Forest State Park. We had to take I-90 for about two miles to reach the park—enough to remind us why we were sticking to back roads. Semis and cars whizzed past, their drivers intent on doing at least 90 mph, and we had a hard time adjusting from an average speed of 45 to double that.

Soon enough, we were off onto another dirty little gravel road. As we pulled up to the building marking the park entrance, we saw some logs lying on their sides, as though someone had begun building a campfire, then thought better of it.

"That's not the petrified forest, is it?" Dawn asked.

It was.

On the trip ahead, we would see a thousand wonder-inducing sights and be constantly dazzled by the state and national parks we would see. This, however, was not a great beginning. For one, we hadn't gotten out of the car since we'd dropped down into Eastern Washington, so we hadn't really noticed the temperature rise. It had gone from the very comfortable upper 70s, where we had started, to the low 90s.

Maybe we just weren't in the right frame of mind, but I felt a little sorry—*petrified*, even—that I had suggested driving an hour out of our way to see chunks of wood that had been turned to stone.

We didn't even bother to go inside the information center. Instead, we backtracked over I-90 and the Vantage Bridge, then immediately got off and dropped down to our comfortable cruising speed of 45 mph.

It was well into afternoon by now and we knew we wanted to make it to Dayton before dark, but it was still summer and dusk was nowhere in sight. So we turned off the main highway toward Palouse Falls State Park. By the time we got there, the sun was getting lower and shadows were lengthening. The road was one of the twistiest we would drive on the whole trip. But we were glad we were going slowly when we came around a turn to find a flock of half a dozen wild turkeys congregating on the road. Big and black, with reddish wattles, they didn't look much like the fat birds advertised at Thanksgiving. They looked like a gang, prepared to rumble with us if we had a mind to. Though unimpressed by us or the Silver Bullet, they were kind enough to let us pass as we nudged forward.

As we approached the park, it was hard to picture where, in this flat terrain, the advertised 200-foot waterfall might be found. How can there be a twenty-story-tall waterfall where there is no mountain? Apparently, by dropping into a hole that rushing water has been carving for millions of years.

Palouse Falls at sunset

Because it was the end of summer, the waterfall wasn't as impressively wide as it is during the rainy season, but the drop was spectacular—a long, thin ribbon of froth constantly plunging to the rocks below.

We walked back through an impromptu campground, where groups of people had set up tents and were gathered around fires and picnic tables, talking and laughing. I saw an acoustic guitar leaning against a table and imagined an eventual rendition of "Kumbaya." This inviting scene made me want to join in, but our reservation at the Weinhard awaited.

We made one last side trip before we called it a day, in Starbuck, Washington. Never heard of Starbuck, or think I was just misspelling the coffee chain? Don't worry. Anyone who has never lived within 100 miles of Starbuck is unlikely to have heard of it. With a population of 129, as of the 2010 Census, there's not much to recommend it to outsiders. In fact, in the town's Wikipedia entry, the photograph of the town is a grain elevator. Not a huge, historic grain elevator; just a normal, smallish grain elevator. That should tell you most everything you need to know about Starbuck.

So, why did we want to drive through Starbuck? I was hoping to exorcise a personal demon. I had lived in Starbuck over the summer of 1968. My mom had just remarried, after my dad had died in 1965, and my new stepdad was a construction worker. I have no idea what he could have been helping to build in the area in 1968, but we lived first in Starbuck, then Dayton.

This second marriage for Mom was not great, and all the not-greatness, at least in my memory, traced back to Starbuck. We had rented a tiny little single-wide trailer, almost a travel trailer. The trailer was cramped, the summer air was hot, and tempers were hotter still. One night, I had been lying across the bed, reading a comic book, when I heard a crash. Like any curious eight-year-old, I ran to see what caused it.

What had caused it was my step-dad hitting my mom hard enough to knock her into the little refrigerator, which had flown open and disgorged its contents of ketchup bottles, milk, and pickles, with a crash. I didn't have a chance to say a word, before my step-dad picked me up and threw me back into what passed for a bedroom.

My mom shouted, "Shawn, he's killing me! Run and get help."

I bolted for the back door, feeling like I had evaded further violence by the merest of whiskers, though I don't know if he even noticed I had left. I jumped off the back porch and looked desperately left and right. There were no houses near us, but there was a large field of tall grass behind the house. I ran and hid in the grass, feeling as helpless as I ever would in life, and berating myself for being a coward.

Eventually, I worked up enough courage to stand up and saw the two of them sitting on the back steps. I approached cautiously. I saw Mom had a cut on her forehead, and my step-dad had the beginnings of a bruise on his cheek. They were both holding

Rainier Beer cans against their abrasions.

"Sorry," my step-dad said. "Things just got a little out of control. This will never happen again."

Mom sat beside him, nodding.

It did, of course. It happened regularly, although rarely involving me. Usually, they just beat up on each other. And though it happened in every house we lived in, I always associated the ongoing violence of my childhood with the town of Starbuck. We moved to Dayton shortly after that, and I hadn't returned to either in the forty-eight intervening years. But it had loomed large in my nightmares.

Now, probably twenty years older than my step-dad had been at the time, I returned to the scene of the crime. Dawn turned down the side streets and we drove around in long, slow loops. We had lived in what was, even then, an old trailer. I knew it was almost certainly gone. I hoped to recognize something, though— some landmark, that big empty field perhaps—so I would know where "home" had once been. I wanted to let it go.

That kind of easy closure was not to be, though. I recognized nothing. We saw closed-down businesses, old houses, people quietly going about their lives, but nothing that looked even the slightest bit familiar. We made one last loop through town, driving at 20 mph. I had always demonized this place, associated it with hell. It wasn't, of course. It was just a tiny dot in a map where my parents launched the first skirmish in a war that went on for decades.

I turned to Dawn and shrugged. "It's not so much. I can let it go, now."

And I did.

In my memory, there was some distance between Starbuck and Dayton, but the grown-up reality was different. Before we knew it, we were on the outskirts of Dayton.

The first thing I saw was a shiny new Best Western hotel. That didn't bode well for being able to remember much in

Dayton, either, as there had been nothing like that years ago. As soon as we hit downtown, though, everything fell into place. The Liberty Theater was exactly where I remembered it, looking completely unchanged. As I peered up Main Street, it was the same, too. Most of the businesses I remembered, like the Bulldog Den, where the young hoodlums hung out, or the five-and-dime store, were gone. But the vibe was exactly the same.

Unlike Starbuck, I had loved living in Dayton. The whole town gave off good energy then, and it hadn't changed.

We found the Weinhard, a century-old building that looked nothing like a hotel, really. I asked the young girl at the front desk if she had ever heard of the Bulldog Den. She looked at me as if I were an ancient prospector wandering in from the desert.

"Just a minute. I'll ask my dad."

Dawn said, "Really, Shawn?" Our bags were puddled around our feet and she obviously wanted to get to our room and relax. Too late. A man and woman who appeared a few years older than me came out of a back room.

"Bulldog Den, eh? Was that the place with the pinball machines?"

I nodded. *Pinball machines, and all kinds of other little machines that would eat all your nickels and dimes, if you let them.*

The gentleman and his wife had a long discussion about where it might have been, deciding finally that it might have been located right in the building we were standing in, before it was converted to a hotel. Or, maybe down about half a block. No one was certain.

Thanking them profusely, and avoiding the look I knew was on Dawn's face, I hustled our bags up the long flight of stairs to our room. Stairs, no elevator. We had each packed a duffel bag with our clothes, plus a small backpack with bathroom necessities and a suitcase for dirty clothes, plus one more packed with other items I thought we might need on the trip. When it was all stacked in one place, I looked like a Sherpa, preparing to mount an expedition to the top of Everest.

Our room was beautiful, decorated impeccably in the style of a hundred years earlier. But everything felt new. We threw our bags down and trekked back down the stairs, which felt a lot shorter when I wasn't schlepping the luggage, and inquired as to local restaurants.

The man and woman both glanced at the clock, then sucked on their teeth and looked slightly stricken at the paucity of options.

"If you hurry," the woman said, "you might find one place open down the street."

We hustled down the charming, old-timey feeling Main Street and did indeed find one place open. It was a bar, but they had food, according to the sign. It was immediately obvious that this was the local watering hole. Everyone there seemed to know each other.

The bartender assured us it wasn't too late to order food and the place would be open for some time. While we waited, we had a chance to look around at the crowd having a nightcap. They were all about my age. Since I went to third grade here, I knew it was vaguely possible I had gone to school with some of them. But I couldn't think of a way to ask without looking like a fool, so I didn't.

Soon, one table group after another stood up, paid their bill, and left. The bartender looked at the suddenly emptying bar and asked if we wouldn't mind taking our order to go. We were pretty dead after our first day, so we were glad to take our sandwiches back to our room.

We immediately discovered something about life on the road: Every hotel has a different shower system and cable television setup. We spent twenty minutes trying to get the DirecTV setup to work, then gave up. Which was fine. We had a lot of miles ahead of us.

Day Two

Have I mentioned how little concrete planning I did for this trip? I had some general concepts, such as wanting to hit all four corner states—Washington, California, Florida, and Maine—and seeing as many national parks as possible. I was intent on sticking to smaller roads, but I didn't have a "point A to point B" agenda. That offers a lot of freedom, though I realize it might drive some people crazy to not know where they're going.

I went to sleep that first night figuring that we were going to wake up and drive to Crater Lake National Park in southern Oregon.

As we were packing, Dawn asked, "Are we going to drive down the Oregon coast?" Having left to me what little planning was to be done, she was flying blind.

"Umm, hadn't really planned on it," I said, envisioning the map of Oregon with an arrow pointing down the middle, toward Crater Lake.

"Oh. Okay. I was hoping to put my feet in both the Pacific and the Atlantic on this trip, but no big deal."

I flipped the map open and saw that we could indeed make it to Crater Lake with a hard day's driving, without a lot of side trips. But that's not what this trip was really about, was it?

"I like the sound of that. Let's do it. But we're clear over in Eastern Washington. That means we'll have to drop down and backtrack all the miles we did yesterday."

"Is that okay?"

"Of course it's okay!"

One simple conversation changed the next two days of driving. That's the kind of trip we were on, and I'll admit I liked it.

When I was young, I had hitchhiked up and down the West Coast, and I had always wanted to ride my thumb all around the United States. Other obligations had arisen, so I had never gotten the chance. Now, with serial killers apparently roaming every inch of highway, not to mention that I was a lot older and liked a comfy bed, I knew I would never thumb across the country. I still had that anarchic spirit, though.

We took a twenty-minute tour of Dayton, looking for the house I had lived in there. I was sure I'd found the right street, but there were no houses that filled the bill. It had been almost fifty years, and the place wasn't exactly upscale, so there was every possibility it had burned down or been torn down. I was glad we had spent our first night in Dayton, though. It was gratifying to see that my childhood memories held true, and it's still a pleasant little town.

We drove south on Highway 12 toward Walla Walla, bragged of as "the town so nice, they named it twice." I have a small confession: Along with other quirks, I have a slight mental problem. (This may not be news to you.) When I hear a sound pleasing to my ear, I tend to repeat it. It's one of those habits that to others seems funny at first, then gets annoying, then provokes homicidal thoughts. That happened with Walla Walla, Washington. Try it yourself.

Isn't it pleasant, the way it rolls off your tongue?

Walla Walla, Washington. It's best if you run it all together, like there isn't a comma there, but if I leave the comma out of Walla Walla, Washington, my editor will have a conniption fit. See, I'm kind of doing it now, in print, aren't I?

In any case, you can see how this might get old if you were stuck in a car with me, driving 40 mph past the same scenery we'd been passing for the previous half-day. Dawn says I'm "special," but I think she means the *other* kind of special, not the good kind.

I used to go to Walla Walla, Washington, (last time, I promise) for work back in the early 1980s, but everything looked different to me this time. Cities do not simply sit still, frozen in time, and wait for me to come back through on Reminiscing Road. WW, W— is that better? worse?—has actually shot up quite a bit, but it still has the look of a small prairie town that's been pumped up like an overinflated tire. Businesses are densely packed together along the main drags, but there aren't many buildings more than a few stories tall.

And then you see it, just down the street. Towering over the town like Wilt Chamberlain playing a pick-up game with a bunch of grade schoolers: the Marcus Whitman Hotel. It is twelve stories tall, twice the height of any other structure in town. The namesake, Marcus Whitman, was a doctor who led one of the first major wagon trains on what became known as the Oregon Trail. He also set up an outpost for others passing through and met a bad end, but more on that in a bit.

We admired the Marcus Whitman Hotel as we drove past, as we knew we would not be staying anywhere nearly that special at any point in our journey. We gassed up the Silver Bullet and got back on Highway 12, heading west this time, exactly the opposite direction we had come the day before.

We hadn't gone far when we saw a sign pointing toward the Whitman Mission National Historic Site. History, tragedy, and a failure to communicate: How could we pass that up? As became our habit everywhere other than the petrified forest, our first stop was at the information center. Throughout our trip, we found every single ranger at these centers to be dedicated, knowledgeable, and eager to share what they knew. They told us a bit of the history, then set us free to wander about what had once been one of the most important outposts of western settler civilization, now reverted mostly to prairie grass.

Here's the condensed story of what happened to Marcus and Narcissa Whitman: Marcus Whitman dreamed of being a minister, but instead became a physician, and practiced in New York state and Canada. His faith was a great motivator, though, and after hearing a speech imploring good people to come west and be missionaries to the indigenous people of the west, he and Narcissa did.

They brought some medical and technological advances and developed a mission in a Cayuse settlement just south of where Walla Walla would eventually spring up. The problem is that along with positive things, they also brought illness; specifically, the measles, a European disease to which the settlers had some immunity but the indigenous people did not. Dr. Whitman did what he could to save as many as possible, but over half the tribe's population died, and nearly all their children were wiped out. A generation lost.

Between the massive loss of life and a general unease at the Christian message the Whitmans were bringing, the Cayuse grew increasingly unhappy with their presence. On November 29, 1847, the Cayuse, under the leadership of Chief Tiloukaikt, killed the Whitmans and eleven other settlers in what became known as the Whitman Massacre.

Looking at it from the perspective of 170 years later, it is easy to see why the Cayuse reacted as they did, though violence is never a good answer. They were living happily in a land that had been theirs for centuries. Then, new settlers appeared, asking them to adapt to their beliefs and way of life. Then the Cayuse started to die in great numbers, creating suspicion that they had been poisoned.

The event became a rallying cry for those in the eastern United States who wanted to be more aggressive against the Cayuse and other indigenous people. The Cayuse War was the result, and in the end, the Cayuse were so decimated the few survivors merged with the Nez Perce Tribe.

We walked through the grounds of the former mission with heavy hearts. The buildings are gone, but the caretakers of the historic site have outlined with stones where each stood, so you can get an excellent idea of what daily life was like in the settlement. On a hilltop directly above the mission is a memorial to those who died that day. It's a bit of a hike, especially on a hot August day, but I recommend it.

We had our picnic lunch outside the information center, eating peanut butter and jelly sandwiches and slices of cheese, and talking about what had happened on that spot. It was one of those tragedies where both sides believe they are doing the right thing to protect or propagate their way of life. When communication broke down, so did everything else, and all parties paid a heavy price.

May I point out that those last two sentences can be applied to many conflicts happening today?

For most of the rest of the day, we followed the Columbia River, sometimes on the Oregon side, sometimes on Washington's. What Dawn had thought looked like a little stream when we first spotted it now really was the Mighty Columbia—broad, swift-moving, and powerful, heading toward the Pacific, as were we.

The mighty Columbia

We drove on the Lewis and Clark Highway for most of the afternoon. With the rolling brown hills surrounding us, and the deep blue of the Columbia below, it was a memorable drive.

Have I mentioned that I like quirky? Thank goodness Dawn also likes quirky, as that may explain why she married me. Our second stop of the day fell on the high end of the quirk spectrum— the Maryhill Museum of Art.

But first came Maryhill Stonehenge. Before leaving on this

trip, I'd had no clue that there are Stonehenge replicas all over the country. This particular copy of the famous prehistoric stones of England was ordered built by Samuel (Sam) Hill, the businessman who had the vision of what Maryhill could become. He built it as one of the earliest tributes to the soldiers of World War I. In fact, at the time it was christened, in July 1918, the war was still going on. Sam Hill, a pacifist Quaker, thought that since the original Stonehenge was believed to have been used as a place of sacrifice, his version would honor the sacrifice of the soldiers who had given their lives in the war.

This Stonehenge is built of concrete, which makes for a formidable if somewhat unimaginative memorial. Sam Hill himself is buried on a small ledge just below the replica but above the Columbia River. Once upon a time, his Stonehenge sat in the middle of the town of Maryhill, but the old town burned down, leaving only the stones remaining.

The Maryhill Museum is a few miles farther down the road, sitting right on the bank of the Columbia and offering stunning views. What's odd is that anyone would place such a massive mansion in the middle of nowhere. Most museums are in locations likely to attract droves of people. We were driving on a lonely little ribbon of road. Our GPS told us we were getting close, but we couldn't believe it, as there was nothing but hills and the river in sight. And then, off to the left, there it was: a beaux arts mansion built as the personal residence of Sam Hill and his wife, Mary, after whom the museum is named.

Construction was started in 1914 but halted after America entered World War I, when materials became scarce. The building wasn't opened to the public until 1940—yes, just making it under the wire for yet another world war. Sam Hill was a visionary character. In addition to the Maryhill Museum and the Stonehenge replica, he played a major role in constructing the Peace Arch in Blaine, Washington, on the Canadian border. He also had a lot to do with improving Oregon's highways.

He envisioned Maryhill as a kind of utopia, a place where Quaker farmers could come together to form a community. That never got off the ground, as he was the only Quaker to ever live in the area. He also never lived in the Maryhill mansion. He died in 1931, before it was completed. Before his passing, he had decided Maryhill should become a museum, not a residence, and so it has been since 1940.

The museum itself is impressive, with an entire section dedicated to Auguste Rodin, famous for sculptures such as *The Thinker*. My personal favorite is a small piece of the overarching masterwork *The Gates of Hell*, called "Fallen Caryatid Carrying Her Stone," which shows exactly that. I have no idea why a few statues, like this one, leave me breathless, while 98 percent of what the world thinks is amazing doesn't register.

Fallen Caryatid Carrying Her Stone

The museum fills three floors, and we spent a few hours wandering its halls. In what would become a recurring theme on the trip, we could have easily spent more time there, but when we looked out over the Columbia from one of the observation areas, we saw that the sun was dipping again. We hoped to make it to Tillamook for the night, and that was a long drive still, so regretfully we pulled away, noting that we'd like to come back when we had a full day to spend. Since we have moved to Seaview, Washington, it's a pretty easy daytrip.

We got back on the Lewis and Clark Highway and shot west toward Portland. Checking my maps, I could see there was no realistic way to make it through the city without hitting a freeway. As it was now several hours past rush hour, we gritted our teeth and hit I-5 for a bit. We lucked out: Traffic through the Rose City was moving, and we were soon on Highway 6, headed toward Tillamook.

We had chosen Tillamook because it was on the Oregon coast and as far as we thought we could reasonably drive that day. That proved correct, as it was dark when we pulled into a roadside motel for the night. Neither Dawn nor I do well driving strange roads after dark, so we were glad to have arrived, safe and sound.

Day Three

If you've read my first memoir, *Feels Like The First Time,* you might remember that one of my wedding vows was that I would always bring Dawn her first cup of coffee each day. At home, that's no worry. I set the pot up the night before, set the timer, and everything is ready when I want it. On the road, I was already discovering things were a bit more difficult. This hotel had coffee in the lobby, of course, and powdered creamer. I can no more imagine taking Dawn a coffee with powdered creamer in it than I can picture myself dunking a basketball.

I jumped into the Silver Bullet and found, typical of the Pacific Northwest, three coffee kiosks in less than a mile. I grabbed her the classic cinnamon hazelnut latte, extra hot, and made it back to the room before she woke. When my first words to her are, "Here's your coffee," I've noticed how much better the day runs.

If you recognize the name Tillamook, it might be because you've seen it in your dairy case, on cheese, ice cream, yogurt, and so on. We had driven through Tillamook on our honeymoon six years earlier and toured the Tillamook Cheese Factory. I know that doesn't sound like the most romantic of honeymoons— "Where did you go?" "Oh, it was exciting! We visited a cheese factory!"—but we were pretty broke then, and a free, interesting tour was definitely on our agenda.

If you ever find yourself within an hour's drive, a tour of the cheese factory is well worth the trip. They still make cheese the old-fashioned way, and it involves a lot of steps. When you do a self-guided tour, you can follow the whole process, from watching the trucks pull up full of milk to the final step of wrapping the cheese for sale. It's a bit like watching a Rube Goldberg machine, where 200 actions take place just to crack an egg.

We completed the tour but thought it would be rude to leave without buying some cheese and at least *trying* the huckleberry ice cream, right? I tried two full scoops to be *extra* polite. Highly recommended.

It was pushing noon and hot before we left Tillamook, looking for the ocean. The Silver Bullet's thermometer said it was already 90 degrees. I rolled my window down, filled the car with hot air, and immediately rolled it back up. It was an air-conditioning kind of day on the road.

After driving through road construction for several miles, we came to a point of decision—turn left and head south, or veer right and take the more scenic route, nearer the ocean. I don't even have to mention the way we went, do I? As we moved closer to the ocean, the temperature began to drop. When we caught our first glimpse of the deep green of the Pacific, it was down to 78 degrees. This is why we moved to the coast—I love the cooler weather.

Some things can be expressed as facts: Five-thousand, two-hundred and eighty feet make a mile. The circumference of a circle is a string of numbers that never repeats. The freezing temperature of water is 32 degrees. Then, there are opinions: Something is always the new black. Some new age is always the new thirty (or forty, or fifty). And so-and-so is *the most beautiful place in the world.*

I can't state with full accuracy what the most beautiful place is, but of the places I've visited, I remember a few contenders: A pristine meadow in the Matanuska Valley in Alaska. A spot in Maui where I looked down on the ocean crashing into the rocks, which took my breath away. However, for me, the Oregon Coast probably tops the list.

It may be because I was born and raised in the region, but there's something about driving Highway 101 down the Oregon Coast that relaxes and feeds my soul. The 101 doesn't track the

Pacific on its whole length, but where it does, it is beyond spectacular: Huge haystack rocks, rising up from foaming water, waves crashing against them. The water turning from blue to green, depending on how you look at it. The sun, playing against the water in constantly evolving patterns and shapes.

We did not make good time as we drove, because every few miles we pulled off, breathed in sea air, and just looked. My wish for you would be that you could someday take two entire days and spend it driving from one perfect spot to another on Highway 101. Interstate 5 gets you from Washington to California quickly. Highway 101 can restore your belief in beauty and the perfection of this third rock from the sun.

The Oregon Coast

Just south of Lincoln City, we found a small state park and pulled over for the picnic lunch portion of our day. We sat on the edge of the park nearest the ocean. The waves crashing below us were a perfect soundtrack. The seagulls were not afraid of humans. As we finished, one landed on our table within a foot of me, calm but apparently hungry. He looked at me, unblinking, until I parted with a small piece of bread. He flew away, only to be replaced immediately by another. I had a hunch they could have played this game with me all day, so I tossed a few crumbs onto the grass and made my getaway while they were occupied. I hate being guilt-tripped.

I did a little math and figured out that in four hours, we had made sixty miles down the coast. Nothing wrong with that, but we knew that if we were going to make Crater Lake by tomorrow, we would need to do better. We did make sure Dawn got to dip her toes in the Pacific, (one down!) then turned to the serious business of driving.

It got easier to put more miles under our wheels once we left Highway 101 and turned inland, first on Highway 38, then south on Highway 138. Yesterday, we'd spent the day running alongside the Columbia. We spent the late afternoon on this day tracking the Umpqua River. Where the Columbia is powerful and dramatic, the Umpqua is gentle and meandering, winding through the lovely and verdant farmland of southwestern Oregon.

I would love to tell you which highways and dirt roads got us to that night's destination, but I'm not sure they all even have numbers, and I'm fairly certain a few were actually someone's driveway.

Once again it was after dark when we arrived at our safe haven, in the lovely little Maple Leaf motel, in the aptly named town of Shady Grove, just south of Crater Lake.

Day Four

Not early enough I've mentioned before that I'm an early riser. I tend to wake up around 6 a.m. every day, no matter what. Dawn is at the other end of the circadian rhythm scale. She's really just waking up at 10 p.m., and would naturally stay up until 2 a.m. if she could. At home, that's not a big problem. I get up and write early in the morning, when the house is quiet, and she often stays up three or four hours after I go to bed. On the road, though, we were going to need to sync up a little more. My solution had been to let her sleep in a bit on mornings when it wasn't important that we hit the road early, in exchange for being allowed to roll her out while it was still dark when we were on a schedule.

Today, we were up and at 'em early. Okay, truth be told, I was up and at 'em. Dawn was up, with resistance. We left Shady Grove not too long after the sun peeked over the hills and headed north on Highway 62 toward Crater Lake National Park.

This is a good time to offer a quick travel tip. If you're going to do a fair amount of traveling around the United States in a given year, I recommend getting an America The Beautiful annual pass. That will get you free entry into every U.S. national park with the exception of Mount Rushmore, which I'll talk about when we get there. Since many of the national parks cost upwards of $20 per car to enter, it doesn't take long to pay for itself. It's only $80, and we got at least $200 value out of it. The pass also ensured that cost was never a consideration when we were deciding whether to hit a park or not.

When we embarked on our travels, we had just a few "must-sees" in mind—The Alamo, Key West, a lighthouse in Maine. Crater Lake fit that category, too. When you talk to people who have seen it, they often get a faraway look in their eyes and say something like, "You've just got to see it for yourself." We intended to.

This had the makings of another scorching-hot day, which would be a constant theme on this trip. Before we left our motel that morning, our host had said, "If you're heading up to Crater Lake, be sure to stop for breakfast at Beckie's Café on the way." He said some people use a visit to Crater Lake as an excuse to have breakfast at Beckie's.

We both love breakfast, so we pulled in. It's across the street from a rustic lodge and, yes, was crowded. The presence of an overflow parking lot is usually a good sign. The food was great, the service friendly, and we even got a free floor show.

Halfway through our pancakes and french toast, we heard a man say, "I've got to run out to my car to get my wallet. I'm not gonna run off on ya." I leaned across to Dawn and said: "That's exactly what I'd have someone say in one of my books if they were gonna run off."

The man was loud, and obviously a little drunk at 9:30 in the morning, so every eye in the café was on him as he weaved to his truck. I kind of forgot about him, but then I heard someone behind me shout, "He's runnin'!"

Sure enough, the guy had put his truck in gear and was hustling down the road. Around the café, jaws dropped in disbelief.

"I'll be go to Hell," the waitress said.

After the excitement died down, we called her over to our table and asked if we could buy the guy's breakfast. We didn't care about the escape artist, but we didn't want her to get docked for his malfeasance. She shook her head and said, "You're the third table to offer that, but it doesn't work that way here."

Just as we were getting ready to leave, the door swung open and the same man walked back in, a little red-faced. "I told ya I wouldn't run off on ya!" he said, fishing his wallet out of his pocket. We didn't know if he had grown a conscience, or figured out that someone in the café knew who he was, but he was back. Beckie's got paid, and we got a free show to go with a breakfast so big and good that we knew we wouldn't have to worry about eating for the rest of the day.

Before I tell you what we saw, I have to ask: Do you know any of the history of how Crater Lake was formed? If you do, please skip the next couple of paragraphs. If not, stay with me, because it's interesting.

Approximately 7,700 years ago, a blink of an eye in geological terms, Mount Mazama, estimated to have been 12,000 feet high, had a terrible case of heartburn and eventually erupted. It didn't just blow its top like Mount St. Helens did in 1980. The eruption caused cracks to form around its entire perimeter. In just a few hours, the top of the mountain collapsed down on itself, forming a huge volcanic depression, or caldera. Over time, that caldera filled with rain and snowmelt, as the area receives an average 44 feet of snow per year.

Side note: I sometimes write time-travel stories, like *The Unusual Second Life of Thomas Weaver*, so I think a lot about going back in time. I can't help but imagine how amazing it would have been to hover over Mazama in a nice safe helicopter, at a nice safe distance, and watch *that* show.

The indigenous Klamath people have an oral tradition, passed down for thousands of years, about the collapse of the volcano and creation of the lake. Today it is known as Crater Lake, and has been a National Park, and thus protected, since 1902. That partially explains why it is the pristine ecosystem it is, with crystal-clear water with visibility to depths of more than 100 feet. It also explains its vivid blue color.

Some have called Crater Lake the Great Silencer, because your first glimpse tends to drive all words from your mind. It did mine. Driving into the park from the visitor's center, Dawn and I caught little glimpses here and there, but when we were able to pull off the road and hike a little to a clearing that looked out over the lake, we were mesmerized. I am rarely at a loss for words, but it did indeed silence me.

A thirty-mile road circles Crater Lake. At least in the summer, it is an easy, relaxing drive. You can take as much or as little time as you like, with the road offering you opportunities to see it from different perspectives.

Crater Lake

One pleasing thing we noted was the plethora of languages we heard spoken by other visitors. I am not a linguist, but I heard French, German, Spanish, and any number of languages I couldn't identify. Obviously, people around the world recognize what a rare treasure Crater Lake is and go well out of their way to see it.

As we drove away from the park on Highway 64 East, we knew that while many wonders awaited us, we'd never forget Crater Lake.

Gasping at the beauty and wonder of Crater Lake took a lot out of us, but I had one more stop on our agenda for the day. After all, I wanted this trip to be a mixture of elements: natural wonders, historic sites, funky little roadside attractions (I was focused on finding the world's biggest ball of twine before the trip was over) and obscure, nearly forgotten footnotes in history.

Our second stop of the day fit into that last category.

When Americans think about the fight against Japan in World War II, two things typically come to mind: Pearl Harbor and the War in the Pacific Theater. But, did you know that Japan actually launched weapons at the U.S. mainland?

During the six months from late 1944 to April 1945, the Japanese military launched about 9,000 "fire balloons," relying on the Pacific jet stream to carry them toward their targets. The Japanese plan was to land bombs on the mainland and cause devastation. Had they been lucky, they might have hit a populated area or started a forest fire. As military actions go, it was a long shot, and almost all the balloons were a complete whiff. Three hundred of them were reported found but did no harm.

Except one. That balloon resulted in the only casualties on the U.S. mainland during World War II. On May 5, 1945, Archie Mitchell, a minister from Bly, Oregon, took his pregnant wife, Elsie, and five Sunday School students on a fishing trip. While unpacking the picnic lunch, Mitchell reported, he heard one of the children shout, "Look what I found!" The couple ran to where they heard the call, but an explosion rocked the quiet morning. Elsie Mitchell and all five children were killed in the blast of the firebomb, but Archie survived.

This felt like a vital, if mostly forgotten, part of our national history, so we set off for the memorial site. Highway 62 turned into Highway 140, and we took a late afternoon's tour of the small towns of southern Oregon. We hit towns that barely show on a map—Chiloquin, Modoc Point, Dairy, Odessa, and finally, Bly. Our GPS pointed us toward an empty field, then a small road that ran through it.

Our tires crunched over gravel as our speed dropped to 30, 20, finally 10 mph. As I mentioned earlier, the Silver Bullet is practically a new car—and a Christmas present, to boot. As Dawn maneuvered around one pothole after another, she shot me a glance that said, *I didn't sign up to bring my new car down roads that are pockmarked like a teenager's face.* Or maybe it just meant, *I'm not happy with you.* I often get those two expressions mixed up.

"I'll bet this is just a little connecting road that will have us back on a main road any minute," I said, proving once again just how wrong I can be.

"How much farther to this memorial you want to see?"

I glanced at the GPS on my phone. "Heh. Eleven miles. I'm sure it will get better, though."

Several miles later, not only had we *not* connected to a new road, but the one we were on had deteriorated. Going faster than 10 mph was a dream. Eventually, the gravel gave way to a dirt road. I hoped that would be an improvement, but it was as uneven as the previous incarnation.

A dust cloud materialized behind us and rapidly gained on us. An F250 pickup, towing a fishing boat, blew past us, country music blaring.

Dawn glanced at me. "Don't say a word. I'm not going any faster."

I nodded quick agreement, as I already felt on unsteady marital ground.

That first pickup became a small parade, as half a dozen others passed us over the next few miles, each kicking up new clouds of dust.

"Might have to redub her "The Dusty Bullet," I quipped, unwisely.

"You owe me a car wash."

"Yes, dear," I said, resorting to the two words every husband memorizes early on.

Almost an hour after leaving the main highway, we rolled to a stop at a sign marking the memorial. The first thing we noticed was deep quiet. Pines and firs surrounded us, but not densely. The forest floor was softened by a thick blanket of dry needles, which dampened any sound. It felt like standing in a natural cathedral, its sacredness deepened by our knowledge of what had happened here more than seventy years ago.

The memorial stands in the exact spot where the explosion occurred. On a rock tower erected by the Weyerhaeuser Company, a huge timberland firm, is a bronze plaque listing the six victims of the bombing, with the simple inscription: *In memory of those who died here, May 5, 1945 by Japanese Bomb explosion. Only place on the American Continent where death resulted from enemy action in WW II.*

A tree a few feet away still bears the scars of the explosion. It stands as mute witness to the terrible things humans do to one another. Compared with the incalculable damage America caused when it dropped the bombs on Hiroshima and Nagasaki, this is a small thing. Standing there and so easily picturing what happened made it feel very real.

There's an interesting addendum to the Japanese bomb story. The Reverend Archie Mitchell, the only survivor that day, remarried, and in 1947 volunteered to serve as a missionary in Da Lat, Vietnam. On May 30, 1962, Viet Cong entered the compound where the Mitchells and other missionaries were based, and kidnapped Mitchell and two others. Even though American and South Vietnamese intelligence organizations were able to track the location where it was believed they had been held, they were never found.

The Japanese Balloon Bomb Memorial was beautiful and somber, and it was worth driving out of our way to see, even over those roads.

Once we'd made our way back to Bly, I looked at the map. It was past dinnertime, and there weren't a lot of promising towns ahead that might have a motel for us. We only had two options: backtrack many miles through the same small towns we had just driven through, or push on to Lakeview, in the far southeastern corner of Oregon. We had done a lot of backtracking the day before, so we headed to Lakeview.

Even that town was no sure thing. It was a Friday night, and Lakeview is a town of only 2,200. Small potatoes, unless you were comparing it with what we had driven through earlier. I pulled up my Hotels.com app and saw how many possibilities it listed in Lakeview. The answer was one, and it showed no vacancy. Pulling my Oregon and California map out, I saw there were simply no other towns of any size within 100 miles of Lakeview, no matter which way we drove.

The name Lakeview conjured up images of a wealthy enclave: a few hundred houses sitting in sun-drenched splendor around a sparkling lake, perhaps. The reality? Just another dusty, dry, eastern Oregon small town, with no lake—virtually no water, period. As it turned out, Lakeview did have things to recommend it: great hang gliding and paragliding, a hot-water geyser called Old Perpetual, and alpine skiing in the winter. It also sits 4,000 feet above sea level, one of the highest communities in Oregon.

What it doesn't have is a lake. Or a view. But I digress.

We found the one motel in town, a dusty little two-story affair that looked as if it had seen better days. Still, I was cheered by the fact that the vacancy sign was on. I almost ran inside to ask about a room.

"Yep, still got one left," the lady behind the counter said. "You want it?"

Typically, I inquire as to rates before I commit, but with no desire to drive another three hours looking for a bed, I said: "We'll take it."

The room, on the second floor and down as far from the stairs as possible, was nothing special. But it was a bed. And, across the street, was a laundromat.

We were going to be on the road close to eight weeks. The Silver Bullet's trunk was spacious, but we still had to pack intelligently, which meant that we needed to do laundry every fifth day or so. We pulled out The Magical Mystery Bag, which looked a little less magical after we'd been grazing out of it for three days, and rooted around for dinner.

Then, I hustled across the street and started our laundry. I am the type of person who throws everything into a couple of machines, then leaves the laundromat. Dawn is a little more conscientious, so I stayed and watched everything cycle through. Eventually, Dawn crossed the street and relieved me so I could go back to the room and write up our daily blog.

By 10 p.m., on our first Friday on the road, we were lights-out, in more ways than one.

Day Five

Being free as a bird on a trip has a lot to recommend it. But I also discovered that it led to a lot of early-morning decision making. Starting out in Lakeview, Oregon, we had a lot of options. We thought about heading west again and hitting the coast of Northern California. That would allow us to go through a lot of the places we love—Monterey, Santa Clara, the gorgeous Pacific Coast Highway—but that was the problem. We loved those areas because we've already been there several times.

We were eager for new sights, new sounds, and new roadside attractions. So, we got on Highway 395, heading south out of Lakeview. We'd still hit California, which would mean we'd have made an appearance in all four corners of the continental United States.

I haven't made mention yet about how we occupied ourselves while we drove. The Silver Bullet has satellite radio, which is helpful on long journeys. I remember driving across the country in the nineties and the frustration of the radio station fading out every fifty miles or so. Satellite radio almost never failed us, unless we were in deep canyons or mountains where land masses blocked us on every side.

So, we listened to satellite radio a lot. One of my favorite things was that the channel '70s on 7 played old Casey Kasem *American Top 40* shows in their entirety. On this day, they were playing one of the shows from 1977, which is right in our wheelhouse. Driving over the border into California, listening to the music (and the voice) I grew up with, my best girl by my side, made for a perfect moment.

Just south of Alturas, California, we saw a sign for the Modoc National Wildlife Refuge. We pulled off and looked around but, aside from some ducks and geese, didn't see much. I'm sure if we had explored the preserve more fully we would have seen more, but our goal for this day was to put miles under our wheels, so we kept driving.

Like southeastern Oregon, northeastern California didn't offer a lot in the way of scenic vistas or sites to stop and goggle over. There simply are no highways in the northwestern corner of Nevada, so we stayed on 395 all the way down to Truckee. I waited for a Grateful Dead song to come on to commemorate the occasion, ("Keep on Truckeein'") but none did. We were forced to get onto a freeway to work our way around Tahoe and Reno, but we were glad to be back on Highway 95 South until we could catch Highway 6 East.

Mostly, all we did on this day was drive. We made over 500 miles, all in the service of getting to one place—The Clown Motel. About six months before the trip, a post had popped up in my Facebook feed about something called The Clown Motel, in Tonopah, Nevada. The name mostly gives it away, as it is a rundown little motel painted in circus colors and featuring clown décor everywhere. That post was followed by a series of dozens of people simply saying: "Nope."

I knew we had to stay there.

Pulling into the dusty gravel parking lot, it was everything I had hoped. A garish sign quoted rates of only $42.50 per night, $2.50 per extra person. I suspected The Clown Motel was not the destination of Dawn's dreams, so I leaned over and said, as romantically as I could, "You're worth every bit of the extra $2.50 you're gonna cost us here."

It's a wonder she stays married to me.

I promised Dawn a nice dinner out if she would just come into the lobby with me.

Let me set the scene. Picture a typical roadside motel lobby—small and cramped, with aging, dirty carpet and a difficult-to-nail-down odor. Now, dump 500 clowns in all shapes and sizes into that lobby. That's what we saw.

The lady at the front desk seemed to be in on the joke. After all, her weekly paychecks said "The Clown Motel" in the upper left corner, so I assumed she had some kind of a sense of humor. I had called early in the day to make a reservation because I didn't want it to be full when we got there. In retrospect, I needn't have worried. There were only about half a dozen other brave travelers staying at The Clown Motel on this night.

We checked in, got our key and headed to our room—me giddy with excitement, Dawn shaking her head at the fact I was giddy. I admit the room was a bit of a letdown. It was just a typical ugly roadside motel room from the early eighties. The only thing that marked it as clownish was a single small print over the bed.

The stuff of nightmares for many

Can't have everything.

Oh, did I mention that The Clown Motel is attached to what is purported to be a haunted cemetery? Unfortunately, it was getting dark, so a tour of the graveyard had to wait until morning, as we didn't have a flashlight with us.

I delivered the promised dinner by stumbling on a little gem called the Tonopah Brewing Company. As wonderful as the place was, it wasn't crowded, which I guess I understand. Although it was a Saturday night, it was in Tonopah. We had great barbecue, including something they called their Nuclear BBQ sauce. Highly recommended, if you have a cast-iron stomach, as I do. We also tried their craft root beer. Very strong and different from anything you'll find in a grocery store, but after the third sip, we didn't miss A&W Root Beer at all.

I should mention something for anyone who might want to follow in our footsteps and stay where we stayed. There are some odd rumors about The Clown Motel—rumors of it being as haunted as the cemetery next door. One friend messaged me as we were getting ready to go to sleep to tell us that another friend had become obsessed with The Clown Motel and then committed suicide under unlikely circumstances.

Me? I am a skeptic in all things I do not see with my own eyes. Yes, I'm one of *those* people. I slept like a baby. Considering how truly awful the mattress was, I would still say it was among the best night's sleep I had on the whole trip.

Day Six

One of the things we wanted to do from the road was send postcards to our grandkids from each state. That led to this conversation with the nice lady behind the counter at The Clown Motel:

Me: "I'll take these six postcards."

She: "That's one dollar, please."

Me: "Wait, I have six of them, and they are 50 cents each." (I hold out three dollars to her.)

She: "I'm overstocked on them and want to get rid of some of them."

Me: "Yes, but I was already going to buy these six. Here's my three dollars."

She: Reaches out, takes one dollar bill, and says, "Thank you."

Just when you think every person in the world is out to shake you down for your last buck, things like this happen.

Before we left Tonopah, we visited the ostensibly haunted cemetery next door. First, I want to say that this was the first of many cemeteries we were planning to visit on the trip. Dawn loves cemeteries. It doesn't matter who is buried there; she wants to stop and wander through. She likes the way she can find stories in almost every one. One thing we've noticed over our years of cemetery-peeping is that if the wife in a long-married couple dies first, the husband usually follows soon after. If the husband dies first, the wife often lives many years afterward. I guess that says something about what each of us brings to the relationship.

The Tonopah Cemetery is creepy. It looks exactly like what a Hollywood set builder would design if the project was a horror movie set in the Old West. There's no grass at all, just dirt and dust, with the occasional patch of weeds. The graves are all marked by fist-sized stones in the shape of a burial plot. The vast majority of the headstones aren't stone at all, but wood.

The cemetery told us a story: Tonopah has suffered. First, there was a mining disaster in February 1911, when seventeen men lost their lives. There was also something called the Tonopah Plague, which in 1902 killed a good portion of the populace.

The cemetery hasn't had any additions in over a century now, and it looks as though anyone who had relatives there has either died or fled to greener pastures. There didn't seem to be a lot of upkeep. The few stone markers or statues were in terrible disrepair, leaning one direction or another, or simply cracking apart.

We walked around the cemetery for an hour, covering ourselves in a fine layer of Tonopah dust, hoping the plague that had once visited the town was long gone.

As we drove out of Tonopah, we had to decide whether we wanted to drive farther south on Highway 395, or continue east on Highway 6. I'd read about a town that had a collection of bottle houses (literally, houses made out of old bottles) to our south, and I wanted to see that. However, if we went that direction, it was inevitable that we would have to head to Las Vegas as well.

Dawn and I have no objections at all to Vegas. In fact, we've gone at least once a year since we've been together. But this trip was to be about new experiences, discovering places we've never seen. We'd never seen eastern Nevada, so that's where we headed.

After a few hours, we turned south eventually on Highway 373, quaintly known as the Extraterrestrial Highway. We had seen eastern Nevada. So much so, we felt no need to see any more. And yet, eastern Nevada still came.

It was just like one of the old *Road Runner* cartoons, in which Wile E. Coyote chases the roadrunner at top speed, while the same background whizzes by, over and over. That, in a nutshell, is eastern Nevada, in our experience.

The Extraterrestrial Highway was dubbed that because it

skirts around Nellis Air Force Base, which includes the notorious Area 51. According to legend, Area 51 is where the government keeps all the little green men (or gray men, if you prefer) captured from alien crash sites. There are several reported UFO sightings in the area each week. Again, I am a skeptic but always glad to be proven wrong.

Calling the deserted stretch of road the Extraterrestrial Highway is excellent marketing on the part of the State of Nevada. If the state hadn't been so clever, I might have driven another road and seen something other than unbroken desert and the occasional Joshua tree.

By the way, thanks to a sign placed by the helpful State of Nevada's Department of something or other, I learned a lot about the Joshua tree. For instance, that it's not just the namesake of a great album by U2. I learned that Joshua trees and yucca moths are in a symbiotic relationship. The yucca moth is perfectly suited to pollinate the Joshua tree, which it does by laying its eggs inside the flower and accidentally spreading pollen around. Meanwhile, its offspring will eat some of the tree's seeds to survive infancy. Neither would survive without the other. It's absolutely stunning how nature evolves in this way.

My main complaint with the Extraterrestrial Highway was that it wasn't crammed with tourist traps every few blocks, selling tchotchkes, postcards, and other useless memorabilia at incredible markups. We did finally come to a building that looked like an old army surplus warehouse. It was completely mundane, aside from the thirty-foot-tall statue of an extraterrestrial that stood in front of it. We stopped both there and down the road and satisfied our tourist lust by buying all sorts of embarrassing alien knickknacks. We even bought something called Alien Jerky, so I can settle the age-old debate. ET does not taste like chicken. It tastes just like regular old beef jerky.

Leaving the Extraterrestrial Highway, we turned east on Highway 93 toward Caliente, one of my favorite names for a

47

town so far. I speak no Spanish, but I remember seeing signs at Seattle Mariner games that said *Edgar es Caliente*, speaking of our great hitter, Edgar Martinez. Whatever that meant, I was sure it was something good.

From Caliente, we turned north toward Pioche, which turned out to be the highlight of our day. If you're like me, you may never have heard of Pioche, but don't let that stop you from visiting some time.

Pioche is what they call a "living ghost town." In other words, it ain't what it once was, but it's still kickin'. There was a time when Pioche was a going concern. At one time, its population was more than 10,000. Today, about 900 people call it home.

It's been said that in the mid-nineteenth century it was the meanest, baddest town in all of the West. At least one website says 72 people died and were buried in Pioche's Boot Hill before anyone had a chance to die of natural causes. *That's* a tough town.

They buried all the bad men in one section of the cemetery, then fenced them off so their remains wouldn't infect the good name of the righteous townspeople of Pioche. Their version of Boot Hill was one of the top three cemeteries we would see on the whole trip. There are normal, sedate cemeteries elsewhere in Pioche, with elegant tombstones, graceful carved angels, and lovely sentiments carved into granite, but we loved the rough-and-tumble Boot Hill.

The bad-man section has plain wooden markers that say things like "Shot by Sheriff 5 times," or "Killed in a dispute over a dog." My favorite was: "Shot by a coward as he staked his claim before anyone could find out his name." Kind of gives you the flavor of what it was like to live in a gold-rush town in the 1860s.

We stopped in at the Lincoln County Museum just before it closed. The displays were haphazard, disorganized, and fun to look at it. Browsing through the heaps of memorabilia, it occurred to me that it resembled the inside of my mind: lots of

48

stacks, no organization, but you never know where you're going to find something cool.

Our last stop in Pioche was at the Million Dollar Courthouse. We drove right past it at first, because it certainly doesn't look like a million-dollar anything. It is a decaying old brick structure that is a testament to greed and mismanagement. The courthouse was originally built in 1872 at a cost of $72,000. That was a lot at the time. However, as things often go with bureaucracies, it got worse. The original contract to build it was broken, and the county ended up farming out various jobs to different contractors at a much higher cost. The county issued a bond, but at about that time the local mining industry took a nosedive—and there went the county's tax base. The Nevada Legislature stepped in next, because things always improve when you get congressmen involved, right? The upshot was that the final bill for the courthouse ended up at more than a million dollars, back when that was still real money. Here's the kicker: When the debt was finally paid off, in 1938, the building was deemed unsafe, so they built a new courthouse across town.

It's done pretty well for a building that was thought to be unsafe more than seventy-five years ago. It's still standing, mute testimony to what happens when you set out to get something done by a committee.

Leaving Pioche, we got on Highway 56 and crossed over into Utah. I was feeling a little bad about making Dawn stay in The Clown Motel the night before, so I searched ahead for a nice place to stay, and found one in Cedar City, Utah. The Abbey Inn calls itself a motel, but it was several cuts above where we had been staying of late. From the time we walked into the lobby until we checked out the next morning, we felt welcomed, pampered, and cared about. Staying in southwestern Utah? The Abbey Inn gets two big thumbs up from us.

Day Seven

I need to start with an apology to all of Utah. I am really, sincerely sorry. I've been making fun of Utah for most of my adult life, saying it was the most boring state in the union. I shake my head at myself. How could I have been so dumb? I based this opinion on several drives from Arizona to Washington over the years. I made those drives by hopping on I-15 somewhere south of Utah and never getting off until I was well north of the state line.

I did 80 mph the whole way and never got off the interstate for anything other than gas and grub. That is no way to see a state. I know that, but I made my shallow judgments anyway. Thus, the apology. *Mea culpa.*

I have grown to love Utah now. It is a state so full of spectacular landscapes and natural phenomena that only a complete dunderhead like yours truly would dismiss it out of hand.

We started our day by regretfully leaving behind the Abbey Inn, with its friendly personnel, huge indoor pool, and wonderful free breakfast—not just a bag of English muffins and some honey-like product dubbed a continental breakfast. We wished there was some way we could bundle it all up and take it with us.

Our first adventure in Utah was Cedar Breaks National Monument. You might ask, *Shawn, what the heck is the difference between a national park and a national monument?*

Excellent question!

Basically, a national park has a variety of focal points, and generally speaking covers more land. A national monument, on the other hand, focuses more single-mindedly on one thing and can cover much less acreage. Here's the easy way to think about it: Yellowstone is a national park. Devils Tower (as seen in *Close Encounters of the Third Kind)* is a national monument.

The road from Cedar City up, and I do mean *up*, to Cedar Breaks is magnificent on its own. It twists and winds and has plenty of places to stop and look out over vast expanses of ridiculously photogenic scenery. All those times I stuck to I-15 I saw nothing but desert. Climbing up to Cedar Breaks, we saw thousands of acres of forests, albeit a different kind of forest than we were used to in Washington.

When we rolled up to the Information center for Cedar Breaks, I realized just how far we had climbed. We were more than 10,000 feet above sea level. I saw some European tourists roll out of their rental car dressed as though prepared for an assault on Everest—bundled up like Randy in *A Christmas Story*. I briefly wondered if I had badly miscalculated my own wardrobe for the day, which consisted of jeans and a t-shirt. The temperatures were in the mid-50s, though, so I managed just fine. I think they might have just been a little on the "over-prepared" side.

Cedar Breaks is focused on a huge natural amphitheater. To my eye, it looked a bit like Crater Lake, minus the lake. That it's not filled with water means you can see Mother Nature's handiwork on the sides of the cliffs, which more than makes up for the missing lake.

We got lucky on our very first viewpoint. In addition to a stomach-churning drop down into the amphitheater below, we saw a furry creature just ahead, sunning itself on a rock.

"Oh, look," I said to Dawn. "It's a yellow-bellied marmot, genus and species *Marmota flaviventris*."

Okay, okay. That's not what I said at all. What I really said was: "What the heck is that?" We didn't find out what he was until we got back to the information center and found a stuffed version. He was adorable—perched comfortably on a rock, facing certain death with any misstep. He was not concerned. He posed for us for quite some time, then confidently disappeared into the abyss below.

Marmota flaviventris, but you knew that

Again like Crater Lake, Cedar Breaks has a road around this dramatic hole in the ground that you can drive in a circle, enjoying different perspectives. After finishing the loop, we descended by way of the same road we had come up. Along the way, I tried to plan the rest of our day. So far, I had relied almost exclusively on my trusty paper maps and atlas, using GPS only at the very end.

✓ Today, I decided to experiment. I wanted to visit Arches National Park the next day, an incredibly popular tourist destination, so I called ahead to reserve a room at a little motel in Moab, just south of the park. That left us the rest of the day to work our way there, while catching as many of the sights as we could. I punched into the GPS what I thought would be a good first stop, folded my maps and just followed blindly.

En route, we took little side trips. We drove through Coral Pink Sand Dunes State Park and stopped at an area where you can look out at the blowing dunes, which are, indeed, coral pink. Off to the left was a little trail promising an easy half-mile hike with lots of informative signs along the way.

"C'mon, it's only half a mile. How bad can it be?"

This sentence is proof that I have still not learned when it would be better to keep my mouth shut.

With some trepidation, Dawn agreed, and we set off. The first thing we noticed was that the sand was not just pink, but also incredibly powdery. It was like trying to walk on talcum powder. That was bad enough on the semi-level path, but when we got out into that place that pilots like to call *the point of no return*, we discovered that walking through entire dunes made up of the stuff was nearly impossible.

I looked at my beautiful bride—red-faced, huffing as though she might pass out at any moment.

"Shawn?"

"Yes, dearest?" I've often found that an innocent demeanor is the best response, especially when I can't think of anything else.

"The next time you get the harebrained idea to take a two-month trip that involves hiking, let's not sit on the couch and eat snacks for the previous year."

"But doesn't a snack sound good right about now?"

"Throwing up sounds good right about now."

I'm happy to report we both survived the half-mile hike, which Dawn swore was mismarked and was actually a two-day, ten-mile hike over treacherous terrain.

We continued to follow the GPS instructions, maps tucked securely under my seat. That led us right past the Best Friends Animal Society shelter. Since Dawn loves animals more than anything besides our children and grandchildren (yes, I know which side of the line I occupy) we swung in to take a look.

Unfortunately it was too late in the day to catch a full tour, but we did have a chance to look around the facility a bit, then drive through the grounds. Best Friends is a no-kill sanctuary of hundreds of acres that saves horses, pigs, dogs, cats, birds—

whatever needs saving. If you spend five minutes with any of the volunteers, you'll know that they do the work out of love for everything that walks on four legs. There is a pet cemetery on the property that moved Dawn to tears while we walked through it. My steely reserve got me through, but I did catch a bit of dust in my eye a few times.

When we left Best Friends, I noticed it was getting to be late afternoon.

"Shouldn't we be getting to the next national park?" Dawn asked.

A reasonable question. One any navigator should be able to answer. I checked the GPS, pulled the state map of Utah out and mumbled to myself for several long minutes. I realized that I must have plugged the wrong destination in to the GPS, and we had spent the entire afternoon driving in exactly the opposite direction from where we wanted to be.

"Baby," I said, "I've got good news and bad news." I've played this game too many times with Dawn, though, and it seems to have lost a bit of its charm with her.

"What's the good news?"

"The good news is, we got to see an entire section of Utah that we were going to miss."

"So, you're saying we're lost."

"Yep!"

"How lost?"

"Well, we have a reservation to stay in Moab and ..." I did a little measuring with my finger on the map, "we're about 300 miles away from there."

"It's 5 o'clock, and we've got to drive 300 more miles before we can sleep tonight."

"Your grasp of the situation is unerring."

"Unlike your navigating."

I hate it when she uses facts against me.

We turned around and spent hours going backwards over the

same ground we had just covered. If we wanted to get to Moab at any reasonable hour, we would have to use 1-70 for at least part of the trip.

When we left our little back road for the I-70 on-ramp, it was a shock. The speed limit, which for us had been 45 mph all day, was suddenly 80 mph. It was getting dark. I-70 through this part of Utah is a little quirky. The speed limit changes from 80 mph down to 55 mph to go through bends, then pops straight back again. After a few of these ups and downs, Dawn pulled across the rumble strip onto the shoulder, and looked at me.

"I'm done."

I drove the rest of the way, a fitting punishment for my navigational ineptness.

"I hate this freeway," Dawn said. "They want you to go 80, then 55, then they tell you this is a deer crossing for the next eighteen miles, but they still want you to go 80 in the dark. How can you watch for deer when you're going 80 and can't see ahead?"

I had no reasonable answer, so I turned up the music and drove.

We pulled into Moab about midnight. I've rarely been as glad to see a crappy little roadside motel as I was the Bowen Motel. It wasn't much, but we made it.

Day Eight

I'm not sure what the city motto of Moab, Utah, is, but I think it might be something like, "Hey, we're really close to Arches National Park. Like, really, really close." There didn't seem to be much else to Moab. Cool name, though. I think I'll save that for a character name.

I'm not sure why several people had told me things like, "Oh, don't worry so much about Arches. The other national parks are much cooler. It's overrated."

This is one of those things that is completely subjective, but I can't imagine what they were thinking. Arches National Park, to me, is mind-bogglingly cool. This may be one of those situations where something becomes so popular that eventually there is a backlash against it.

When we pulled off Highway 191, we entered a long line of cars, SUVs and motorhomes waiting to take the steep, winding trail up to the park. We were once again glad for our America the Beautiful pass, as the Arches entrance fee is $25 per vehicle. Even at full price, it's a great deal.

As cool as Crater Lake and Cedar Breaks are, the visitor experience basically consists of driving around, seeing the same thing from different angles. Arches is more like a zoo with lots of exhibits, and the animals are all made out of rock. I may have taken that example too far.

We planned to spend the bulk of our day at Arches, knowing that we still would only get to see a portion of it. We set our priorities, then threw them out the window and just took things as they came.

✓ Here's the easy lowdown on Arches. It's a series of rock formations in shapes you don't see much anywhere else. Our first stop was to take in the breathtaking vista. Did those formations have names? I'm sure they did, as everything in the park seemed to have a name, but I totally missed most of them.

Balancing Rock, though, is an easy one to remember. As you drive up to it, you think: *Surely that big heavy rock isn't balanced on those much smaller rocks below?*

From the road, it looks like an oblong sitting delicately on a column, as though a good stiff wind might send it tumbling down. Of course, I wanted to take the little hike to walk directly beneath it. A path leads you in a circle around it, and as you get underneath you see Balancing Rock is partially an optical illusion. It's not really an egg set on its end, as it first appears. There's more to it than that, but it's just not visible from most angles. Knowing the secret of it did nothing to detract from the wonder of seeing it.

Balanced Rock

Next we stopped at one of the most famous formations—Delicate Arch, which looks just as the name implies. There's a picnic area there with enticingly shaded tables, so we hauled our Magical Mystery Bag from the car. It was stinking hot already, in the mid-90s, but every table had at least one occupant. So we approached an older gentleman and asked if he minded if we sat down with him.

He smiled assent, so we spread out the sleeping bag we used as a tablecloth and unpacked. One of the things we had bought along from the Extraterrestrial Highway stop was a container of garlic-infused pistachios. As thanks for sharing his table, I gave a small handful to the man, who seemed a touch surprised when he ate the first one. No one expects garlic pistachios.

A moment later, his family returned from their walk and filled out the rest of the picnic table. From the looks of them—sweaty, wrung-out, exhausted—it seemed to me he had been the smart one. They told us they were from Japan and were visiting as many of the national parks as they could get to. It gave me an odd sense of pride that so many people come from such distances to see what is in our backyard.

I offered the garlic pistachios around. Neither we nor the older man gave the others any warning as to the additional flavoring, and we enjoyed watching their reactions. They shared some candy that brought back old memories of visits to a restaurant called the Bush Garden in the International District in Seattle. When I told them that, they insisted on giving me most of what they had with them, no matter my protests.

They had made the hike all the way up to Delicate Arch. Forewarned is forearmed. We opted to visit the viewing area just a short hike away, and were limp with the heat just from standing around. We couldn't imagine hiking a mile or more in each direction just to get a slightly better view. Our capacity to justify our laziness knows no bounds.

One of our reasons for doing this trip is to stretch and grow a bit. Dawn did a lot of that on this day. She is deathly afraid of heights, but she climbed up on a slightly tilted rock, with a massive drop-off just a few feet behind her, and stood triumphantly with her arms in the air. It's my favorite picture of the trip.

Dawn, triumphant

We spent several more hours driving and hiking around Arches. We saw the South Window, the Double Arch, and the Park Avenue Trail. Even after giving the bulk of the day to Arches, we knew we had just scratched the surface. It's like listening to a beloved band's greatest hits. Great stuff, yes, and what they are famous for, but there's so much more if you care to dig.

✔ Some of the memories we made on this trip are indelible. Arches National Park is absolutely one of those.

We left the park with a few hours of exploration time left, so we made our way to Dead Horse Point State Park. Here's a good travel tip for you: if you pay to get into a state park in Utah (and many other states) save your receipt. It will get you into other state parks for several days afterward, which saved us $10 getting into Dead Horse.

Why do they call it Dead Horse Point, instead of something lovely and more tourist-friendly like Rainbow's Vision State Park? It's because of the history. Legend holds that cowboys would drive wild horses into blind canyons, where they would fence off the only exit. Then, they would pick and choose the horses they wanted to break, and left the others behind to die. There was no PETA in the Old West. The horrible thing about the legend is, if it's true, those horses died of thirst within easy sight of the Colorado River.

Speaking of the Colorado, it's responsible for the loveliest sight in the park. For millions of years, it has wound this way and that and formed a snaking canyon that is stunning. In fact, you've very possibly seen it without knowing it.

If you saw the movie *Thelma and Louise*, starring Geena Davis and Susan Sarandon, you probably remember the ending (*spoiler alert!*) where the two stars hurtle off a cliff at 100 mph, freezing in mid-air like Butch and Sundance. In the movie, that was supposed to be the Grand Canyon, but the scene was filmed at Dead Horse Point State Park. The more you know.

Dead Horse Canyon State Park

Looking down at the Colorado so far below, it's impossible not to be moved by the power of water, time and nature's patience.

Seeing Arches and Dead Horse Point was a full day, but we

decided to cram in one more stop. We drove through Canyonlands National Park. Perhaps being worn out or seeing Arches first left us less impressed by Canyonlands. If we'd seen them in reverse order, I'm sure it would have dazzled us. After the rock formations of Arches and the magnificent canyon at Dead Horse Point, it didn't have the same impact.

After a quick drive through and a few stops for pictures, we got back on Highway 191 and drove south with the setting sun on our right. There weren't a lot of big towns in our immediate future, so we pulled off in the small town of Blanding, which reminded me of the old Cary Grant movie, *Mr. Blandings Builds His Dream House.* My instinct is that Mr. Blandings would not have built his house in Blanding, which is a completely nondescript town, but it did have a motel with a vacancy.

Once again, we were given a room on the second floor, as far from any staircase as possible. Dawn set about getting the room ready, while I carried the bags in, which took three trips. On my Sherpa's journey, I couldn't help but overhear a conversation two couples were having outside the door of a first-floor room.

A pair perhaps in their mid-sixties were sitting in plastic lawn chairs, with a cooler between them. Another couple, maybe a decade older, greeted them and asked where they could find the nearest store to grab a six-pack.

The younger man said, "Nowhere in town. Blanding is dry." (If you're not familiar with a "dry" town, it is one where no alcohol is sold. It can be consumed, just not purchased.)

The older, white-haired man let loose a stream of invectives.

"Don't worry," the seated man said. "This ain't my first trip through this little shithole. I've got enough cases stacked up in the room to keep us and you and your wife happy all night."

"Well, that's mighty nice. I do appreciate it. It'll just be me drinking, though. Ruth don't drink no more since she had her surgery. She ain't right in the head since then."

I peeked over the railing to make sure I was hearing the

conversation correctly. Ruth, apparently, was in complete agreement with this. She nodded her head and said, "Yep. I'm not right in the head anymore." She seemed undisturbed by this analysis.

I dropped the first round of bags off in the room and hustled back down to see if I could catch any more tidbits. By the time I got back downstairs, there were four plastic lawn chairs huddled around the life-giving cooler, and they were in deep conversation, as though they had known each other for years. The conversational grease that is a cold beer had worked once again.

Day Nine

Waking up in southeastern Utah, the road forked ahead of us. We could go south, then west, and hit the Grand Canyon and everything else Arizona had to offer, or we could head east to Colorado.

At the beginning of the trip, Dawn had said she really wanted to see the big hole in the ground that is the Grand Canyon, so I left the decision in her hands. She concluded that seeing the canyons at Dead Horse Point and Canyonlands the day before was good enough for now, so we lit out for Colorado instead.

Being us, though, we didn't take the most direct route. A few miles outside Blanding, we saw a sign that pointed in the opposite direction of our chosen route: *Natural Bridges National Monument, 30 miles*. Since that required heading west when we'd intended to go east, that meant a sixty-mile round trip just to get back to where we were now. How could we resist?

Ten miles down that road, we saw another sign, reading *Butler Wash Indian Ruins, 12 miles*. Yes, going in yet another wrong direction. We were starting to jump around like a long tailed cat with ADD in a rocking-chair factory, but who doesn't want to see Indian ruins? Off we went.

Twelve miles down that road, we found another sign, saying that Butler Wash Indian Ruins was an easy one-mile hike thataway. I looked at the Silver Bullet's dashboard. A toasty 94 degrees outside. A mile-long hike over uneven surfaces? Sign us up!

We were learning that although every mile is 5,280 feet, there's a big difference between walking a mile on a nice street, or walking up, down, around and across an old wash. At first, the trail was well marked and easy to follow. After a few hundred yards, that petered out and we lost it entirely for stretches. We also realized we had left our water bottles back in the car.

Eventually, we came up over a rise and could see a viewing area ahead in the distance. Even without a marked trail, we could figure out how to get to it.

As soon as we got there, we knew the whole dusty, thirsty hike had been worth it. We were able to look down directly into cliff dwellings built by the Anasazi people a century or so before Chris Columbus crossed the Atlantic. It was fascinating, getting a glimpse into the way they built their shelters, getting an idea how they had lived.

On the hike back to the car, we didn't have the advantage of spotting the viewing area to mark our route. All we saw was unbroken desert and tiny little lizards. After about ten minutes of hiking up a dry wash, we realized that we were totally lost. No trail, no clue.

Dawn started to panic a little. Being the genius I am, I said, "It's fine, it's fine. Don't panic."

That is exactly like telling her to calm down when she is mad at me. In other words, not good.

We realized that we had left all our water in the car. The sun was beating down on us.

"Two tourists found dead ten feet from highway at Butler Wash," I said.

Dawn remained unamused.

Finally, I climbed to the top of a hill, got my bearings on where the dwellings had been, remembered which way we had come, and found the trail. Another crisis averted.

On the way back to the car, we crossed paths with two young guys. They were athletic, suntanned, properly attired, and each carrying a water bottle. They smiled sunnily at us as they passed us at a steady jog. We hated them both.

We drove on to Natural Bridges National Monument.

And that was when we knew we had overdosed on gorgeous Utah scenery. We drove around the park, stopped at all the viewpoints, and realized that they just weren't having the impact

on us that Arches and Dead Horse Point had the day before. It
was time to move on.

We backtracked to where we had started the day and turned
toward Colorado.

Before we crossed the state line, we made one more stop, at
Hovenweep National Monument. There was something about the
name itself that grabbed ahold of me and wouldn't let go.
Hovenweep is a Paiute/Ute word that means "deserted valley."

On the way up to the Butler Wash Indian Ruins, I had
tweaked my ankle a little bit and told Dawn that I thought I would
lay off hiking for the rest of the day. When we got to the
Hovenweep visitors center, a park ranger who appeared to be
about twelve handed us our map and pointed out various possible
hikes. As she looked at me – slightly sunburned, gray-bearded,
and overweight—her pen hovered over the 60-yard walk out to
the observation deck, as opposed to the two-mile walk around the
entire perimeter, which included hiking down and back up the
valley. That was probably the only thing that could have inspired
me to hike those two damn miles at that moment, but it was
enough.

Once again, it was completely worth the hike. Yes, it was
90-some degrees, and the sun was melting us, but this time we
remembered our water and loved what we saw. This was another
example of Anasazi architecture from 800-plus years earlier.
Though these ruins were from that era, there is evidence the
Anasazi were living in the area as much as 8,000 years earlier.

America, especially the western half, is so young that we
don't often get to see buildings this old. It was a little boggling to
look at these stone structures and realize that when they were
built, Genghis Khan was still running roughshod over the world,
and King John was being forced to sign the Magna Carta.

As I mentioned earlier, the hike took us down the steep side
of a canyon, across the canyon floor, then back up the other side.
By the time we made it back to the top, we were sure we had to

be almost done with the hike. In fact, we were less than halfway.

Somehow, even as out of shape as we are, we survived. Our lips were chapped and our legs had turned to jelly, but we proved wrong that young girl who didn't think we would make it.

Pretty sure she didn't notice.

We finally crossed over into Colorado and stopped for the night in Cortez. I hadn't made a reservation, so we just drove down the main drag, looking for a place. Off to our left, I saw a sign for something called The Retro Inn. Do you remember the Lucille Ball movie *The Long, Long Trailer?* There was a slightly shrunken version of their trailer parked out front. A statue of Elvis Presley sitting beside it, as cool as The King can be, clinched the deal for us. We were home for the night.

Day Ten

My phone had been acting up a bit. Not wanting to take a charge, shutting itself off, and so on, so we stopped in to a Verizon store in Cortez before hitting the road. I'd been waiting for the new Note 7 to come out and had meant to get one before we left, but all the kerfuffle caused by finding a new house at the last minute and losing my wallet meant I hadn't gotten it done.

Two related things happened in short order. The Verizon clerk told me I was too late—the phone had been selling quickly and the store's supply was exhausted. Disappointed, we returned to the car. I opened one of my news apps and learned that the Note 7 had been recalled because the phones were exploding when charged. Sometimes unanswered prayers are the best kind.

One reason we had chosen to stay in Cortez was proximity to Mesa Verde National Park. We had really enjoyed seeing the ruins at Butler Wash and Hovenweep the day before and wanted to see more.

A quick aside: I grew up on movies with John Wayne, Glenn Ford, and Clint Eastwood. I also grew up in the most white-bread environment imaginable. I didn't meet any minorities until I moved away from Mossyrock, Washington, population 400, to Seattle in the late seventies. Coming out of that environment, I believed what was fed to me—that the cowboys (and European explorers before them) were the heroes who had brought civilization to the untamed wilderness. I left a lot of that way of thinking behind with other childish things, but this trip really forced me to consider a new perspective.

When I see that societies and civilizations were existing quite happily here for millennia before the Europeans hit the Americas, then had their lifestyles forcibly taken away in the name of "progress," it hurts. My ancestors came from Europe. My family helped to settle the West. The more I see of the way the First Nation lived, though, the more my perspective changes.

End aside.

Mesa Verde National Park has a well-deserved reputation as *the* place to see Ancestral Puebloan cliff dwellings. Unlike all the other national parks we've toured so far, all the excursions in Mesa Verde require participation in a park ranger–guided tour to see the cool stuff.

As soon as the tour started, I understood why. In Butler Wash, by comparison, we were standing at a viewing area, looking down into the cliff dwelling 50 yards away or so. At Mesa Verde, we got to go right inside the cliff dwellings. Humans being what they are, if these groups weren't supervised by sharp-eyed rangers, there would soon be Snickers wrappers everywhere, and someone would have spray-painted *Joanie loves Chachi* or something across the historic dwellings.

We chose the Cliff Palace tour and hooked up with Ranger Rick. By the way, the tours cost extra, but the price is very reasonable —about $5 per person. When I commented on how affordable they were, the ticket seller said, "Yeah, it's almost like we want you to take them." Everyone is a comedian.

Rick was all business about protecting the historic site, but he was also a fount of information and a pretty funny guy.

Ranger Rick and Mesa Verde ruins

One other word of caution about the Mesa Verde tours. They all are rated "strenuous" by the park service. They all require some hiking, and most require you to climb up and down ladders and over a few hundred very uneven steps. As Ranger Larry said, "The Civilian Conservation Corps built these steps, and it might have been their first day, because they didn't do a very good job."

One woman who had signed up for the tour saw the first ladder, said, "Nope," and disappeared back the way we had come. Still, the rangers give you plenty of time to rest, and shade wherever possible. Dawn and I had no trouble with any aspect of our tour, although my understanding is that one of the other tours would have required us to essentially crawl through a long, dark tunnel. I didn't even ask Dawn about that one.

The First People who lived in these cliff dwellings didn't have a written language, so there is no written record of their day to day life, but of course they left many clues behind for today's researchers to interpret. One of the interesting things Ranger Larry shared was that the average lifespan was very short, probably only thirty years.

Why? Because their diet consisted primarily of ground maize, which is much different from today's corn —tougher, harder to eat and digest. Many members of the tribe spent the bulk of their day grinding the corn into meal, placing the maize on a flat rock and pounding it with another rock. This action also ground the rock itself, leaving traces of it in their food, which destroyed their teeth and contributed to their short life spans.

We left Mesa Verde in mid-afternoon and, without plans for other stops, just drove, seeing what we could see.

One of our favorite things is to follow a country highway to a small town, then drive around it, trying to get a feel for what life is like in, say, southern Colorado, northern Florida, or western Maine.

One of these little side trips took us to Mancos, Colorado. As far as we could tell, not much of historic significance took place there, and there are no real tourist attractions. But we loved this little town. We drove by what turned out to be the oldest operating high school in Colorado—a three-story building that appears to be made of local stone and immaculately maintained, right down to the bell tower straight out of an Alfred Hitchcock movie.

Mancos High School

There was a little farmers market going on. We had farmers markets every Friday when we lived in Orting, Washington, but those were mostly arts and crafts booths. This felt more like a legit farmer's market, with lots of fresh, local produce. We wished we had more room for food storage. We even bought a chocolate brownie for dessert later.

Dawn said, "Wait a minute. We're in Colorado. Marijuana is legal here. You don't suppose it's *that* kind of a brownie, do you?"

"I don't think they're selling dope brownies for a buck each, or there would be a longer line."

It was delicious, by the way.

Our last stop in Colorado was Durango, birthplace of Apollo

14 astronaut Stuart Roosa and Tom Tully, who was nominated for an Oscar for his role in *The Caine Mutiny.*

I was excited to see Durango and much of the surrounding environs: Silverton and the Animas Canyon. Why? Because I am a music geek, and I grew up listening to C.W. McCall. If you remember C.W. at all, it's probably because of his hit that helped spark the CB craze of the seventies, "Convoy." I never cared much for "Convoy," but I bought and loved his album, *Black Bear Road.* One of my favorite songs on the album was called "The Silverton," about a train that ran right through this area. It was a thrill for me just seeing the place I had heard and dreamed about so much as a kid.

We stopped off at a city park and saw another train there—the Emma Sweeney. If that name doesn't ring a bell, you're forgiven. It was the train that starred in the 1950 movie *A Ticket to Tomahawk.* She had been left to rot in some Hollywood back lot when someone got the idea to bring her to Durango and restore her, which they did. She now lives out her days in pristine beauty, surrounded by tall hills and sunshine.

We crossed over into New Mexico, the seventh state of our trip so far, and made it as far as Aztec. There was another national park we wanted to see, but it was too late in the day by the time we arrived, so we found a kitschy little motel called the Step Back Inn. The idea being that it is a step back in time, I believe. It does have an almost Southern plantation vibe to it. Each room is named after an early settler. Nice place. Terrible wi-fi.

Day Eleven

The three-day Labor Day weekend was bearing down on us, and we knew that would mean more crowds everywhere—in the national parks, in the hotels and motels, and especially on the highways. So we decided to pick a nice little spot to spend a couple of days and let all that pass us by.

Today and tomorrow, though, we still have driving to do!

We started at Aztec Ruins National Park. What first surprised us was its location. Most national parks are, geographically speaking, pretty lonely. This one is right in the city of Aztec. Our second surprise was that the Aztec Ruins have nothing to do with the Aztec people. In fact, they were left by essentially the same people who built behind Mesa Verde to the north and the Chaco ruins to the south. However, the early settlers thought their structures looked like Aztec ruins, so the name stuck, both for the park and the city.

We'd had such a great guided tour at Mesa Verde that we decided to do the same here. Our guide was a volunteer named George. How can you not love someone who gives up his free time to take tourists through a national monument for free? He wouldn't even accept a tip at the end, and asked us to donate at the box inside instead.

The Aztec Ruins, about 900 years old, were once a great center of activity. This was the largest of the ruins we toured, with more than 100 rooms. George showed us how the buildings lined up so the sunlight was focused in a particular way on the first day of summer and the first day of winter, like a mini-Stonehenge.

He also showed us how the ruins combine architectural styles used in Mesa Verde and the style of the Chaco buildings. Essentially, there was a merger of different peoples, and Aztec Ruins shows how their building styles merged and evolved over the years. To us, Aztec looks like a single ruin, but this group of people lived there for 200 years or more. Just as the houses we build today don't much resemble those of the early 18th century, methods changed in this community. Building styles came and went as the years passed.

There are several kivas here, rooms used for ceremonial functions. Kivas served many purposes—for learning, training, religious ceremonies, and so on. We spent an information-packed hour wandering through the ruins with George. One thing I noticed is it seems people were a lot shorter back then. I'm a bit over six feet tall, and I had to stoop to go through several passageways and almost kneel to get through another. Dawn had no trouble with any of them. There advantages to being vertically challenged.

The highlight of the Aztec Ruins, at least for us, was a completely restored Great Kiva. A Great Kiva differs from a normal one not just in size, but in access. A typical kiva was entered via a ladder from the ceiling. A Great Kiva has a door providing a front entrance, making it accessible to everyone. The restored Great Kiva is not original, but everything possible was done to ensure its accuracy, working from photos that Earl Morris, the original archaeologist at the site, took early in the 1900s. Standing inside the kiva felt like standing in any holy place. It was somber, quiet, and deserving of respect.

One last piece of information about the Aztec Ruins. Some sections have been left unexcavated deliberately, and there are no current plans to dig there. They will remain untouched for at least a generation, allowing archaeological technology to advance enough to allow a more thorough, less damaging dig. If the whole site had been dug when first discovered, it would have meant destroying many important artifacts, just because the technology had not yet been devised to save them. That will continue to be true as archeology moves forward and new methods are invented. This idea really impressed me, as it runs contrary to how we humans tend to investigate—to charge ahead and let the chips fall where they may.

We left the Aztec Ruins and drove southeast, toward Clovis, New Mexico, where one of the true highlights of our trip waited.

On the way, we passed through Albuquerque, New Mexico. Albuquerque looks like any other medium-sized city. Bustling freeways, mile after mile of strip malls and big-box stores, and traffic. Did I mention the traffic?

We contemplated turning north to visit Taos and Los Alamos, because there were things we wanted to see in both places, but it was important we make it to Clovis for the night, so we passed, saving that for a different Lap Around America, perhaps.

After several days of staying happily on the backroads of Utah, Colorado, and northern New Mexico, the few miles we had to spend on I-25 through Albuquerque were enough to last us. Soon enough, we were on Highway 60, which was much more our speed. We passed through small New Mexico towns— Mountainair, Willard, Vaughn, Fort Sumner, Melrose. Many seemed to have been hit hard in the economic downturn of 2008 and hadn't yet recovered.

Along with cemeteries, we love to find old abandoned buildings and walk through them, if it doesn't feel as though we are trespassing. We found an old church just outside a town called Yeso that had a great vibe to it, sitting back off the road with both front and back doors standing wide open. The entire interior had been stripped clean, and there was evidence of an interesting battle between a spray painting vandal and someone who seemed to represent the church. The vandal would paint graffiti in the form of prayers, while the other would come and paint over them. There was quite an exchange between the two.

Site of the great graffiti battle

It was fascinating to me to compare our own ruins, like this church, which was less than a century old, with the 900-year-old buildings we had seen earlier in the day. We think of ourselves as modern and master builders, but I think those ancient indigenous people had something on the ball, too. I wonder if anyone will wander through our own ruins in the year 3000, wondering what killed us all and why we abandoned our cities. Sorry. These are the thoughts from the overactive imagination of a writer, I suppose.

When we were still about fifty miles from Clovis, I was doing what I normally did as we drove—looking out the side window and daydreaming—when I heard a little "thump."

"What was that?"

"I don't know. It almost looked like a spider. Please tell me there isn't a spider big enough to make a thump when we run over it?"

"Thank goodness for Google!"

I opened my browser and searched to see if New Mexico has

tarantulas. It turns out that, not only are there tarantulas, but August is their mating season, which makes them much more active. Which means they often wander onto highways and get run over.

"Well," I said, "Good news and bad news. The bad news is, yes, that was probably a tarantula."

Dawn shuddered, but didn't say anything.

"The good news is, we probably killed it. As long as we didn't just piss it off, so it picks the car up and throws it into the ditch, we're all right."

"I'm not getting out of the car again until we're out of New Mexico."

Of course, that was an exaggeration. As deathly afraid as Dawn is of any spider, let alone a spider that makes a thump when you run over it, I did persuade her to come into the hotel with me in Clovis.

Day Twelve

You might be coming into this book cold, not knowing much about me. So, I have to share just a small bit. I was born on February 3, 1960, exactly one year after what Don McLean called "the day the music died" in his epic song "American Pie."

Because I was born on the first anniversary of Buddy Holly's death, and because I had three older sisters and an older brother in the house, I've heard and been fascinated by his music, life, and death since I can remember. I have strong memories of dancing around the kitchen with my mom and sisters while "Maybe Baby" or "Peggy Sue" played on our old turntable. As I grew up and my musical tastes evolved to include The Doors, The Beatles, Led Zeppelin, and Pink Floyd, I never lost my love of Buddy's music.

That's why, after I published my first two memoirs, when I decided to write fiction, I wrote a book called *Rock 'n Roll Heaven* It was the story of a small-time rocker named Jimmy "Guitar" Velvet, who described himself as "not a has-been, but a never-was." Jimmy dies early in the book and is transported to Rock 'n Roll Heaven, where he meets Buddy Holly and the other icons of fifties, sixties, and seventies music.

Here's my confession. I wrote that book just so I could bring Buddy Holly back to life in some small way. I wanted to spend time with him and pay homage to what kind of a person and artist I believe he was.

When we were planning our trip, then, my number one goal was to hit a few of the Buddy Holly sights. His hometown of Lubbock, Texas, yes, but also Clovis, New Mexico, where the Norman Petty Studios are. That's the place where Buddy cut the vast majority of his greatest hits, like "Oh Boy," "That'll Be the Day," and "Not Fade Away." The soundtrack of my childhood.

Visiting the Norman Petty Studios is a unique experience. It has more early rock memorabilia than many museums, but it's not set up that way. Instead, it's a completely interactive tour with no off-limits areas, and no velvet ropes keeping you from standing where the great early stars of rock 'n' roll stood.

Our hosts for the tour were Kenneth Broad and his friend Jay, a much younger man who helps out around the studio as a labor of love. Kenneth was a longtime friend of both Norman and Vi Petty, and before she passed, she asked him to serve as caretaker of the historic studio. He agreed and has done just that. He makes himself available to lead tours of any size through the studio.

A small entrance area features dozens of framed photographs of all the artists who recorded here, including Roy Orbison, Jimmy Gilmer and The Fireballs ("Sugar Shack"), and many others. I glanced toward the corner where an old fashioned Coke machine stood. Kenneth slipped me a wink and nodded.

"Is that the same Coke machine that Buddy and the Crickets would have used?"

"One and the same. A bottle of Coke was a nickel back then."

Straight ahead was a large picture of Norman and Vi Petty that mostly covered a window. I peeked around the picture and looked straight into the master control room for the studio. This is where I learned we weren't simply in a museum. Jay saw me peeking in and said, "Want to go in and have a look around?"

I nodded. Of course I did.

Jay flipped the lights on and I found myself standing in the room where Norman Petty twisted the dials and created the Clovis Sound, which launched the careers of Buddy Holly and The Crickets and many others. There was an old mixing board, a master tape reel-to-reel for playback, and the aura of history. Sitting casually on top of the board was a pair of ancient headphones.

"These were Norman's," Jay said. "Why don't you put them

on and sit down in his chair?"

I did. Dawn took a picture of me sitting there, in Norman's chair, in his master studio, wearing his headphones, thrilled. Stunned, but thrilled.

Shawn, in his own rock 'n roll Heaven

Jay pulled another rabbit out of his hat. "Would you like to hear the original master recording of "Heartbeat"?

I did.

When he played that song, which just happens to be one of my top three favorite Buddy Holly songs, from the original master tape, through the original studio speakers—I admit it, it was so beautiful, so overwhelming, it made me cry.

That would really have been enough, but we were just getting started. Kenneth and Jay introduced me to another older gentleman named David Bigham, who was a member of The Roses, and who sang on many of the great recordings made there.

We went into the actual studio where Buddy Holly, Roy Orbison, Jimmy Gilmer, et al, recorded their music. Many of the original instruments are still there, including an organ, celesta, and guitars, and the actual microphones used to record the hits. Kenneth offered to let me play something if I wanted, but all my musical talent is in my ears, so I demurred.

After we toured the studio, he led us to another area clear in the back—a small apartment with a kitchen, bathroom, bedroom, and living room. Norman Petty didn't believe he could put a time clock on creativity, so instead of charging by the hour, like most studios, he charged by the finished songs they produced. So he made this small apartment at the back of the studio available to the artists while they were recording.

It felt surreal to sit in the chair Kenneth pointed at, saying, "That's where Buddy liked to sit and drink his coffee to wake up." In the living room is an old couch and coffee table. On the coffee table is a book with a picture of Buddy and the Crickets sitting on, yes, that same couch. As I said: surreal.

I glanced at a clock and noted that we had already spent two hours in the studio. It had passed in a blink. I knew I could happily stay there for many more hours, but I was aware that Kenneth and Jay had a music festival coming up that they needed to prepare for. I never felt they were hurrying me along, but I wanted to respect their time, so we got ready to leave.

Before we did, Jay took one last picture of Dawn and me, standing in the middle of the recording studio. I was wearing a smile that would need to be surgically removed.

I want to take a moment and thank Jay, Kenneth, and David for sharing the history of the place and music they love with fans. It filled my heart and spirit to overflowing. By the way, the tour of the studio is completely free. However, there is a discreet box that sits in the room you first enter that accepts donations for the upkeep of the studio. I happily contributed.

I walked out of the Norman Petty Studios in a happy daze, wonderful music ringing in my ears.

We climbed into the Silver Bullet and got on Highway 70,

heading south. We'd been traveling and sightseeing for almost two weeks, and we were ready for a little break. A small vacation from our vacation. We had spent a dozen nights in crappy little roadside motels, so I found a nice hotel in Roswell that we could stay in for a couple of nights. It would be a nice break to not have to carry the bags in and out for a day.

On the way to Roswell, we drove through Portales, which had the best "Welcome to ..." sign we saw on the entire trip. It said, *Welcome to Portales, Home of 17,000 Friendly People (And three or four old grouches*.) Of course, I've never been very bright, so I turned to Dawn and said, "If we moved here, they'd have to change the sign." The look she gave me told me I didn't need to explain further. Grouch.

I think that spending almost two consecutive weeks cooped up in the car might be taking a toll on us. Time for a little break!

Day Thirteen

If the name "Roswell" is burned into your consciousness, it's probably because of the Unidentified Flying Object that ostensibly crashed here. On June 8, 1947, the *Roswell Daily Record* ran a headline that read, "RAAF Captures Flying Saucer on Ranch in Roswell Region." If that's not an attention-grabbing headline, I don't know what is.

Shortly after that, the government stepped in, displayed portions of a downed weather balloon, and a million conspiracy theories were born.

Did a UFO actually crash on a Roswell ranch? Were there little green men, or tall gray men found? I have no way of knowing, but by nature I remain a skeptic.

However, our first stop in Roswell was the International UFO Museum and Research Center. That's a pretty serious name for a place that was a lot of fun. Yes, there are a few cheesy exhibits, (the alien autopsy springs first to mind) but there's also a lot of straightforward information—newspaper clippings, signed affidavits from the principals of the 1947 crash, etc. If you wander through with an open mind, it isn't out of the realm of possibility that there was at least some kind of a cover up.

There was some kind of a UFOlogist convention going on while we were there, so there were quite a few people wandering around who had forgotten more about the whole event than I will ever know. And, they are willing to tell you their theories, if you give them a chance. Sometimes, even if you don't give them a chance—simple eye contact can be enough encouragement.

It was nice spending as much time as we wanted walking through the exhibits. One thing we've found is that even though we were taking two months for this trip, we still felt pressure to keep moving. We wanted to make it all the way to Key West, Florida, then up to Maine before heading toward home, so we knew we couldn't dawdle too much.

The rest of the day, while Americans everywhere were enjoying the third day of their weekend with barbecues and road trips, we retired to our little hotel room, which had a kitchenette, good cable television, and a swimming pool. It even had laundry facilities, so by Monday night, we were refreshed and ready to hit the road again.

Day Fourteen

On many days, we try to cram two, three, or four stops into our itinerary. This day, we had just one: Carslbad Caverns. One of my favorite writers is Kurt Vonnegut, and in his book *Player Piano,* he wrote that Carlsbad Caverns was sacrificed to build EPICAC XIV, the supercomputer that ran the world. Ever since I read that as a teenager, I wanted to investigate the caverns for myself, looking for some trace of Vonnegut's computer.

We got to the parking lot a little before noon and thought we might want to have our picnic lunch before we descended into the caverns. There was a single picnic table at the end of the parking lot, but as soon as we stepped out of the car, we were blasted by the 90-plus degree heat. We looked at the picnic table, baking in the direct sun, with no shade available anywhere, and got right back into the Silver Bullet and turned the AC on high. We sat perched on the edge of the parking lot, looking down at the open vista that graces the area surrounding the national park.

While we had lunch, we watched two brown hawks riding the wind currents. I had no idea if they were hunting or just enjoying the freedom of flight, but they rode the wind currents with unmatched skill. In fact, in the 30 minutes we watched them, they didn't flap their wings a single time. It was like watching a master class in piloting.

When it comes to the caverns, there are choices. You can hike down through the natural entrance, then turn around hike and back up, or you can ride an elevator both ways, or walk one way and ride the other.

We elected to compromise and walk down through the natural entrance, then ride the elevator back to the top. A few things to keep in mind if you plan to visit Carlsbad: It is 56 degrees inside, year-round. We read that in advance, and so we took our jackets. Even though that sounds cool, bordering on chilly, we found that because of the humidity and working up a sweat by hiking, we didn't need them. So, we carried our jackets with us the whole way for nothing.

You should also be aware there is a strong odor that most people find unpleasant, or worse. I saw a few people with weaker stomachs gagging a bit when they hit the entrance. Others, I saw, had sprayed something on a handkerchief and covered their mouths and noses with that. Me? I just breathed through my mouth after that first pungent inhale. That solved the problem for me.

We assumed that the smell is produced by piles of bat guano, but a park ranger later told us that's not correct—that the cave swallows that live in abundant numbers at the front of the cave cause the smell. Whatever it is, it's potent.

The path to the bottom is steep, dark, and in some spots, a little slippery. The hike is about a mile and a quarter from the natural entrance down to the Big Room. (By the way, every time I refer to the Big Room, I first call it the Great Room, then have to go back and fix it. Must be too many years as a Realtor.)

As I mentioned earlier, Dawn has a few minor phobias. Darkness, enclosed spaces, heights and spiders are on her Mount Rushmore of fears. It was too dark to see if there were spiders there, but otherwise, the inside of Carlsbad was three for three. She was a trouper, though, and did great. The trails were pretty wide in most places, and the lookouts all had railings you could hold onto.

You'd think walking down would be easy, and it is at first. Eventually, though, your thighs and calves tighten up from trying not to go too fast. From then on, it's a bit of a battle with gravity. By the time we got to the bottom, we were fairly well worn out.

At the bottom, a sign offers two choices: get on the elevator back to the surface, or take another mile-and-a-quarter hike around the Big Room. The interior is dank. The epic size of the caverns had been cool to see, but we weren't sure we would get that much more out of walking around the Big Room.

Finally, after we stood there contemplating our sore feet for a minute, Dawn said, "C'mon, let's go. When are we ever going to get back to the bottom of Carlsbad Caverns?"

Good point. Off we went. I'm so glad we did. The best parts of the tour were there within the Big Room. One was seeing the remnant of a rickety old ladder nailed to the side of a cliff that early explorers used to descend parts of the cavern. We both agreed that if we had needed that ladder to see what was there, Carlsbad Caverns would remain unexplored to this day.

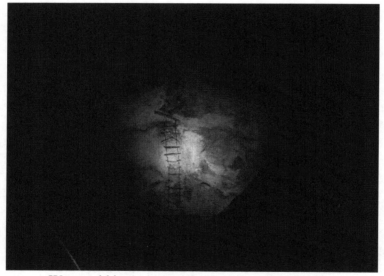

We would have never been caught on this ladder

Just how big *is* the Big Room? A little more than eight acres, the largest single cave chamber in North America by volume. There are incredible displays of stalagmites and stalactites all around, forming into a million different shapes and sizes. I constantly told myself: *Stalactites come from the ceiling, because the name has a "c". Stalagmites grow from the ground, because the name has a "g".* The things we learn in childhood that somehow stick with us.

The parks service has the elevators well organized. They are slightly cramped, though, because as many people as possible are put on each trip. You make a smooth trip up through solid rock. Not that Dawn would know; her eyes were closed the entire time.

Once we made it to the surface, we hit the gift shop—I probably haven't mentioned Dawn's magnet habit, but it's akin to any addiction—then wandered down for the day's last highlight, to wait for dusk, when the Brazilian free-tailed bats come pouring out of the bat cave. After the long hike, we were more than happy to sit in the shade of the comfortable amphitheater and wait. About half an hour before the bats appeared, a park ranger gave us another highly informative talk about the flying rodents. I am thankful for all that I have learned from park rangers.

I didn't take any pictures as the bats emerged, for a very good reason. The rangers insist that all electronics – GoPros, cellphones, video cameras—be turned completely off, as they bother the bats. It was an unusual experience to sit with a large group of people, all of them living in the moment, none of them videoing or Facebook Live–broadcasting the event. It was really nice.

The bats were the stars of the show. The caverns house several hundred thousand bats that are waiting to migrate to Mexico at the end of October, and they come out at dusk every night. They emerge in a silent school, swirl together in a counterclockwise double helix to gain altitude, and take off on their nightly hunt. In the air, they are not nearly as graceful as the hawks we watched earlier in the day. In fact, to my eye, they looked to be laboring a bit, but they will travel 30 miles or more to feed and drink before returning to the cave to sleep and care for their offspring. And in a black cave with hundreds of thousands of other occupants, how do they locate their own offspring? The ranger said it was through memory of where they left them, and recognizing the smell of their own. Nature is a beautiful thing.

Walking up the trail back to our parking spot, where we had watched the hawks soar, it felt like we had been gone a very long time. We were bone-tired. Although we had entertained the idea of driving into Texas after the caverns, we realized we wanted nothing so much as a bed for the night. So, we made the short drive back to Carlsbad, found a pretty awful little roadside motel, and crashed.

Day Fifteen

New Mexico had been a pleasant surprise for us. When we daydreamed about the trip, we thought of seeing Texas, Florida, and Maine, but New Mexico never crossed our minds. Having spent a few days there, though, it made our list of places we'd like to visit again.

However, the southeastern corner of the state doesn't have a lot to recommend it: flat, sandy scrub and muddy rivers are the only features as far as the eye can see. We'd been on Highway 128 east toward Texas about half an hour before we noticed that the only vehicles sharing the road with us were semis and company pickups. The entire length of that highway, we never saw another car. We soon understood why. Anyone driving Highway 128 risks having their fillings jarred out of their head at several points. The joys of driving back roads! There is so little non-commercial traffic heading into Texas on that road, there wasn't even a sign welcoming us to the state.

Once in Texas, we turned north toward Lubbock. Since our number one destination in the state was San Antonio, this was a bit out of the way. This trip has never been about the strategically optimal route, though, so why start now?

The impetus was the Lubbock Flash himself, Buddy Holly. After our great visit to the Clovis studios where he recorded his greatest music, we wanted to wrap up the Buddy part of our tour with a visit to his hometown.

Lubbock honors its favorite son with The Buddy Holly Center. Relatively new, it has a permanent Buddy Holly wing and other parts that offer rotating exhibits on other artists and topics. The day we visited, the center was paying tribute to women in rock. A worthy subject, and one I am interested in, but honestly, it didn't do much for me. It was basically just pictures of Patty Smythe, Chrissy Hynde, Stevie Nicks, and Deborah Harry. Cool enough as far as it went, but not a lot of interesting facts or stories about them.

Likewise, the eighteen-minute movie about Buddy Holly that is constantly playing was well done, but if you're a Buddy fan, there's not much new to discover.

The museum part was something else again, though. Being in Buddy's hometown and having access to the Holley family obviously had its advantages. Please note that the spelling in the previous sentence is not a typo. Buddy Holly was born Charles Hardin Holley but changed his name when he went into music.

The Holly exhibit is worth the price of admission. I was mesmerized by several exhibits, including the glasses Buddy was wearing on February 3, 1959, when his plane went down in an Iowa cornfield. The lenses were thought to be destroyed in the crash, and the frames themselves were lost for many years. About twenty years after the crash, a Cerro Gordo County sheriff in Iowa was cleaning out an evidence locker, found the tagged glasses and returned them to the Holley family. It was a tangible connection to rock 'n' roll's first great tragedy.

There were also photos I'd never seen before, some of Buddy's guitars, and one item that was special to me. In my book *Rock 'n Roll Heaven,* I had described a specific guitar strap Buddy had made and hand-tooled himself. I knew it existed because I'd seen a picture of it, but now it was right there in front of me.

I could have spent hours in the museum staring at all the Buddy memorabilia, but we had one more stop to make in Lubbock, and it was already getting late. When we'd entered Texas earlier in the day, we had joined the Central time zone and lost an hour on our clock.

Before leaving Lubbock, I wanted to visit Buddy's grave and pay my respects. He had fired my imagination and given me so many happy hours of music, I couldn't leave without doing that.

We found the cemetery with no trouble, but had a heck of a time finding Buddy's grave. I think I had expected something big and grand, but there is just a tiny headstone that reads: *In loving memory of our son, Buddy Holley.* His family name was restored in death, as I believe he would have wanted it. He is buried right next to his parents, who have similar headstones. On this trip, we would see some grand and awe-inspiring headstones, but Buddy's impressed me with its modesty.

Buddy's grave, lovely in its simplicity

I was feeling somber when we left the cemetery and drove through the outskirts of Lubbock, so I looked for something more cheerful before we left town.

I found it in the form of Prairie Dog Town. Prairie Dog Town was the brainchild of a gentleman named K.N. Clapp, in 1935. Clapp was concerned that the black-tailed prairie dog was in danger of extinction. So, he trapped two pairs, built an enclosure, and oversaw the growth of the operation until his death 34 years later. Forty-seven years after his death, his dream of Prairie Dog Town is still thriving.

Those original four prairie dogs have bloomed into hundreds of the cute little buggers. They have tunnels and holes over several acres where they pop up and down like a real-life game of whack-a-mole. We were walking along the fence line to get a better look when the skies opened up and a Texas gully washer dropped on our heads. Where we come from, you usually get a little warning before it rains, but this was like someone turned on a shower overhead.

We ran to a roofed picnic area, but the wind was bringing the rain in sideways, so we sprinted to the car and waited the storm out. We were already learning that these downpours don't last long, and five minutes later, it was done. We spent another half hour watching the prairie dogs, then got in the car to leave.

On the way out of the park, though, we discovered that several of the little critters had managed to tunnel their way out of their enclosures and were sitting up alongside the road, looking at us hungrily. I'm sure there are rules against feeding them, but I'd like to see someone explain that to Dawn when she has a chance to feed a prairie dog. I am not the right man for that job, I can tell you.

She grabbed a box of raisins and within a minute had one particularly hardy fellow, whom I named Fred, literally eating out of her hand. We'd been on the road for fifteen days and had covered thousands of miles and much of the western portion of the United States, but Dawn said that was her favorite part of the trip so far.

That's one of the lessons I'm taking from this trip. The big, planned events are cool, but it's the unexpected little moments that sneak up on you out of nowhere that stick with you.

We got on Highway 87 South and made it about a third of the way to San Antonio before we gave up and found another in what had started to feel like an endless series of roadside motels, in Big Springs, Texas. Everything is big in Texas, but we never saw any springs as we passed through.

Day Sixteen

It had been hot the entire trip. We got a little break driving down the Oregon coast, but as soon as we turned inland, the temps climbed back into the 90s and we'd hit at least that mark every day since. It hadn't been that bad, though, because we'd been in desert in Utah and New Mexico. Now, we were in Texas, and a different kind of heat: Oppressive. Wet. Blech. I suppose that if you were born here, it would feel normal. For me, as a native Pacific Northwesterner, it was pretty awful.

Looking ahead, I saw Louisiana, Alabama, Florida, and Georgia on our itinerary, with no real hope of cooler weather any time soon. So, we prepared to spend a lot of time in the air-conditioned Silver Bullet, dreaming of the cool autumn days we knew were coming in Maine and Vermont.

My friend Al Kunz, of the Big Al's Books and Pals website, told me before we left that we were probably making a mistake by driving counterclockwise around the country. His logic was that if we drove clockwise, we would scoot through the northern part of the United States in August or early September, long before the bad weather. Plus, it would be a little cooler for our drive through the southern part of the country. I couldn't argue with his logic, but if we had done that, we would hit the northeast corner of the United States in early to mid-September, and we wanted to be there for prime leaf-peeping season, which doesn't start until October. So, we were rolling the dice and taking our chances with snowstorms in Michigan, Minnesota, or Wyoming, and suffering the heat for now.

Today was mostly about the drive. We wanted to get to San Antonio by nightfall, so we didn't have a lot of big stops planned. I'm not sure we could have stopped a lot even if we'd wanted to. There's just not much around this part of the country but back roads, long, flat stretches of nothing, and the occasional small town. One of my blog readers said this part of Texas is so flat you can throw a ball, stand on a sardine can, and watch your dog run for days.

We passed through one of those small towns, Sterling City, population under a thousand. It didn't have much to recommend it, other than the fact it is the county seat for Sterling County. About ten miles outside Sterling City, we saw an arched sign for a cemetery. We pass cemeteries every day, but this one was unusual. Cemeteries are attached to towns. Montvale Cemetery was in the middle of nowhere, without a building or other road in sight.

Intrigued, we pulled in. Eventually, we located a sign that told the story of the cemetery without a town. Montvale had been formed in 1884 and grew to be a prosperous town. The first school opened in the late 1880s. Then, in 1889, a local businessman, R.B. Cummins, decided to start his own town five miles over and named it Cummins. Of course he did. Why else would you start a town if you didn't want to name it after yourself? Between some of the population leaving for Cummins and the rest for Sterling when it was founded in 1891, Montvale was deserted. Except for the cemetery, of course, which now stands lonely amid flat fields and scrub brush.

Nature is slowly reclaiming the cemetery, despite someone's efforts to keep it at bay. Long grass and sapling trees are pushing up everywhere. In another half-century or so, when the sign inevitably falls, it's likely there will be no trace left of Montvale Cemetery.

Some of the headstones are better maintained than others, so we were able to wander through the waves of heat and humidity and find small stories that are told in few words. Here's one that touched my heart: *Virginia M. Holloway, Born November 26, 1885, Died June 6, 1897. Sweet Virgie unto earth/A little while was given/She plumed her wing for flight/And soared away to heaven.* It may be because I lost a granddaughter named Aubrey

Ruth when she was just a baby, but grave markers for little ones tear at my heart.

We made one small side trip on the way to San Antonio. We drove to Comfort, Texas, to see another memorial that marks a little-known event in American history. The Japanese Balloon Bomb memorial in Oregon was sad and somber because it was so unlikely, such a tragic twist of fate. The memorial in Comfort is more about what man is capable of doing to man. It memorializes the loss of 40 German-American lives in the Battle of Nueces, or the Nueces Massacre, depending on which side of the issue you stand.

Long story short, there was a large settlement of Germans in the Hill Country of Texas at the start of the Civil War. They were, overall, not friendly to the idea of slavery. When Texas voted to secede from the Union, many of the "no" votes came from them. This put them under scrutiny and suspicion. When the war started outright, some of the German men decided to ride into Mexico, then across to Union-controlled New Orleans, where they could join the Union army.

Understandably, Confederate forces were not crazy about a group of local men joining the other side, and so set out to stop them. On August 9, 1862, the Confederate forces caught up to the German Texans along the Nueces River. A battle followed, with the Germans taking the heaviest losses.

Eventually, the remainder of the German forces broke and fled. So far, so good, as far as calling it the Battle of Nueces. However, after that, the surviving prisoners and those who fled into the river were hunted down and killed as well. A point toward calling it the Nueces Massacre.

I don't pretend to know the truth of the situation, but this memorial presents a powerful picture of loss and grief. Several of the remaining German Texans bought a lot and had this memorial built by local stonemasons in 1865.

Where the Japanese Balloon Bomb Memorial is hidden in a

forest, the Nueces Massacre Memorial is right in Comfort, alongside a quiet residential street and right across from a church. One thing that caught my eye is that the flag flying above the memorial only has 36 stars—the same number of states as were in the Union the day the memorial was dedicated.

Between Comfort and San Antonio, we were attacked by a horde of moths. All right, "attacked" might be a bit dramatic, especially since we were the ones doing the killing, but we couldn't help it. No matter how slowly we traveled, clouds of the little things threw themselves at our front grill. We killed so many, we felt as though we were wiping out the entire population of the state of Texas. Not so, though, as there was apparently an infinite supply of the wispy, white-winged little bugs.

By the time we pulled in to San Antonio, it was a little after 5 p.m.

"Good timing," Dawn said. "The only city we're going to hit today, and we manage to time it right at rush hour."

It wasn't bad, though. We're used to Seattle traffic, which is slow-and-go or a parking lot at almost any time of the day, seven days a week. The traffic in San Antonio, at least on this day, was mellow and manageable. I had found a nice hotel downtown and near the Riverwalk that had a good rate, so I booked us in for two nights.

We threw our bags into the room and went for a walk around San Antonio. We immediately got the dichotomy of the city. On the one hand, it is a modern, booming city. On the other, there are remnants of history everywhere. Old churches, restored buildings, and historical markers abound.

As tourists in the city, we knew we had to do three things— see the Alamo, visit some of the old churches, and eat some Texas barbecue. We saved the first two for our full day, but walked along the Riverwalk until we found the third. If you're not familiar with Riverwalk, it is a network of walkways along the San Antonio River, which flows below street level through the heart of the city. In 1921, the river flooded, killing fifty people. A plan was put in place to build dams and otherwise redirect the river so it could be controlled. Now, Riverwalk is a tourist attraction in its own right, like a lower-key, classier version of New Orleans' French Quarter.

We walked along it for a mile or so, until our noses drew us to a barbecue place called The County Line. We threw caution to the wind and ordered the All You Can Eat Whole Mess of BBQ. It wasn't just all we could eat; it was much, much more than we could eat. It was delicious, but we had to ask for several doggy bags to carry the bulk of it back to our room. Happily for us, the room came with a refrigerator, so we had another meal for the next day.

Overall, we didn't get lost often on this trip, at least while on our feet, but we got totally turned around in San Antonio. GPS was no help. Finally, about midnight, Dawn spotted an old building we had stared at on the way out of the hotel. We had been wandering around lost about two blocks from the hotel. JRR Tolkien said, "Not all who wander are lost." Typically, that applies to us, except in downtown San Antonio.

Day Seventeen

Another blessed day when we were not driving, so we didn't have to pack up before leaving for the day. We were becoming skilled at packing and loading, but it still felt good to put down roots in the same place two nights in a row. It was also nice to leave the Silver Bullet parked in the garage.

We set off on foot, heading for The Alamo. If you've never been to San Antonio, you might not be aware that The Alamo is literally in the middle of the city. The city grew up around it, and now has it surrounded.

We weren't in any hurry to get there straight away, so we took one of our typical circuitous routes, which led us past a museum we didn't know existed: the Briscoe Western Art Museum. We were just walking down the street when we noticed an eight-foot statue of a cowpoke busting a wild bronco. Kinda hard to miss.

Among the impressive pieces on display were Santa Anna's parade saddle, Pancho Villa's sword, and personal items of the heroes of The Alamo—Davey Crockett's bear knife and comb, for instance, were proudly displayed. There was a scale model of The Alamo, featuring tiny figures. Seeing the little model before the real thing gave us perspective on exactly how outmanned the Texas troops were that day.

Accompanying the historical exhibits was a wide display of western art. The museum doesn't look big from the outside, but it manages to display a massive number of paintings, statues and other displays inside.

After killing 90 minutes in the museum, we forced ourselves back into the humid 95-degree weather and made our way to Misión San Antonio de Valero, more commonly called The Alamo. The downtown location makes for some strange bedfellows—there is a Fuddruckers and a Ripley's Believe it or

Not! Museum within a block or two of the famed landmark.

There are two ways to tour the Alamo. You can plan your visit and book a tour with one of the knowledgeable park rangers, or you can be us. Maybe I should say *me*, as I am the one in charge of planning. Either way, I had not planned ahead, and all the ranger-led tours were booked for the day by the time we arrived. Happily, there is also a self-guided audio tour.

Never to be forgotten

Here are a few things we learned: The Alamo is not as big as it once was. The main buildings are still standing, but the small settlement around them once occupied a lot of what is now valuable downtown real estate. The buildings and rooms themselves are also smaller than I would have guessed from the movies and TV shows I've seen. Also, although The Alamo is hallowed ground to Texans, the defenders came from all over the world, not just Texas. I learned that some fighters from Ireland gave their lives, which is where I trace my own heritage.

Of course, it's the story behind the Alamo that has stirred

imaginations ever since Santa Anna overran it. You can feel the weight of that history while walking around the grounds. There are several memorials in the walls, but my favorite was the one that recognized the sacrifice of the men from Gonzales, Texas. While Santa Anna was gathering his forces and establishing his lines, the men inside The Alamo, knowing how badly they were outnumbered, sent messengers to seek help. In most cases, this was futile, but thirty-two men from Gonzales volunteered. They helped reinforce some of the weaker defenses in the fort. All thirty-two died in the final attack.

The grounds and buildings that remain are somber and lovely. In several spots, we just sat and reflected on what had occurred there so long ago. It wasn't hard to do. That seemed to be the mood of the visitors. Yes, there were the inevitable selfie sticks and the kids running around, not understanding what had transpired there, but the adults seemed to feel the weight of it.

After a few hours in The Alamo, we walked back to the hotel. Our Fitbits told us that we had completed our 10,000 steps by early afternoon. Here's something odd we noticed about Texas, or more specifically, San Antonio. We had always heard about Texas hospitality and friendliness. Sad to say, we didn't see much of that in evidence on our trip. I'm the kind of person that smiles and says "hi" to just about everyone. I love to engage with people. In San Antonio, that wasn't returned much, if at all. Time after time, I would nod, smile, and say hello to someone we met. Each time, without fail, they looked away and didn't respond. Maybe they just didn't like the cut of my jib.

We had one last San Antonio sight to visit—Mission San José y San Miguel de Aguayo, or, as it is more commonly known, the Mission San José.

Walking through these two sites, I realized how important the Catholic Church had been to the development of the Mexican territories, including what we call Texas today. The driving forces were the Spanish hunger for gold and riches, and the

Church's desire to spread its doctrine. Signs of Catholicism are strong everywhere in San Antonio, hundreds of years later.

✓ We have learned the value of watching the movie whenever we go to a visitor's center. I'm glad we did that again at Mission San José. The film presented a history not just of this specific mission, but of the whole mission era in Texas. The Mission San José, being a bit more on the edge of San Antonio, is more complete than The Alamo, and we were surprised by the size of the grounds. We were able to walk hundreds of yards over grass and through trees before we ran into a wall.

It's easy to lose track of time wandering around the immense mission, where there are things to see and learn everywhere. We spent a few quiet, sweaty minutes inside the church itself, imagining what it must have been like to attend services there.

I learned a lot at this stop, much of it relating to how the Catholic Church related to the First People who had lived in the area for 10,000 years. The Catholics thought of the natives as "savages" and wanted to "civilize" them. The Spaniards and the church brought much more than their version of civilization, though—they also brought European diseases to which the natives had no immunity. Many of the native people gave up their hunter/gatherer way of life to join the Mission lifestyle. After a century or so, both the Spanish and the church proper left the area, and a new culture emerged—a blend of Spanish and native culture known as Tejano.

We were hoping to accomplish a lot on this trip. We wanted to see things we'd never seen, get new perspectives on our country, and learn the kind of history that doesn't jump out at you from a book. So far, so fine.

We found a carwash on the way back to the hotel and did the best we could to wipe the bugs off the front grill of the Silver Bullet and restore her to something resembling her initial glory. Assuming, that is, a Hyundai Sonata can ever be glorious.

We were dead on our feet by the time we got back to the room, so we collapsed on the king-sized bed and went to work on the leftover barbecue from last night. There are a lot of things we're going to miss about Texas, but barbecue tops the list.

Day Eighteen

In many ways, it felt like this whole trip had its genesis when I went to Austin, Texas, back in March. If I hadn't attended the Smarter Artist Summit there, I might very well have still been back in Enumclaw, selling real estate. So, it felt important to me to take Dawn through the city that started it all.

We drove straight through to Austin, where we met two of my writer friends, Marlayna Sanders and Bobby Adair, for lunch. It's not much of a drive, so we got there early. Austin has evolved into a non-traditional Texas city. Most of Texas is conservative by nature, but Austin lives by the unofficial slogan, "Keep Austin Weird." I'm sure there are parts of the city that reflect more typical Texas values, but the part I've seen is markedly more liberal. Austin has become a hotbed of artistic activities. Every March, it hosts the SXSW (South by Southwest) Festival, during which musicians and filmmakers from all over the world descend on the city.

We parked on Commerce Street and walked up and down looking at the funky little shops and businesses. It reminded me of Broadway on Capitol Hill, back in Seattle, which I always loved.

Eventually, we hooked up with Bobby, Marlayna, and her husband, Alan. Here's a word of advice: If you'd ever like to get a word in edgewise, it's probably better not to sit down at a table full of writers. We swapped stories for about ninety minutes, and I would swear a few might even have been true.

Back in the Silver Bullet, I pulled out the atlas and realized we had a problem. By the time we were much down the road, it would be late Friday afternoon. Houston lay dead ahead. Any number of people had warned me to avoid Houston and its traffic if possible, but whatever I did, I was never to hit it during rush hour. I'm sure doing so on a Friday wouldn't improve our chances. So, I set about finding us a route that bypassed Houston.

Typically, it's pretty easy to miss a city, but Houston is truly sprawling. As a tourist, I had no idea where the bad traffic would start, so I wanted a route that gave a wide berth to the whole mess.

At the same time, we wanted to end our day's travel in Galveston, just a short drive to the southeast of Houston. You might be asking, "Why, Shawn? Why did you want to spend the night in Galveston?"

A reasonable question. There are three answers, really: Glen Campbell, a great disaster, and my step-dad. Glen Campbell, of course, had a big hit with the song, "Galveston." I grew up loving it, though in itself that's not enough to get me to drive out of the way to see it. Dawn and I had watched a documentary a year or so before that had told the story of the incredible storm that had hit Galveston in 1900. Finally, for some reason, my step-dad had spent time there, and he always got a funny look in his eyes when he talked about Galveston. He often brought it up, and it had come to take on a mythical connotation in my mind. I admit it's possible that he had just gotten lucky there once, and that was the reason for getting all misty-eyed, but I digress. Add all three of those together, and we were heading to Galveston, whether it made sense or not.

We followed a winding route, making so many highway changes that I can't come close to remembering them. Eventually, we found Surfside Beach and saw the Gulf of Mexico for the first time. We turned north toward Galveston Island, keeping the gulf on our right as we drove. We immediately began seeing an architectural style that would become old hat over the next few weeks: houses built on stilts. Not just a few of them, but essentially all of them.

We don't have a lot of houses built to withstand floods like this in Washington state, so it looked slightly foreign to our eyes. We felt as though we were a long way from home. The first chance we got, we pulled off onto a side road leading to the beach.

The first thing we saw was a sign that warned *Alligators may be present.* Uh-huh. That's a new one on us. We don't typically see alligators on the Washington coast. That wasn't the only thing that felt strange. On the west coast, the sun sets over the ocean. Here, peering out at the Gulf of Mexico, it was setting somewhere off to my right. It felt a bit like my world had shifted on its axis.

See ya later, alligator

I haven't written much about hotels, motels, bed and breakfasts, and the cost of staying at them, because it's mostly a personal decision. For this trip, we were on a budget, so we were mostly staying in modest accommodations. Here's something I've learned, though: The cost of a place doesn't have all that much bearing on how nice it is.

Our stay in Galveston was a perfect example. Galveston is a tourist town. We were hitting it on a Friday night. We were past the prime tourist season, but the town was still crowded and bustling when we drove through. Most hotels and motels had *no vacancy* signs lit up. So, our equation for a Galveston room looked something like this: Friday night + tourist town + lots of no vacancies = Shawn and Dawn spending a lot to stay in a pretty terrible place.

Do you remember the quote from Leo Tolstoy that goes, "All happy families are happy in the same way, but each unhappy family is unhappy in its own way?" Right. I think the same holds true for lodging. Great hotels are great in the same way, but awful motels each seem to find a way to be awful in their own unique way.

This one was awful in that it just felt … wrong. There were odd smells in what passed for a lobby, but the family who owned and operated the place were very kind. In fact, they had a turtle tank in one corner and got into an extended conversation with Dawn about how best to care for turtles. That's important to us, because we have a turtle named Kumar. We used to have a turtle named Harold, too, but he ran away. (How does a turtle manage to run away? That's probably the subject for another book.)

In any case, they gave us what I'm sure was their equivalent of the Presidential Suite. It had an odd vibe about it. Dawn gave me her look that said, "You owe me one," and I gave her my look that said, "I know, I know." This is the great thing about being married for a few years; you can have entire conversations without speaking.

Day Nineteen

One thing I've noticed is that the worse the motel, the earlier Dawn wants to get up and going early in the day. Silver linings. One last thing about this awful little motel, which I have not named because I really did like the owners: This would not be even close to the worst spot we would stay during the trip. More on that when we reach the Upper Peninsula of Michigan.

We had arrived in Galveston late enough Friday that we wanted to spend at least half a day or so cruising the town. Our first stop was at the memorial for the 6,000 people who died in the 1900 hurricane that ravaged the island. It wasn't the loveliest memorial we saw on the trip, but it was moving. It depicts a man with his arm raised in the air, pleading with God, and a woman holding an infant against her chest.

I've mentioned the humidity we'd encountered since we crossed over into Texas, but nothing matched what we felt in Galveston. It felt like it was raining even when it wasn't. And, on this Saturday, if it wasn't raining, it was about to rain.

We had parked the Silver Bullet on the opposite side of a busy four-lane road to see the Galveston Memorial, so on the way back, we stood waiting for all four lanes to clear. I felt a single raindrop. I turned to Dawn to say, "I think maybe it's about to rain," but she couldn't hear me because buckets of water from somewhere were being dumped directly on our heads. I've never seen or felt rain like it. We could not have gotten any wetter if we had jumped directly into the Gulf of Mexico.

We made it safely back to the car, but all the windows fogged up immediately. We almost bagged Galveston right there, but we are made of stronger stuff than that.

Our next stop was in front of the Beach Break store, where an eight-foot shark with legs stood holding a surfboard. I could see Dawn was immediately drawn to him, for his outstanding abs, if nothing else. I named him Bruce and did my best not to be jealous as Dawn asked me to take twenty or thirty pictures of her posing with Bruce.

After letting Dawn spend a few more quiet moments with Bruce, we took the Galveston Tree Tour. When Hurricane Ike tore across the island in 2008, it took many of the island's proud old trees with it. Many of the residents took that strong blast of lemon and did their best to turn it into lemonade by hiring sculptors to carve the dead trees into something beautiful and meaningful to them.

That's when I learned something else: There is a lot of old money in Galveston. We saw some of the most elegant mansions of the whole trip on our little tour of carved trees.

We chose to leave the island by taking a trip on the Galveston–Port Bolivar Ferry. The ferry operation is a well-oiled machine. Even with the weekend rush, boarding and exiting was smooth and fast. We enjoyed the ride and wished it had been a little longer. The cool ocean breezes went a long way toward drying out our still-wet clothing.

When we got off on the other side, we considered driving up to Port Arthur, Texas. It's not exactly a happening place, but it is where Janis Joplin was born and raised. I poked around the Internet, though, and saw that there wasn't a lot of Janis left to be seen there. The home she was raised in has been remodeled so much that almost all that's left of her there is a set of handprints in concrete. The local museum claims to have a display, but most of the online comments were along the lines of, "Hey, why don't you have more of Janis's stuff?" In the end, we decided to pass.

Instead, we drove quiet back roads up eastern Texas and over into Louisiana. I know I insulted Texans a couple of days back when I said the people we ran into there weren't friendly, but we found just the opposite in Louisiana.

Just after crossing the state line, we pulled off to get gas and refill our ice chest. Before I could add more ice, I had to drain the water. As I was wrestling the ice chest to the ground, a guy fifty feet away saw me and shouted, "Hey, you need some help with that?"

Dawn said, "I already like Louisiana better." And, she was right. Everywhere we met, people were friendly, said hello, and went out of their way to make us feel welcome.

That includes the bugs. It was in Louisiana that we met odd black bugs, everywhere. Called lovebugs, they look like they have two heads, one at each end of the body. I soon got into the habit of cleaning lovebugs off the grill every time I cleaned the windshield.

We drove straight through to Lafayette, Louisiana, for the night, because I had a couple of things planned in the area before our departure for New Orleans. Also, we hadn't been able to do laundry in about six days, and our pile of dirty clothes was reaching critical mass. So we checked into our little motel, which had a laundry room, and I volunteered to do the honors while Dawn relaxed. I took the pile of clothes and my laptop, so I could write my blog while the machines did their thing.

This, of course, is where I experienced my near-death experience that I related at the very beginning of the book, which left off with both Dawn and our desk clerk weak with laughter, and me gasping for air. My day started in Galveston with an involuntary second shower and ended with me almost dying in a tiny laundry room. Since Dawn had ultimately decided to rescue me, I forgave her flirtation with Bruce, the tall, well-built land shark in Galveston.

Day Twenty

We awoke in Lafayette with a busy day before us. For one thing, it was 9/11, and even though we were nowhere near Ground Zero in New York, I had found a place where we could mark the occasion and pay our respects.

The Lafayette 9/11 Memorial is very cool. The city asked for a steel beam from World Trade Center buildings 1 and 2, and New York sent them down. They stand 13.5 feet tall, matching the WTC buildings at exactly 1/100 scale. The base of the memorial has five sides to represent the Pentagon, which was also hit that day. Finally, the soil in the base was brought in from the field in Pennsylvania where Flight 93 went down.

It's not huge, but it is well done and thoughtful. A perfect place to mark the 15th anniversary of the tragedy. We thought it might be crowded, but the little plaza was almost empty. There were a few police present, and the local fire department had brought a truck down, but that was about it. It was early, though, so maybe there were ceremonies scheduled later in the day.

When we got back into the Silver Bullet to head toward New Orleans, I glanced at our odometer and realized we were past due for an oil change. Sundays in Lafayette are not great for finding businesses open. In fact, all the oil change places were closed, except for one—Walmart. We've been trying to avoid huge corporations wherever possible, but I didn't want to go another day or two without changing the oil, so we toddled off to Wal Marche.

Ever-efficient, they promised to have the oil change done in thirty minutes.

Ninety minutes later, I was still sitting in their waiting area, wishing I had left this whole chore for another day, another town. There were two sweet young girls working the counter, though, so we talked with them while we waited. Mostly, we talked about food, because it was getting to be afternoon and we hadn't eaten a bite.

"So, if you had company coming, and they were going to be in town for just one day, where would you take them?"

They looked at each other, smiled, and in unison, said: "Laura's."

By the time they were done telling me about Laura's, I was glad our car was done, because we were ready to start eating the tires behind us. There's something about hearing someone describe food in such loving detail that makes my stomach growl.

Their recommendation more than made up for the slow service. Laura's turned out to be one of the most memorable meals of the whole trip, though the restaurant itself, located in an unattractive strip mall, looks inauspicious.

When we walked in, I knew we'd found a winner. The first clue was the intoxicating smell. The second was the line, which was prodigious. Laura's serves soul food, and whatever wonderful image that just conjured in your mind, the reality was better. They open at 11 a.m. and close when they run out of food. They never have to stay open late, because the flocks inevitably descend.

They don't have a set menu, but just cook whatever they want on a particular day. This day was barbecue day. Dawn ordered what was described as ribs, but she didn't get a lot of rib. Mostly, the meat had been marinated and cooked until it fell off the bone. I got barbecue sausage, along with coleslaw, baked beans and rice with gravy. I'll just say this: If you ever find yourself in Lafayette, Louisiana, do yourself a favor and track down Laura's. Get there early, though—Dawn got the next-to-last serving of ribs, and there were a lot of disappointed people behind us in line.

As it was Sunday, a lot of customers had come straight from church. There were many Sunday dresses and men's suits on display, albeit with the ties loosened. Football games flickered on a couple of televisions scattered around the restaurant, but nobody paid any attention. I didn't see a single cellphone, either. Everybody just talked and laughed and ate. We felt like we had stepped back in time about twenty years.

On our way to New Orleans, we took a one-hour detour to hit Abita Springs, Louisiana, a town that, like so many we passed through, didn't have a lot going for it. Abita Springs has just a little more than 2,000 people and, aside from a small local brewery, there isn't a lot of commerce. The reason we drove an hour out of our way is the UCM Museum. While you're trying to puzzle that out, I'll tell you it's a play on words. If you pronounce it out loud, it sounds like "You See 'Em Museum." I knew I had to see any place willing to subject itself to such an awful name.

The UCM Museum, also called the Abita Mystery House, might just be the very best or very worst stop on any tour of America. Once upon a time, John Preble, on his own tour of America, stopped at the Tinkertown Museum in New Mexico. Preble thought to himself: *I would love to have a place just like this.*

And now he does.

It's hard to describe the Abita Mystery House to anyone who hasn't been there. It is housed in what looks like an old gas station that has been added to over the years. The admission is as reasonable as you could hope for—just three dollars. In the gift shop you can do all your Christmas shopping for any eccentric friends you might have. I was impressed with the "In Case You Touched Your Genitals" hand sanitizer and "Understand What Your Dog is Thinking" breath spray. I can't speak as to the efficacy of either item.

I'll be honest. I'm not sure the UCM Museum is for everyone. Or even, for most. For that small minority that loves Americana and kitsch, though, it's a dream come true. The displays are offbeat and unique. For instance, the world's largest display of paint-by-numbers paintings adorns an entire section of the museum. Preble says inflation has struck the paint-by-numbers painting industry, but he is holding firm at a $1-per-painting acquisition price.

You can also see a bassigator and a dogigator, and a miniature jazz funeral, and ... well, by this point, either your eyes have glazed over and you've skipped on to the next section, or you're already sold on a stop at the Abita Mystery House, so I'll just stop there. I will just say that I absolutely loved the place, and Dawn was a good sport about it.

With my need for funky roadside attractions momentarily satisfied, we lit out for New Orleans. As it happened, our route called for us to go directly across Lake Pontchartrain on a bridge about as long as Rhode Island is wide. Not quite, but surprisingly close: Rhode Island is 37 miles across; the Lake Pontchartrain Bridge is 23-plus miles. Dawn, who is occasionally nervous about driving across bridges, drove it, in her words, "Like a boss."

I agreed with her as I sat silently, white-knuckled, in the passenger seat.

We'd been looking forward to seeing New Orleans since we started planning the trip. As with San Antonio, we knew we needed to dedicate some time there, so I made a reservation for two nights at what billed itself as a bed-and-breakfast.

I say "billed itself as" because it was not like any B&B I had ever seen. The Marigny district, where our temporary home was located, is old. And, when you say "old" in New Orleans, that can mean something different than it does in say, Seattle.

This B&B wasn't a quaint little house, with an apple-cheeked matron serving a piping hot breakfast every morning. Instead, it was a series of leaning buildings next door to a small bar. The bar served as the lobby as well as a source of refreshments.

Our room was at the top of three narrow, rickety flights of stairs. At least, the first trip up the stairs was three flights. By the

time I was on my third and final trip with the bags, that had
magically extended out to twelve or thirteen flights.

The room itself was fine. The building had obviously served
other purposes over its 130 years of life, as the rooms were all at
odd angles to one another, and the "kitchen" in the room was
smaller than our closet back home. Still, the bed was comfy, and
if you didn't mind the heat and humidity, there was a cute little
balcony outside both the bedroom and the living room.

I thought the whole place was old and dilapidated. Dawn
loved it. When I arched one eyebrow at her, she said, "You should
be thankful that I love things that are old and decrepit." She
always knows how to put things into perspective for me.

The best part, really, was that the Marigny neighborhood is
a great location. It was close to everything we wanted to see and
do while we were in NO. In fact, we were able to park the Silver
Bullet and give her a well-deserved rest for a few days.

We changed into clean clothes, a necessary step in southern
Louisiana as you will sweat through at least three or four sets of
clothes each day, and headed for Frenchman Street. New Orleans
has so many things to recommend it: history, an unmatched
artistic community, wonderful food, and music. I couldn't wait to
hear the jazz.

We walked for three or four miles and listened to three jazz
bands. I swear if I lived in New Orleans I would never get any
writing done, because I would be hanging out, listening to music
all day and night.

Finally, it got dark, and we realized we hadn't eaten
anything since Laura's. When we'd left, we thought we might
never eat again, but the aroma that wafted through the air outside
the restaurants changed our minds.

✓ I had one thing on my mind: red beans and rice. It had been
twenty-five years since I had been to New Orleans, and I had been
dreaming about that dish ever since. Dawn ordered shrimp. Of
course Dawn ordered shrimp. She loves the little buggers and

114

orders them every chance she gets. She just had never had the chance in New Orleans before.

When the food arrived, she found her order staring back at her. Granted, the eyes were dead, but they were definitely looking in her direction. Everything was present and accounted for: the head, the tail, all parts in between. There were curly little whiskers everywhere. Dawn looked a little green, but dove in like a soldier. She peeled and ate every one of them. She didn't say it this time, but I will: like a boss.

Long before midnight, we gave up and trekked back to our room. Had we arrived here thirty years earlier, we would have stayed out late, shut the places down, and likely been looking for an after-hours club. Instead, we were back in our B&B-that-is-not-a-B&B, fast asleep, before the witching hour struck.

Day Twenty-One

Since we got to bed at a decent hour the night before, I woke up at my usual time: 6 a.m. After being with Dawn for a little more than seven years, I have learned that she never, ever, under any circumstances, wakes up at 6 a.m. So I killed a few hours on my phone, checking out things we could do in New Orleans. By 8:30, I felt like a six-year-old on Christmas morning. I couldn't wait any longer to open the presents that New Orleans had for us. I shook Dawn awake and told her I was going to go and find her coffee somewhere.

"What is that beeping?" she asked.

"Beeping?" I heard no beeping, mostly because there are a lot of things I don't hear. I was a disc jockey for ten years, with headphones slammed over my ears, listening to loud music. I've been to more than a hundred rock 'n' roll concerts, including seeing KISS from the front row seven times. In other words, I'm at least half-deaf.

"You can't hear that?" Dawn was shaking her head. She seems perpetually surprised by my deafness.

"I think you're imagining things." I am perpetually surprised when she hears things that I cannot.

I opened the door to the stairs and then even I could hear it. A smoke alarm. An *industrial strength* smoke alarm. The door to our room must have been heavy to have kept that sound out. I shut the door again. Quiet, at least to my ears.

"Okay, you're not crazy. There's a beeping out there."

Dawn dropped her chin and gave me the look that said both, "You are a moron," and "Why am I awake and do not have my coffee yet?"

I laughed, because she is so cute when she is mildly ticked off, opened the door and headed downstairs in search of coffee. When I got to the bottom floor and onto the sidewalk, I shut the door behind me, grateful for some momentary peace. Leaning up against a railing was a young guy of maybe thirty. His hair was a mess, and he had bags under his eyes.

I smiled, and said, "Man, it's a bit noisy in there."

He gave me a haunted look and said, "You don't have to tell me. That's coming from my room."

"How long has it been going on like that?"

"Since a little after midnight." He had what veterans refer to as a thousand-yard stare.

"Non-stop?"

"No, it's almost worse than that. It would blare like that for an hour or ninety minutes, then it would go quiet. We would finally just get back to sleep, then it would start up again."

"Did you call the manager?"

"Of course. They are across town and said there was nothing they could do."

I said a silent prayer of thanks that this had all happened to him and not us, then fixed a sympathetic expression. "Sorry, man. That is truly awful."

"You don't know the half of it. My wife wanted to stay in a different place downtown, but it was more expensive, so I booked us in here." He grimaced and glanced up at the second floor.

I followed his gaze and saw a woman in sweats and no makeup, with bags that matched his, looking daggers at him.

"My sincere condolences. Can I suggest roses, or possibly diamonds?"

He nodded, disconsolate. "Would have been cheaper to stay downtown."

Like any married man, I knew that it he wouldn't be paying for that choice just today, but in hundreds of future conflicts. Every time he made a suggestion, she would remind him of this disastrous night in New Orleans. He would pay a heavy price, but there was nothing I could do for him. His fate was set, so I hustled off and found Dawn's coffee. No sense in both of us having unhappy wives.

By the time I got back, Dawn was showered and ready to go. We left our room looking for a quieter environment, which would have included anything up to an active gun range.

As we walked toward our first activity of the day, we found the reputation New Orleans has for friendliness and quirky residents is well earned. Everywhere we went, people stopped and talked to us. Once, a lady with a well-dressed poodle walked alongside us for several blocks, chatting, only to say, "Well, I was really heading the other way, but I was enjoying talking to you." Nice folks.

As we got to the edge of the Marigny district (pronounced MAR-uh-nee, kind of like marinate) we saw a lovely park that covered most of a city block. There were huge trees offering shade, which was attractive to us. It didn't matter what time of the day or night, it was too damn hot in New Orleans.

Inside the gates of the park, we goggled a bit, as we saw what appeared to be a wild pig frolicking in the grass. As it turned out, it was no wild pig, but the very civilized Snuffleupagus Dawson. Snuffy is a pet pig, more civilized than many people. By the way, I know he is civilized, because he has his own Facebook page, which you'll no doubt find if you search for Snuffy the Pig. Like all animals, myself included, he was immediately attracted to Dawn. Having a chance to feed Snuffy a treat and scratch his Brillo-pad head was a great start to the day. It's hard to be in a bad mood when you've been befriended by a pig.

We walked toward the French Quarter and had a great lunch. I'm sure it's possible to get a bad meal somewhere in New Orleans, but I never have. I had jambalaya with andouille sausage, while Dawn had calamari. It was great, and she was more than pleased that it came with no eyes staring back at her.

After lunch, we boarded a tour bus to visit one of New Orleans' most famous graveyards, St. Louis Cemetery. For hundreds of years, people could just drive there and wander around to their heart's content. Be warned: That is no longer the case. Too many incidents of vandalism have led the church to close the cemetery to anyone not with a certified guide. It didn't really matter to us, because I wanted the guide anyway, to provide perspective on what we were seeing.

If you've never seen a New Orleans cemetery, you may not know that burials are handled differently here. New Orleans is often referred to as The City of the Dead, but the dead are not buried six feet under. Instead, they're interred in above-ground tombs. Built on what was once a swamp, New Orleans has an exceptionally high water table. So objects put into shallow ground may not stay there. Floating bodies, or corners of caskets sticking up out of the ground, are not good for anyone, so an intricate burial system was developed in which bodies are not given their own shelf, but rather stacked inside. They're left to decompose and make room for other bodies to come.

One of our first stops was at the grave of Voodoo Queen Marie Laveau, the most famous practitioner of Louisiana voodoo in New Orleans. By the way, if what you know about voodoo comes from Hollywood, chances are you've got it wrong. As with most things, Hollywood went for what worked for a story, not the facts. Voodoo is described as another spiritual pathway to communicate with the unknown—not all that different from many other faiths and religions.

St. Louis Cemetery is like all cemeteries in one way—it has a definite caste system. Some of the vaults are large, well-decorated, and look like little cities. Others have fallen into disrepair and are crumbling and in danger of falling down.

Nicolas Cage once owned a lot of real estate in New Orleans, but when he ran into financial difficulties, he sold it all, with one exception. That exception is a striking white pyramid vault right in the middle of St. Louis Cemetery. To my eye, it looked like it might have clues to where the treasure was buried in *National Treasure.*

Nic Cage's last piece of New Orleans real estate

Seeing the cemetery was cool and historic, but the temperatures were once again in the mid-nineties, the humidity was set to "sticky," and everyone on the tour was wilting. There was virtually no shade, and even our guide seemed thankful to get out of the sun and back on the tour bus.

Once the bus dropped us off, we hiked to a bar in the French Quarter that had lots of shade and misters. Dawn reinforced herself with a margarita. For the ten-thousandth time in a row, I did not have an alcoholic beverage.

We finally spent some time walking up and down Bourbon Street. I think it's a law that when you go to New Orleans, you must visit Bourbon Street. I admit, I didn't enjoy it. Imagine if Disneyland was for adults, not kids. Now, imagine that they have not cleaned Disneyland in several decades. That would still be cleaner and smell better than the Bourbon Street. The heat and humidity, mixed with garbage, sweat, bodily excretions and God only knows what, form the French Quarter funk. If I never smell it again, I will be happy.

Also, let's be honest. A lot of people come to New Orleans to do one thing: drink. We saw a lot of glazed eyes. I hope they took a lot of pictures, because I have a hunch that's the only way they will remember their trip. There are also hundreds of sad, homeless people and neon signs with hucksters out front doing everything but grabbing you by the collar to get you to come inside. All in all, as much as I love this city, I don't know that I ever need to come back to Bourbon Street.

Once outside the French Quarter, the charm of the city reasserts itself, though. The architecture is varied and there are any number of stunning old buildings to gawk at and photograph.

Have I mentioned that Dawn is a great lover of the macabre? Her favorite books are all true crime, Ann Rule is her favorite author, and if something famously bad happened somewhere, she wants to see it. So, we looked up the address of the LaLaurie Mansion and walked to it. It is beautiful, with graceful arched windows and a balcony that runs its entire width. It's also infamous, which is why we sought it out.

The first sign of trouble at the LaLaurie Mansion was in the early 1830s, when a slave girl was chased along the upper balcony by Delphine LaLaurie, who was brandishing a bullwhip. The young girl leapt off the corner of that balcony, trying to get away. Unfortunately she got tangled in the ironwork and fell head-first to the pavement, killing herself. The LaLauries were fined $300. You read that right: no jail time, $300 fine.

The next Very Bad Thing happened on April 10, 1834. Mr. and Mrs. LaLaurie were attending the opera. A fire started in the kitchen and the police and fire departments were summoned. They found a dead girl chained to the stove, burned to death. While the police were investigating, some of the other slaves begged the police to investigate the "third floor, where the bad things happened." They did, and they found a horrifying room where the LaLauries had been torturing and killing their slaves for many years.

The LaLauries were tipped off that the jig was up while they were still at the opera; they separated and fled. Mr. LaLaurie disappeared, never to be heard from again. Mrs. LaLaurie fled to France, where she lived until her death.

The LaLaurie Mansion was among the pieces of New Orleans real estate Nicolas Cage owned. Legend holds that Cage was disappointed because he had believed he was buying a haunted mansion, but never heard so much as a piece of furniture go bump in the night.

LaLaurie Mansion

I knew there were a lot of other macabre sites in the city, so at dusk, we signed up for a walking ghost tour. As I've mentioned, I am a skeptic in all things. If I haven't seen it or touched it, I probably don't believe it. Even if I have, I need to take into consideration that I might have been drugged and my perceptions altered. I'm a tough guy to convince. Dawn, on the other hand, is a true believer, because it makes her happy. If someone tells her a convincing ghost story, she believes.

The good thing about the New Orleans Ghost Tour is that it was perfect for both of us. Our tour guide, Daniel, was funny, self-effacing, and chock-full of interesting stories and historical tidbits. It didn't hurt that he had graduated with a degree in History.

Thus, I took a History Tour of New Orleans, and Dawn took the Ghost Tour. Perfect. Daniel knew the ins and outs of every legend, ghost sighting, and murder. He also chatted with me about the epic history of New Orleans as we walked between stops.

When the tour was over, I thanked Daniel for going over and above for us and slipped him ten bucks. He glanced down, then smiled and said, "I knew you were my favorite."

I knew it too.

The witching hour drew near, and I checked my Fitbit app, which showed we had walked ten miles that day. No wonder our feet hurt. We limped back to our room and were happy to find dead silence in the building, with no sign of the chagrined couple down the hall.

Day Twenty-Two

After our epic march through the streets of New Orleans, we were ready for a quiet day of driving. The downside of visiting large cities is that there is typically no way to get out of the city without driving on a freeway. As soon as humanly possible, though, we take an exit ramp and look for a winding little highway with farms and small towns.

Today, we were lucky to find Highway 90, which runs along the bottom of Mississippi. I had been to Mississippi before, but only the northern part of the state. I'd never seen what it looked like along the Gulf. I now know that I had been spending time in the wrong part of the state. Southern Mississippi is filled with gorgeous white sand beaches that rivaled any we saw on our trip. Even better, they were all empty. Several times, we pulled off and took our shoes off to walk in the warm sand, or dip our toes in the water. We never saw another human being on any of these beaches.

Still, we were hoping to cross the border into Florida before we slept, so we pushed on through. We did make one stop in Biloxi, Mississippi, because it had played an unwitting role in Shawn and Dawn Part One—our romance when we were kids.

Dawn and I had come to a point at the end of 1978 where we wanted to be together more than anything else on Earth. Dawn's parents were equally convinced that was a terrible idea. They were so sure, they had forbidden us to see each other at all. I was a freshman at the University of Washington at the time, and Dawn was still going to Mossyrock High School. That's when I came up with the brilliant idea that we should elope.

The problem was that Dawn was only fifteen, and we couldn't get married without her parent's permission. I'm an optimistic guy, but even I was pretty sure that permission was not forthcoming. So, I looked for a state where we could get married without parental permission. I found only one state where that was possible: Mississippi.

The only town I knew of in Mississippi was Biloxi, again because my stepdad had spoken about it in glowing terms. So, that was my plan. We would get on an airplane in Seattle, fly to Biloxi, get married and return as husband and wife.

I never said I was mature or bright, did I? What would have happened to Dawn and me if we had carried out my harebrained scheme? I have no idea, but it never came to pass.

Still, all these years since, Biloxi has lingered in my mind, somehow legendary as the path not taken. When we rolled into town, I saw a sign for a national cemetery there. We try never to pass up the opportunity to pay our respects to the men and women who made the ultimate sacrifice for our freedom, so we turned in. As they always are, the grounds were impeccably maintained, permeated with a sense of somber duty.

I was surprised, then, when I saw a sign that read *No game playing at Biloxi National Cemetery*. I looked around. There was a solitary woman carrying a bouquet to lay at one of the white crosses, and a groundskeeper mowing the lawn, but the rest was deserted. It was hard to imagine a busload of schoolkids pulling up to play hide-and-seek or something.

I Googled the sign, though, and found the answer. It turns out that Biloxi National Cemetery was some sort of a hotspot for Pokemon Go, and people had been walking the grounds with their phones, trying to capture Pokemon. The very idea boggled me a little. All our national cemeteries are hallowed ground. I can't imagine being so out of touch with that idea that you would enter to play a video game. The sign was evidence it had happened, though.

After our visit to the cemetery, we were ready for lunch. As we rolled through Biloxi, I saw a black station wagon with a pink pig straddling the roof. On the side of the station wagon were the words: "Slap Ya Momma's Barbecue." I'm not 100 percent sure that's grammatically correct, but it was eye-catching, and when I rolled down the window to take a picture, the smell of smoky barbecue did the rest. I was gonna miss Southern barbecue down the road.

The rest of the day was just driving, but what a wonderful drive. We hugged the Gulf coast for most of the day. For the first time, I wished the Silver Bullet was a convertible.

Once again, we managed to hit the only city of any size right at rush hour. It's uncanny how I manage to time this out. Luckily, what they call rush hour in Mobile, Alabama, wouldn't compare with a Sunday afternoon in Seattle traffic. We breezed right through town, rarely having to dip below 45 mph.

Then, something weird: As we approached the Jubilee Parkway Bridge, we saw a sign that warned of fog ahead.

"Really?" I said, looking at the sky. "I think that sign must be left over from winter."

There were a few clouds, but nothing too ominous. It was another hot and humid day, and fog didn't seem to fit the equation.

But as soon as we hit the bridge deck, we also hit fog. And another of those drenching rains the South seems to specialize in. Dawn was driving and I was navigating, but when you're on a freeway on a bridge, there's not much navigating to be done. The few miles crossing the Jubilee Parkway Bridge may have been the worst driving we had to do on the whole trip. We went from sunshine to deep fog to pounding rain, then back to sunshine, all in about ten minutes.

Welcome to the South.

As soon as we got over the bridge, I had Dawn take the first exit. I had no idea where it was going, I just wanted to be away from Interstate 10. As it turned out, that road dropped us into the southernmost portion of Alabama, and it was beautiful. We drove through country that had no cities or towns, just mile after mile of winding highway, farms, and blue skies. We could have made it from Mobile to the Florida state line in less than an hour on I-10. The loopy way we went, it took us two and a half hours. We were much happier taking the long way.

Before we crossed into Florida, I did see one more tourist trap we needed to investigate: Bamahenge. It's just like Stonehenge, except it's in Alabama. Oh, and the "stones" are all made of fiberglass. Other than that, it's just like Stonehenge, really.

This, the second Stonehenge replica of the trip, might just have met our quota.

Bamahenge is the creation of artist Mark Cline, who was commissioned by billionaire George Barber. That's the difference between a billionaire and myself. If I turn to Dawn and say, "I think I'd like a life-size version of Stonehenge in the backyard," she tells me to pound sand. When George Barber says that, he has the wherewithal to make it happen. As crazy as many of my ideas are, it's probably just as well that I don't have billions of dollars. For instance, I'd like a device that will wipe out the part of my brain that remembers my favorite books, so I could read them all over like new again.

We found Bamahenge in the middle of nowhere, and we were the only people in sight. Hard to believe people weren't flocking to this place from all over the world. We had a bit of fun, pretending we were druids dancing in the moonlight. Wait. Check that. *I* had a bit of fun pretending I was a druid dancing in the moonlight. Dawn just looked at me like I had lost my mind. It's an impressive illusion until you knock on one of the stones and it sounds like knocking on a Corvette fender.

The sun was setting on another glorious day on the road, and even though we hadn't seen any major tourist hot spots, this was exactly the kind of day we had envisioned. We'd seen a part of the country we'd never visited, spent the entire day together, and laughed a lot.

We made it into Pensacola, Florida, just as it was getting

dark. I hadn't made a reservation because we weren't sure we would make it to Florida, so we cruised the strip looking for a likely suspect. We found a place at least three notches above the usual motels where we'd been staying, and the vacancy sign was on.

We'd been hitting the sights so fast and furious, I thought it might be nice to have another mini-break, so we took a room for two nights. That meant another day to relax, enjoy the giant swimming pool at the motel, visit the local beaches, and get caught up on our laundry. We were ready for the break.

Day Twenty-Three

And on the twenty-third day, we rested.

I've heard people refer to this part of Florida as the Redneck Riviera. It may be so. I might have a little redneck in me, because I loved Pensacola and the gorgeous white-sand beaches.

No crowds at the Redneck Riviera

When I've gone to Maui, Hawaii, I've always loved the beaches, but they can get a little crowded. In Pensacola, the beaches were every bit as lovely, the water every bit as warm, but they were almost deserted. We spent four hours out in the waves, swimming, bodysurfing, drying off, then going right back to it.

We didn't make any progress on our lap, but we had an excellent day.

Day Twenty-Four

It was probably inevitable that on this trip, with so many different climates and cuisines, that one of us would eventually feel a bit under the weather. Dawn was the lucky winner, as she woke up not feeling great.

It was also highly likely that at some point, the Irish guy with the pale complexion would get sunburned. The previous day on the beach was that point. I woke up looking more lobster than man. I had slathered SPF 30 sunblock all over, a brand guaranteed to survive many dips in and out of water. It didn't. I burned. So, Dawn was sick, I was burned, and neither felt like embarking on a grand adventure.

The philosophy beaten into me in my youth is that you will feel better if you are up and doing something. Dawn's philosophy has often been to tell me to stuff my philosophy. In this case, we took off, anyway.

We've driven through most states on a pretty direct line. Not Florida. We are entering the state in the far northwestern corner, then driving across the Panhandle, down the Gulf Coast, then over to Miami, all the way down to Key West, then all the way back up the eastern coastline. We were going to be in Florida quite a few days and I wanted to get started on it.

We learned almost immediately that the scenic route through Florida wasn't going to be quick. We hit what looked like a small town, according to the atlas, called Destin. The 2010 census says 11,445 people live in Destin. If that's the case, every one of them was on the road this day. It took us nearly an hour to navigate through the town.

Our one tourist side trip was to swing through Seaside, Florida. Have you seen the Jim Carrey movie *The Truman Show?* The majority of that film was shot in lovely little Seaside. *The Truman Show* is about a baby raised completely within an elaborate TV show set, for an audience that witnesses every aspect of his growing up—even watching him sleep at night. Truman is surrounded by actors playing a role 24 hours a day but is blissfully unaware that his reality is a fiction. The producers hunted extensively for a town that could serve as the fictional perfect town but came up blank. They were already constructing sound stages in Hollywood when they stumbled upon the master-planned community of Seaside, whose every aspect had been designed from the start, as opposed to the willy-nilly growth patterns of most cities. Master planning makes for a beautiful, pristine city, but with kind of an odd vibe, like a *Stepford* town.

Dawn said, "I'll bet if you drop a gum wrapper, a robot cop will have you in jail before it hits the ground." She had a point. Everything was so immaculate, it still kind of looked like a movie set. We even tracked down the house the fictional Truman had lived in.

Truman's House

I was glad we'd stopped in Seaside, but in the end, it gave

131

both of us the heebie-jeebies. I don't think we're cut out for living a vacuumed-up, buttoned-down life. We like things a little messy, at least in the corners, where no one but your mother-in-law might check.

We drove the rest of the Florida Panhandle in the afternoon, then settled for the night in tiny little Perry, Florida. If you've never heard of Perry, congratulations: You stand with almost all of the rest of the world.

We had a pleasant conversation with the innkeeper at our roadside motel. He was Asian Indian, as so many of our hosts have been on this trip. He told us he was from Detroit, Michigan, but had come to Perry because he got a good deal on the motel. It was a modest place by any standard, but it was clean, neat, and well-maintained. I could see the pride he took in his business. Having driven through Perry, I also thought he was a pretty good salesman to talk his wife into coming here.

I went through my nightly Sherpa routine with our bags, but it was easy tonight—this was a one-story motel, so no stairs. While Dawn was getting us ready for the evening, I peeped into The Magical Mystery Bag. There was much more bag than there was magic or mystery, so I ran down to the local Winn Dixie to restock our supply of bread, cheese, and trail mix.

I hustled through the aisles of the Winn Dixie, picked up my few items and headed for the checkout, where the young cashier looked so bored I was afraid she might fall asleep before I got there.

We held a conversation that I have almost every time I travel to the Deep South.

"Did you find everything alright?"

"Yes, I did, thank you."

The bored look slipped away, and a light came into her eyes. "You're not from around here, are you?" Every time I go south of the Mason-Dixon, my inherent Yankee-ness seems to roll off me in a cloud, so I'm used to that question.

"No, I'm not," I answered.

She nodded wisely, happy to have her suspicions confirmed. She closed one eye and looked at me slant-wise. "Where you from?"

I knew that "Orting," or "Enumclaw" would only result in a blank look, so I said, "Seattle."

She knit her brow critically, and said, "Wait. You're from Seattle, and you're spending the night in *Perry*?" The way she said *Perry*, it sounded like she had said *black plague*. She was obviously not her town's number one booster.

"Yep."

"Why?"

"It was getting dark, and we needed a place to sleep?"

"That's the only reason I can think to stay in Perry if you don't have to."

Her words rang in my ears as I drove back to our little room. Looking around at the town, I got what she was saying. And yet, I remember my own years growing up in Mossyrock, population 400: In high school, all I could dream about was getting away from there. Away from the tiny dot on the map that had no entertainment beyond a bowling alley. Away from the rolling green hills, lakes, and country roads.

Now, decades later, I remember Mossyrock fondly as the place that helped shape who I am. I don't know if the young girl in the Winn Dixie will ever feel that nostalgia about Perry. But I have a hunch she might. Our hometowns remain our homes, no matter how far afield we wander.

Day Twenty-Five

I'm glad I wasn't expecting the sticky humidity to improve once we got to Florida, because I would have been horribly disappointed. I had started planning on the shortest distance between air-conditioned indoor spaces. I don't think I would ever get used to that weather. I'd swear I could see small drops of moisture hanging in the air, waiting for me to pass so they could attach to me. I was absolutely loving Florida, but I thought I might be happier there in, say, January.

We drove south and straight through the heart of Tampa, not following our usual practice of avoiding big cities, because there was something that I knew Dawn would love on the southern side of the city. Beautiful place: lots of water, bridges, gorgeous views. Still, too much like a city for my liking. We did drive by the Raymond James Stadium, where the NFL's Tampa Bay Buccaneers play. I like their old, uniquely designed stadium, nicknamed The Big Sombrero by ESPN's Chris Berman. This new stadium just looked like a stadium, as opposed to headgear.

Dead ahead was Big Cat Rescue, a facility designed to provide permanent homes to big cats rescued from circuses, closed zoos, roadside attractions, and the homes of people who unwisely believed a full-sized lion or tiger would make a great pet.

Almost all of the feline residents have had difficult, abused lives. One we saw had been found chained inside a crack house. Many have been declawed or otherwise damaged. Having been semi-domesticated, they can't be released into the wild, and they shouldn't be in private homes. So, Big Cat Rescue it is. It may not be their wild environment, but it is as good as the rescue can possibly make it.

We signed up for a walking tour of Big Cat Rescue. It's not free, or even inexpensive, at $36 per person, but every dime you pay goes into the care and feeding of the rescued cats. As you walk through, you pass by many caged environments. It's not like a zoo, though. Each enclosure is designed for the specific cat living there, and there are places they can go when they, like Greta Garbo, want to be alone. As we walked through the maze of enclosures, the guide told the story of each cat and how it arrived here. Many of the stories would break your heart.

We were in central Florida, so as I mentioned, it was hot—probably 90 degrees. It was humid. There was thunder and lightning and intermittent rain. Looking at the magnificent cats strolling casually around just a few feet away, it was easy to imagine we were standing on the African veldt. In fact, it very much put me in mind of the story "The Veldt," by Ray Bradbury, from his book *The Illustrated Man.* Then, you'd look at a 300-pound tiger casually admiring his claws like Shere Khan in *The Jungle Book,* and find yourself feeling glad those cages are secure.

Big Cat Rescue, in my opinion, is doing the work of the angels—taking care of animals that would never receive this level of care anywhere else. The moral of the story is, big cats are not pets and should never be domesticated. As happy as these cats are in the refuge, I know their lives would be fuller in the wild.

We drove down the western side of Florida, hugging the coastline as much as we could, and were rewarded with our first spectacular Florida sunset—a burnt-orange display that filled the sky and shared its colors with the water.

Here's another of my occasional travel tips. If you're going to be taking a massive trip like this, it's a good idea to pick one website to make reservations. Many will give you rewards for booking a set number of nights. We'd been using Hotels.com, which gives you a free night for every ten you book. The price of the free room is calculated by averaging the cost of the ten nights you stayed. Unfortunately, that means that you can't stay ten nights in fleabags, then take a night at the Ritz, but it's a fair system. By now we'd used the website enough to get a free night at a nice hotel in Estero, Florida.

It even had luggage carts and an elevator. Heaven!

Day Twenty-Six

What is it about mankind's periodic attempts at building a utopia that fires my imagination? I am endlessly attracted to both the idea and the attempted execution. Our first pass through one on this trip was in Maryhill, Oregon, where Sam Hill attempted to build the perfect Quaker lifestyle and failed.

Our second was just north of Estero, Florida, in Koreshan State Park. This is not a typical state park, but it has a lot of history attached to it.

In 1869, a young doctor named Cyrus Teed did a series of experiments with electricity. One experiment went awry and knocked him unconscious. While he was out cold, he had a vision that changed the direction of his life. Parts of his vision were incredibly progressive for the time—he believed in complete equality among the sexes, for instance—but some of his beliefs were a little out-there.

In a nutshell, he believed we were all living in a nutshell. Okay, that's not quite right, but he believed that the Earth was hollow and that we were all living on the inside of the crust, not the outside, which he described as "a void." He even conducted scientific experiments that he claimed proved this to be the case. I believe scientists call that "confirmation bias."

He changed his name to Koresh, and formed the religion Koreshanity, which drew a number of followers. He moved to southwestern Florida, bought a bunch of land and started building his utopia. As these things go, it was pretty good. He didn't build the society simply to enrich himself, or take dozens of wives, although there are rumors that he had a way with the ladies.

Everything went along swimmingly until Koresh passed away in 1908. His followers fully expected him to be resurrected. When that didn't happen, the wind went out of their sails. The last of the Koreshans carried on until 1961, when they deeded the land to the State of Florida.

Now, the whole utopia is contained in the state park, and you can walk freely through the grounds and through many of the buildings. It was fascinating to see how they lived more than a century ago, and the things they used to support their belief system. There's even a model that reflects the way that Koresh saw us living—inside a perfect sphere.

Beyond that little quirk, he was a pretty cool guy. The society was essentially matriarchal, as the ruling council was made up of nine women. He knew that wouldn't fly with the outside world, though, so he appointed men to meet with outsiders to carry out the wishes of the women. Fascinating stuff.

One of the unexpected benefits of the trip was the number of ideas it was giving me for new stories. As we walked around the deserted utopia, I wondered: *What would it be like to be the last two people keeping a place like that going?* Once upon a time, they were part of something they believed in. They may have thought they were changing the world for the better. Then, life happened, and people died, or gave up, or moved on. So, what was it like for those last two? I don't know, but I decided to try to find out by writing about it when I got home.

Leaving Estero, we headed south by southeast toward Miami. I wasn't much interested in Miami proper, but there is an attraction that I was interested in—the Coral Castle.

Before we could get to the Coral Castle, though, we passed through the little flyspeck town of Ochopee, Florida, which boasts the smallest post office in the United States. There was a time when Ochopee had a pretty normal, if smallish, post office. But it burned down in 1953. The town needed a replacement, and quickly. After all, the U.S. mail must go through! As a temporary measure, the post office moved into a deserted irrigation pipe shed. Sixty-three years later, it's still in use. You never know when temporary becomes the new normal. I didn't measure it precisely, but the whole building looks to be the size of a very small bedroom. We mailed postcards to our grandkids, knowing they would be postmarked from the tiniest post office in the country. It doesn't take much to make us happy.

We drove through areas boasting wildlife preserves that are supposed to be filled with alligators, but try as we might, we didn't see a single one. We drove down deserted roads, pulling off in spots where they are known to be; we even stopped at viewing areas set aside just for that purpose. Nada. We were not destined to see a gator on this day.

We drove into Miami via a series of small, dusty back roads. When you see pictures of Miami on television, it almost always shows the sparkling water, the glimmering high-rises, and all the beautiful people cavorting on the beaches. The part of Miami we drove through, coming at it from the northwest, was more like an agricultural center. We saw lots of open fields and farms everywhere. It was kind of cool to see this other side of the city.

We stopped at the Coral Castle before turning farther south toward the Keys. The Coral Castle doesn't look like all that much from the outside, but we were pretty dazzled by what we saw inside the fences. It represents a tale of love, obsession, and a total inability to "just get over it." Since I kept a flame burning in my heart for thirty years for the girl I could never get over, I could relate to the project. I'd just longed for Dawn secretly in my heart, though. I never built anything like the Coral Castle.

The story begins in 1913, when Edward Leedskalnin was still living in his native Latvia. He was engaged to the girl he loved, Agnes Scuffs. On the day of their wedding, Agnes reneged on their engagement and told Edward she wouldn't marry him. Life is full of disappointments, but it's always about how you react to them, right?

Edward reacted by moving to North America, where he did manual labor in Canada and the United States until he contracted tuberculosis, which was not a trifling matter a century ago. He moved to Florida for his health and eventually found his life's work: building a shrine to his lost love, many thousands of miles away.

What he built and how he did it is fascinating: Using no electricity and only the most primitive of tools. he moved delicate coral rocks weighing as much as 30 tons to build his castle—all alone, under the cover of darkness. He never revealed his methods. Nearly a century later, there are wildly varying theories about how he accomplished this, but no one knows for sure.

Mysteries abound throughout the site, for example the nine-ton gate he was able to move easily by himself. When it stopped working many years after his death, engineers using modern equipment were brought in to fix it. They could not, and it has been frozen in place for years.

You may be thinking Ed was a huge, hulking man who moved these rocks with brute strength, but he was not. There is a life-sized cutout of the man near the gift shop. Dawn Adele, who claims to be 5-foot-3 (which would have to be when she's wearing heels) was several inches taller. It looked like he might have weighed 110 pounds after a large meal.

Dawn and Ed

Ed himself said he had discovered the secret of how the Egyptians built their pyramids and used the same system. Other theorists suggest he used a strange form of magnetism, or alien technology. Me? I am happy to admit that I have no idea.

Ed's story doesn't have a happy, or even satisfying, ending. He apparently stayed in contact with the girl he was obsessed with for years after he arrived. Eventually she stopped answering his letters. He died alone, having never married, at the age of sixty-three. Now that's stubbornness. Or, a complete inability to move on from past injuries.

As a man who was also in love with a long-lost girl for decades, I can relate. I simply wrote a book about Dawn Adele, though, and resisted building an immense shrine to her. I think I made the proper choice.

We left Miami without ever seeing the part of the city that shows up on television, and we were good with that. We turned onto Highway 1, the only choice you have if you want to drive the Florida Keys.

The Keys consist of a string of small islands curving southwest from the southernmost tip of mainland Florida. They are the stuff dreams and songs are made of. If you remember the old Bertie Higgins song "Key Largo," ("Just like Bogie and Bacall"), that was one of the first we drove through.

We were immediately drawn to the vibe that permeates the Keys. Everyone we talked to seemed relaxed, happy, as though they didn't care much what was happening in the rest of the world—they were good with their little corner.

We saw our first Keys sunset on the way to our hotel. A little side road off Highway 1 pointed west toward the sunset, so we pulled off. We almost gave up taking it when we spotted a sign that marked it as a private housing area, but other sunset-seekers immediately began showing up around us. They clustered in little groups, taking pictures, murmuring quietly and absorbing the wonder of the deep oranges and reds that soon filled the sky.

Two years earlier, I had written a novella called *Second Chance Summer*. The cover for that book showed an idyllic palm tree silhouetted against an island sunset. It looked precisely like what was laid out before us. Glancing to our right we saw a home with a large deck built out toward the water, filled with people watching the sun slowly dip toward the horizon. How nice would it be to have that kind of an ending to each day? I wouldn't mind finding out.

We drove on to our hotel for the night, the Glunz Ocean Resort. It was relatively inexpensive, so I was a little worried it might be one of those places that call themselves a resort when they are ... not. I needn't have worried. The friendliest front desk person we had met on the trip checked us in and seemed genuinely sad that we were only staying one night.

"You're going to love it here," she said.

She was right.

The room itself was pleasant, with a separate bedroom / bathroom / kitchen / living room. Much more space than we were used to on our trip. It was when I threw open the sliding glass door that things got really special. The Glunz's owners advertise it as an oceanfront resort, and they are not kidding. It was pitch-dark by the time we got to our room, but we could see the opalescent moon shimmering over the Atlantic, the water just a few feet below. The soothing sound of rolling surf gently washing up below us was like music. I wanted to lie down and sleep right there on the lanai.

Day Twenty-Seven

When I woke up about 6 a.m., I hustled back to the sliding glass doors. I wanted to get a better view of what I could only glimpse the night before. I was not disappointed. Sunshine dappled across blue waves that stretched to the horizon. The surf continued to roll right below our deck, beckoning. I knew Dawn would be asleep for a time, so I slipped my swim trunks on and headed for the ocean.

Our view from Glunz Resort

A groomed white sand beach that belonged to the Glunz sloped gently into the water. The temperature was already in the upper 80s, but floating happily in the warm salt water, I felt as contented as I had on the entire trip. I'm not sure how long I spent floating the day away, but eventually Dawn joined me and we both swam until we were tired.

When we climbed out, we saw our first iguana, scooting along the beach, casting sideways glances at us as we invaded his space. The woman at the front desk the night before was correct—we didn't want to leave.

But Key West awaited us. Since we had started in the far northwestern corner of the country, reaching Key West, which was as far south as we could go, felt like the halfway point of the tour. The trip was starting to wear us out a little bit, so making that halfway mark looked pretty big. Reluctantly, we left the Glunz and continued on toward the home of Ernest Hemingway and perfect sunsets.

Just a few miles down Highway 1, we saw a sign that read *Turtle Hospital.* That sounded interesting. Dawn Adele loves turtles. She loves all animals, but turtles occupy the top rung on her adoration ladder.

Like everything in Florida, which had been by far our most expensive state to tour, there was a $22-per-person charge, but The Turtle Hospital is a nonprofit, so all the entry fees go back to caring for the turtles. Unlike Big Cat Rescue, which we had visited earlier this week, these turtles don't come from homes they have outgrown but rather a wild environment that nearly killed them.

Turtles are injured in many ways—by ingesting litter from the ocean, by getting run over by boats, or by contracting diseases they cannot survive. Anyone who spots a turtle in distress can call The Turtle Hospital and its staff do the rest. Whoever spots the sick or injured turtle gets to name it. One fisherman has found so many that he has used up the names of all the characters on *Gilligan's Island.* The hospital is serious about nursing these turtles back to health and releasing them back into the wild.

I love the way it all started, as a tourist attraction at a roadside motel. Since that was in the eighties, kids who went through the attraction naturally asked about *Teenage Mutant Ninja Turtles.* When the man who owned the place investigated, he found out he needed to help turtles before he could display turtles. Thanks to a kids' cartoon, The Turtle Hospital was born.

Many patients have been run over by boats and barely lived to tell the tale. They can often be patched up, rehabilitated, and set free to swim once more. Others suffer from an unfortunately named condition: "bubble butt." Bubble butt occurs when turtles get micro-pockets of gases trapped inside their shells. That causes the back of the shell to be lighter than the front, which means it rises in the water, making it difficult to swim. Imagine trying to swim comfortably underwater when you have large pockets of air in your swimsuit, lifting your hind end toward the surface. Eventually, this problem leads to exhaustion, stress, and often death. The hospital places weights on an afflicted turtle's shell to counteract the air pockets and help him swim more normally, but there is currently no cure for the condition, so such turtles aren't eligible for release back into the ocean.

After a few hours gawking at the turtles, I was able to pull Dawn away, and we arrived at Key West in mid-afternoon. We checked into a cute little room in a 120-year-old hotel. I think people were smaller a century ago; I know their hotel rooms were, as there was barely room for a queen-sized bed in the room.

Still, it was in Key West, and it had a sweet little swimming pool that we happily jumped into for our second swim of the day. We could get used to this aspect of Florida living.

Eventually, we got dressed and wandered down to Mallory Square, where there is a celebration of the sunset every night. In a high-tech world, a gathering of people to watch a sunset seems like an anachronism. We saw it with our own eyes, though.

With good reason, they make a big deal out of sunsets in Key West. A huge crowd gathers, and of course, where people gather, merchants gather to sell them things. So, it wasn't quite completely low-key, but it was still nice. We grabbed a shaved ice and watched a few of the performers there, in particular a juggler I found impressive.

Eventually, we found a seat right on the dock, facing dead west. As the sun dropped, a sense of anticipation built. Yes, many people had their cameras out to capture the moment, but there was kind of a contented, happy reverence in the crowd as well.

When the sun finally touched the horizon, the crowd oohed and aahed as though at the grand finale of a fireworks display. When the last bit of sun disappeared, everyone on the pier broke out in spontaneous applause. For just a few moments, I felt a little less cynical and I was proud to be a human being.

We walked back home via Duvall Street, which is to Key West what Bourbon Street is to New Orleans. If, that is, Bourbon Street didn't smell like one of the outer circles of Hell. Duvall was actually nice and clean, with a million bars, restaurants, and ways for tourists to part with their money. Before we knew it, we were back at our hotel.

Dawn turned to me and said, "You know what we just did, right?"

"Saw an amazing sunset?"

"Right. We saw an amazing sunset, then walked past about a hundred restaurants without getting dinner."

It was a fair point. I had been too busy gawking at everything to think about eating. On the corner right next to our hotel room was a small food truck that specialized in gourmet pizzas.

"You go on to the air-conditioned room. I'll order us a pizza and bring it to you in just a few."

"These are the times when I remember why I married you."

I'd like to think that's a constant thought in her mind, but I'll take what I can get.

I approached the window and saw a pretty young woman, maybe twenty-five, taking orders. I ordered our pizza, then glanced at her. Her hair was pulled back, sweat was pouring off her, and she looked like she was about to pass out.

It had "cooled off" to about 90 degrees by that time, but of course it was much hotter inside the food truck, where several pizza ovens were running.

"Do you like this gig?"

"Not really," she said, "but it's worth it to be living in paradise."

I took in her sweat-stained shirt and glazed eyes, and almost asked, "Can any place that makes you look like that really be paradise?" but instead, I smiled and nodded.

The pizza was great, but the air-conditioning in our room was even better.

Day Twenty-Eight

For the first twenty-seven days of our trip, it had felt as though we were moving farther and farther from our home. Today, even though we would be driving first east, and then north, it felt like we had made the turn and were heading home.

Before we could leave Key West, though, I had to stop and tour Ernest Hemingway's house. It was just a short distance from our hotel, but we didn't know that until we were already in the car and had checked out. So, instead of a short walk, we took a very short drive, then paid the price by having a hard time finding a place to park.

Eventually, we found a spot on a little residential side street. I'm sure the locals all appreciate tourists like us taking up their parking spots. *Mea culpa.*

We arrived at the little shed where the ticket taker resides and found that it is $13 per person to tour the house and grounds. I get that. A grand old house like this no doubt has a lot of upkeep to keep it shining. I handed the man my debit card. He shook his head and pushed it back to me.

"Cash only."

I turned to Dawn. "Have you got any cash?"

Between us, we had about $15. Any mugger that hit us was going to be severely disappointed.

I turned back to the man in the booth. "Do you have an ATM?"

"Of course. It is around the back of the house, in the bookstore."

"Okay, we'll just run and grab some cash and be right back, then."

He shook his head. "No, no. One of you will have to stay here." He pointed at Dawn. "She can sit there on the bench until you get back."

I nearly gave up on the whole idea, but I did want to see the house where the master wrote some of his finest works, to see the legendary six-toed cats. So, Dawn sat on the bench in the blazing heat, while I ran as quickly as possible back to the ATM, got some money and sprung Dawn from Bench Jail. Let me serve as a cautionary tale: Do not show up at Papa Hemingway's house without any folding green. They will treat you as a suspect and give you the fish-eye.

As soon as we entered the house, I forgot about everything else. A sense of history swept over me, and we managed to catch one of the tours just as it was starting. About Ernest Hemingway I will just say this: he led a diverse and messy life. Along with having read probably half of what Hemingway wrote, I knew a few things about him, but was no expert. I learned a lot as we toured his home. I didn't know that just a few months prior to his suicide, he had undergone electroshock therapy at the Mayo Clinic. The guide said the electroshocks left him unable to think creatively or write. I don't know whether that's the case or not, but if it is, I can better understand why he took his own life.

Have you ever seen the meme writers like to circulate? It says, "Don't make me angry, or I'll put you in one of my books and kill you off," or some such. Hemingway did exactly that. While serving as an eighteen-year-old ambulance driver in World War I, Hemingway was badly injured and left with hundreds of pieces of shrapnel in his legs. He was nursed back to health by a woman he fell in love with—Agnes von Kurowski. He pledged his love, but she brushed him off, as she was several years older and thought him too immature. In his first bestseller, *A Farewell to Arms*, Hemingway wrote of a similar scenario. In the final chapter, he killed the character of the nurse. That is how a writer gets revenge.

Hemingway's house is beautiful, and when you think of how old it is (built in 1851) it is stunning. The thing I most wanted to see (aside from the cats) was his writing studio. It did not disappoint. It sits at the top of a staircase in a separate building at the back of the house. Since Hemingway created approximately 70 percent of his life's work in the nine years he lived in Key West, he wrote a lot of stories in that private studio. Today, it is set up much as it was then. The walls are lined with bookshelves, his hunting trophies are on the wall, and in the middle of the room is a table with a beat-up old typewriter in the middle. I am betting writers would pay a lot of money to be able to sit in that room, commune with Papa, and write. I know I would.

Papa's writing studio

Cats are everywhere in Hemingway House. Hemingway was given a six-toed cat by a sea captain. He believed six-toed cats to be good luck, so he kept her and she had many litters over the years, passing on the odd gene. Many of the cats living in the house today are descended from that original cat. Papa was, in fact, a kind of crazy cat man; he had as many as seventy cats living with him. If I end up being reincarnated, I would be happy to come back as a six-toed cat at Hemingway House. I'd have lots of visitors to ignore year 'round, and I'd be very well taken care of.

One of the other funky things we loved in the house is a gussied-up urinal from a Key West bar that Hemingway used to frequent. After the bar was moved, the urinals were ripped out. Hemingway told the owner he had poured so much money down the drain of the urinal, he felt he should own it. The bar owner agreed, and Hemingway brought it home, much to the dismay of his wife. She had someone put tiles around it to disguise it, but to my eye, it still just looks like a fancy urinal. Today, it is used to give water to the cats.

We left the Hemingway House and swung by one last tourist stop in Key West—the "Southernmost Point Buoy." The problem is that the buoy that is supposed to mark the southernmost point of the Keys isn't really the southernmost point. The true southernmost point isn't publicly accessible, so, as with so many things, visitors agree to close our eyes to the facts and pretend. Humans, as a general rule, are very good at this game.

We drove by the Southernmost Point Buoy several times while we were in Key West, and the line for tourists to get their picture taken rarely seemed to shrink. Once again, we struggled to find a parking spot within six or seven blocks, but did eventually. Like most everywhere else in Key West, there was a mellow vibe in the line. No one seemed in too big a hurry. People traded information about where they were from, then took turns acting as photographer for the other. Very congenial.

It's a law: You have to get your photo taken here

When you stand at the buoy and look west, you see a large object shaped like a golf ball. That's government land, and apparently, the *real* southernmost point. We were happy just getting our picture taken at the buoy. We pretended, just like everyone else.

I kind of hated to leave Key West. It is my kind of place, aside from the baking temperatures and humidity. Maybe I should say that Key West is really my kind of place ... in January or February.

We got back on Highway 1, heading east toward the mainland, often on narrow spits. The Gulf of Mexico was on our left, the Atlantic Ocean on our right. On cold, blustery days in the Pacific Northwest, I will close my eyes and dream of that drive.

I found another memorial to stop at in Islamorada. It's a memorial to the victims of the Labor Day Storm of 1935. Some people refer to it as The Wrong Way Memorial. Why? Because the carving shows palm trees bent over by high winds. The problem is that the palm trees are shown blowing to the east.

Since the storm came from that direction, the trees should be blowing the other direction. Eh. I think some people could find other things to worry about. I focused more on the fact that the bodies of 300 of the storm's victims are buried near the memorial.

Things were very different in 1935, of course. Transportation wasn't always reliable, and the science of meteorology was crude compared with today. There was no Highway 1 that ran the length of the Keys —the only way off was via boat or train.

On the day the storm hit—Labor Day, 1935—a train was dispatched to rescue a group of veterans who were working on the Keys, along with some civilians. In a comedy of errors that seems almost unbelievable, the train was delayed again and again. Eventually the storm, one of the few Category Five hurricanes to retain that designation at landfall, swept over the Keys, killing almost everyone in its path, including those trying to escape via the train.

So many places we've visited in the South, including the Keys, New Orleans and Galveston, have been decimated by storm after storm. Dawn and I live now on an ocean beach that sits over a famous fault line. If it shifts and "the big one" hits, we will be in major trouble. The odds of that happening in any given year are remote, though, so it is easy to put it out of our minds. It is hard for me to imagine living in an area where it is possible that a storm can change your lives at any time. I feel for the people of the Gulf Coast. They are a brave and hardy lot.

We made it across the Keys, around Miami, and up to West Palm Beach before we stopped for the night. We found the Hotel Biba, self-described as an artsy boutique hotel. After so many years working as a Realtor, I should have been able to decipher what that meant. *Artsy* means weird. *Boutique* means tiny and cramped. Once again, although the room was small, the place was saved by having a fine swimming pool.

It started to rain while we were in the pool. Fat, heavy, warm drops plopped down on our heads and splashed the pool. It was pleasant, even a little romantic, until the thunder and lightning hit, then we headed for the room.

Day Twenty-Nine

We'd been in Florida for nearly a week and had yet to see a manatee, but I had a plan to change that. As Dawn was driving the previous day, I'd found a spot in West Palm Beach that Florida Power & Light had built to highlight the manatees. It's not a zoo, just a peaceful spot for them along their normal route to stop, rest, and rejuvenate.

We knew we'd found it when we spotted the giant statue of two manatees in the parking lot. The impressive information building was modern, full of light, and had many informative displays. Outside, we walked along the waterways, waiting for one of the huge creatures to reveal itself. We waited, then waited some more.

"We must be looking in the wrong place, right?"

"Right," I said. "I'll go ask."

I went back to the lady behind the first counter inside and said, "We've been looking for quite a while and haven't seen anything that looks vaguely like a manatee. Are we looking in the wrong place?"

"Oh, no, you're in the right place, just the wrong time. We haven't had any manatees about for several days."

I broke the news to Dawn, who salved her pain with a lengthy visit to the gift shop. We might not have found a manatee in the flesh, but a magnetic one will adorn our refrigerator forever.

That left us with some unexpected time on our hands, not to mention an overburdened suitcase full of dirty clothes in the trunk, so we sought out a laundromat.

Here's one thing I've learned on our trip: Laundromats are essentially the same no matter where you go. The slightly musty smell, the humidity of drying clothes, the same year-old magazines scattered about, the same broken pop machine.

We nearly had an accident, as Dawn accidentally left her key to the Silver Bullet in her pants pocket when she threw her laundry in. Typically, it's not a huge deal to wash your keys, but because the Silver Bullet is almost new, it has one of those newfangled electronic keys that can do everything but massage your feet for you. Electronics don't like to be washed, tumbled, and rinsed.

As soon as Dawn realized what had happened, I ran to the machine, but it locked automatically while running. The lady who ran the place was able to shut the machine off so it would unlock. Except, she turned off the wrong machine.

That meant that we had to pay to restart both machines we had going—a small price to pay to save the key—but as soon as the water drained away, we retrieved it. I'm not sure how Hyundai builds their keys, but I am impressed. Dripping wet as it was, it still unlocked the doors and trunk. Another tragedy averted.

We found it difficult to plot a sensible route to Orlando without using major roads, so we bit the bullet and took the freeway north. One thing we will not miss about Florida is the toll roads. Every time we turned around, it felt like we were getting dinged for $2 here, $4 there. Eventually, I learned to just keep a stack of bills handy.

Orlando, of course, holds several of the world's most famous theme parks, Disney World and Universal Studios among them. Our friend Knutty Gerry (the "K" is not silent, by the way) works at Universal Studios and offered to give us a day pass to both of the Universal parks. How could we say no?

We met with Knutty and bought him dinner as a thank-you for the passes, then failed to avail ourselves of Orlando nightlife. Instead, we took advantage of staying at The Point Orlando Resort, which was several cuts above our normal accommodations. We relaxed in the spacious room, swam in the huge pool and pretended we were rich people for a few hours. We like how the other half lives.

Day Thirty

I am not the biggest fan of amusement parks. A few too many people all gathered in one space for my taste. Dawn, however, loves them. If we lived near Disneyland, I would have to get her an annual pass. Plus, I love to travel, while Dawn is more of a homebody, so I figured I might owe her a little something.

We'd spent a happy day at Disneyland on our honeymoon, so we followed the same game plan for Universal Studios: get there early, hit as many popular attractions as possible before the park fills to capacity. From there? Stand in line and be patient.

We started at Islands of Adventure, which is next to Universal Studios and connected to it by the Hogwarts Express. Because, of course, Universal is the home of The Wizarding World of Harry Potter.

In the interest of full disclosure, I need to say that Dawn and I are both huge Harry Potter fans. I read the first four books to my girls before they got too big and read on ahead without me. We've both read all seven HP books and seen all eight movies. On trips with my girls, I used to play games such as trying to remember a hundred characters without peeking into the books. It's not easy, but we got there.

The three primary rides associated with Harry Potter didn't thrill us much. They were all very frantic, twisty, roller coaster-ish rides. Neither of us is a big fan of that type of ride. However, there was a lot of The Wizarding World that we really liked. The Hogwarts Express, for instance, could have just been a tram between parks, but it's not. You sit inside compartments exactly as described in the books, and scenes and characters make appearances both inside and outside the train. We loved that.

Also, they got Diagon Alley just right. It's rare for me to see something in the physical world that I've read about and have it match my mental image perfectly, but it happened today. All the shops and pubs that were mentioned in the books were there— The Leaky Cauldron, Ollivanders Wand Shop, Gringots, etc.

In the Harry Potter section of the park, we appreciated most the parts that closely echoed the books or movies. We can ride roller coasters and dipsy-do rides anywhere, but it was very cool to be able to feel like we were stepping into the pages of some of our favorite books.

While we were walking through Diagon Alley, an alarm went off and a large crew of park employees rushed to cordon off half the area. The alarm continued to blare, over and over, for about fifteen minutes while we stood there, waiting to see if we could get into some of the other attractions.

Eventually, we gave up and went elsewhere. Which brings me to a point: It's difficult not to compare Universal Studios to one of the Disney parks. To us, it seemed Universal Studios fell a bit short of the gold standard that Disney sets. When we arrived, we saw that several rides were down for various reasons. Okay, that happens. Later, it was announced that another of the major rides, based on *The Incredible Hulk*, was shut down for the rest of the day.

The worst experience for us was the new King Kong ride. Not the ride itself, which was fun, but the experience of getting there. It's not unusual for the parks to design lines so that you can't tell how far you are from the actual ride. It's all psychology, I suppose.

When we entered the ride area, signs said we were thirty minutes from getting on. That's not terrible, so we got in line. The line twists and turns, ever-downward, in increasingly tight corridors. The good news is, as you head underground, it gets cooler. But you can never see more than thirty feet or so ahead before the route twists away again. This keeps hope alive.

After we had descended down, down, down, into the labyrinth, the loudspeakers announced: "Ladies and gentlemen, the ride is momentarily not working. We are aware of the problem and hope to have it back up shortly," or some such. We stood in place for about fifteen minutes before a second announcement declared that things were A-OK, and we started moving again. Then the first announcement came again. Then the second. It felt like we were doing the Hurry Up and Wait Tango. Then a third verse, same as the first.

As a writer, I'm always observing people and thinking: *How would I write this scene into a book?* We had one of those moments at the King Kong ride. We had finally turned the corner and could see the actual tram we were to ride in. We were to be the next group to go. Then, another round of announcements: "We're sorry ..."

Fifteen feet from the ride, we had no idea how long it was going to be shut down. Five park employees were on the other side of the rope, four essentially doing nothing. The fifth was in a world of his own, play-acting as though he were actually in a King Kong movie, pretend-talking on his walkie talkie, playing the whole scene as though auditioning for a role in *A Streetcar Named Desire.* He twirled his arms, raised and lowered his voice, and desperately tried to get the other employees to play along.

They didn't, but after a while, I thought I could read their minds: *Matthew, you are such a dweeb, you are making us all look bad.* For the first ten minutes or so, I found him mildly amusing, but after that, he veered off into a place where the crowd wanted to feed him to Kong.

In all, we spent about 90 minutes in the dank underground corridors of King Kong. The ride was good once we got on it. It was a great combination of virtual reality, motion-activated monsters and scary fun. Still, I'm not sure I'd have been willing to spend an hour and half in an underground passage for five minutes of fun, if I'd known in advance how long it would take. This is why I am not the ideal amusement park patron.

In the final analysis, we got to the park just as it opened, stayed until it closed, and had a great time. There's no place better than a huge amusement park for people-watching, except maybe McCarran International Airport in Las Vegas, where every face tells a story. It had started to drizzle a bit by the time we got to the bus that would return us to our hotel, and, typical of these storms, within four steps, it absolutely poured on us. Fifty very wet people on a single bus made for a steamy ride home, but we got there safe and sound.

Dawn's natural body clock keeps her up until midnight or later every night. I can count on one hand the nights she falls asleep before me. This was one. I think the excitement of the park and the 16,000 steps we logged on our Fitbits did her in.

Another pleasant vacation from our vacation, but tomorrow, we would be ready to hit the road once again, because we were finally turning north in earnest.

Day Thirty-One

Aside from the humidity, we'd loved our time in Florida. There was so much to see and do. Nonetheless, we were ready to move on and see some different license plates.

Before leaving Florida, we made one more stop, and it turned out to be one of our favorites: St. Augustine. Towns tend to have a personality, a vibe, a culture. The vibe in St. Augustine is wonderful. The streets are clean, the architecture is old, Spanish, and gorgeous, and everyone we met smiled and chatted with us. It goes on our short list of towns we'd like to return to.

One building that made a real impact on us was the Cathedral Basilica of St. Augustine, built in the 1790s. In Washington state, our history just doesn't go back to the eighteenth century. Minutes later, we found ourselves visiting a fort that dated back to the *seventeenth* century.

Construction on the Castillo de San Marcos started in 1672, but it wasn't finished for several decades. The harbor that it guards was strategically well placed, so it saw several battles and sieges. The fort was built by the Spanish while they were still a major world power, to defend the city of St. Augustine. Its walls, made of coral rock, were a strong defense against cannons. When a cannonball hit the coral walls, they absorbed the blow without crumbling. The British, it's said, described attacking the Castillo de San Marcos as being like stabbing a piece of cheese with a knife. Damage, yes, but not devastating.

The fort was as close to impenetrable as any. It was heavily armed with cannons, making it nearly impossible for opposing forces to gain entry by placing ladders against the walls. Because it was built on typically wet Florida soil, tunneling beneath it was also impossible. The cannon defenses also made it difficult for ships to sit in the harbor and shoot at will.

The fort looks essentially the same today as it did centuries ago. It is easy to climb the bell tower, look out into the bay, and imagine living the life of an eighteenth-century soldier. We saw the barracks, too, so I can tell you they weren't exactly living in luxury.

Because the fort was so impenetrable, opposing forces would lay siege to it rather than attack outright. Then the townspeople would crowd within its walls and subsist as best they could until one side or the other gave up.

We spent a few hours walking around the shops and cafes of St. Augustine but knew we needed to head north if we wanted to get to Georgia by nightfall. We got on Highway A1A. Interstate 95 would have been faster, but A1A offered much better views of the Atlantic and gave us our last chance to walk on lovely Florida white-sand beaches. Dawn also found a lot of beautiful shells on the beach, which sat in the cup holder in the car for the rest of the drive.

Those shells are now sitting next to me on my writing desk as I write the book. When I get stuck on a sentence or paragraph, I hold them and seek inspiration.

We made it to Savannah, Georgia, by dark.

Day Thirty-Two

This part of the country is familiar to me again. I lived in the South, briefly, on two occasions, and have spent time in Georgia, South Carolina, and Arkansas. I'd never been to Savannah, though, which is one of the crown jewels of Georgia. Like much of the Deep South, it has a lot of old-world charm, immense mansions, and a feeling of history.

To Dawn, Savannah meant just one thing: *Midnight in the Garden of Good and Evil.* If you've read the book or seen the movie, starring Kevin Spacey and John Cusack, you know the story of a murder that occurred in the Mercer Mansion. Here's a handy historical tidbit: No one named Mercer ever lived in the Mercer Mansion. You might be able to win a bar bet with that one. Dawn loves the movie, so we made reservations for a tour in the early afternoon.

Before we got to the Mercer House, we toured the Savannah History Museum. Overall, it's a pretty typical museum, but there were a couple of displays that caught my eye. One was a full display of old-timey dentist's equipment. It is the complete office setup of Dr. William Bedford, which he purchased in 1919 for $600 and continued to use, unchanged, for sixty years. He finished his last day with the same equipment he started out using in 1919. I might be wrong, but I'm pretty sure there were a few updates in dental technology over those six decades. As I stood staring, I kept thinking of those last patients, and wondering, "Why in the world didn't they find a different dentist?"

Another display claimed to be the bench Tom Hanks sat on in the movie *Forrest Gump.* That would have been pretty cool, but when I read the fine print, I saw that it was just a copy, and that the original bench still belongs to Paramount Pictures. Nothing like going to a museum to see a copy of a pop-culture touchstone.

The rest of the museum was fine, with lots of Civil War

memorabilia, as might be expected. We didn't want to be late for our date with the Murder ... er, *Mercer* House, so we left and began walking toward it.

On the way, we came across another piece of history—the site of the Battle of Savannah. Sometimes it's hard to keep track of the players without a scorecard, and the Battle of Savannah is a great example. In 1779, the British were holding Savannah and were intent on keeping it. They built defensible positions around the city called *redoubts, each* basically a little earthen fort that is relatively easy to defend. On October 9, 1779, the combined forces of American revolutionaries, and French, Haitian, and Irish forces, attacked the redoubts. An hour later, the battle was over, the attacking forces had lost badly, and 800 men were dead. The British continued to hold Savannah and took great cheer from this victory. The Revolutionary War continued for four more years. Now, those redoubts and the historical site sit right in the middle of a heavily trafficked street in Savannah.

A few minutes later, we arrived at the Mercer House. *Midnight in the Garden of Good and Evil* is based on the historical case of the killing of Danny Hansford by local art dealer, historic restorer and bon vivant Jim Williams. It was a case complicated by the reputations of Hansford (rumored to be a male prostitute) and Williams, who was very much a part of upper-crust Savannah society. Over the years, there were four trials, and in the end Williams was acquitted.

Jim Williams continued to live in the house (which he had restored in meticulous detail) until his death by heart attack in 1990. It is a magnificent, if odd, home, and I will say that it was restored to the very specific tastes of Mr. Williams. The interior of the house was decorated in a completely over-the-top manner that couldn't be further from my own taste, so I am not the right person to award style points.

There were a lot of old paintings in gold frames hanging as if in a museum, and a lot of no doubt very expensive furniture and knickknacks, but beyond the perspective of the story, the house didn't do much for me. Because of the age of the house (built during the Civil War) there weren't typical kitchens or bathrooms, so Williams had a bathroom put in just off the main hall. I so wish I could show you a picture of it, but they don't allow photography inside. I will just say that everyone in the tour gasped at the garishness of the red and gold wallpaper and seventies-era fixtures. Clint Eastwood chose to film the movie right there in the house, so if you've seen it, you've already seen the interior, anyway, although I don't remember shots of that bathroom.

It's always interesting to walk around what is essentially the main set of a movie, and the Mercer House is no exception. If you're ever in Savannah, it's only ten dollars to take a tour of the place, worth every penny.

Mercer House

We had a couple of delish Cuban sandwiches for a late lunch, then continued our *Midnight in the Garden of Good and Evil* tour by driving to Bonaventure Cemetery. Bonaventure was also featured in several scenes in the movie, but as soon as we got to the cemetery, we forgot all about the film. Massive oaks scattered throughout the graveyard, dripping with Spanish moss, somehow give the place a proper Southern Gothic vibe. Naturalist John Muir described that moss beautifully: "It drapes all the branches from top to bottom, hanging in long silvery-gray skeins, reaching a length of not less than eight or ten feet, and when slowly waving in the wind they produce a solemn funereal effect singularly impressive."

We walked through as much of the cemetery as we could. I'm sure we didn't see more than a small percentage of its 160 acres. It's a place we would very much like to return to and spend an entire day.

We left Bonaventure and lit out for South Carolina. As usual, we stuck to the back roads. Late-afternoon drives like this were one of my favorite parts of the trip. We'd so often find ourselves on quiet, twisty back roads in that golden hour before the sun set. We'd be tired, and even I was usually talked out, so we'd just listen to our music and let the miles slowly roll under our wheels. I'd watch the wheat or cotton fields, or the winding river, and wait for the sun to dip below the hills. Dawn was beside me. Life was good.

This day, midway between Savannah, Georgia, and Aiken, South Carolina, we saw a small, abandoned church and cemetery off to the side of the road. The church wasn't much to look at, but we paid in blood to see the cemetery. More accurately, Dawn paid in blood sacrifice to the mosquitoes, but they ignored me. She's much sweeter-tasting than I am.

The abandoned graves looked like the opening shot of a horror movie, just before the zombies rise to eat the spleens of the interlopers. It was an old cemetery—many graves dating to the 1780s or 1790s— with typically heartbreaking stories in evidence. It's easy to forget how common child and infant mortality was just a century or two ago, but such cemeteries bring it back into focus.

We made it to Aiken just as darkness was falling. I'd lived in Aiken for a little less than a year back in 1990. Twenty-six years later, I recognized nothing. I honestly don't have many memories of Aiken, and the two places I worked when I lived there are out of business now.

I do have one offbeat memory of it, though. In the summer of 1990, I was working for Blockbuster Video and legendary singer James Brown was serving a six-year sentence for leading police on a two-state chase. I passed the prison every day on my way to work, and after months of looking, I finally spotted Mr. Brown in his prison jumpsuit, out in the yard. That was probably the highlight of my year in Aiken, which may tell you something about my life at that time.

Day Thirty-Three

It felt odd to be waking up in a roadside hotel in Aiken, South Carolina. I had lived there for a year, but there was really nothing I cared to go and check out for old time's sake. No favorite restaurant, or hangout, no cherished piece of scenery. My only good memories of living there were playing with my daughters, who had been two and four years old at the time. The funny thing was, although I had lived in Aiken in 1990, and Dayton, Washington, twenty-two years earlier, my memory of Dayton was so much sharper than what I remembered here. Memory is a funny thing.

We gassed up the Silver Bullet and Dawn said, "Okay, this is your town, so where do you want to go?"

I had a one-word answer: "Away."

So, away we went. Sorry, Aiken. I'm sure you're a lovely town.

Since we were in the South, I thought it was important that we visit a plantation and get a feel for what that life was like. Of the several options, we chose Redcliffe, which had been a well-known, working plantation for many years, until the fortunes of the family that owned it declined over the decades. When the fourth generation inherited it, they couldn't afford the upkeep or taxes and donated it to South Carolina. The state took ownership in the 1970s and has maintained it as a historic site ever since.

The plantation was originally owned by James Henry Hammond, famous for his "Cotton is King" speech to Congress in 1858, in the lead-up to the Civil War. What he said was, "Cotton is king." What he *meant* was, "Don't mess with our right to own slaves." Hammond was one of the most vocal of all the pro-slavery Southerners. Oh, and he seemed unashamed to have had sexual relationships with his four nieces. He nonetheless went on to be elected a U.S. Senator, a position he resigned as soon as Abraham Lincoln was elected. Meanwhile, those four teenage girls were thought to be "tarnished," and never married. Hammond goes on the list of people karma seems to have missed, at least in public view. Knowing his history, and the fact that he owned 300 slaves at one time, put a dark cloud over the whole plantation for us, but we took the tour nonetheless.

Though it was only mid-morning, it was already above 90 degrees again, so the interior of the house was sweltering. From a historic standpoint, I was glad to have seen it. Knowing that every floorboard, painting and vase was bought and paid for through the labor of slaves made the whole tour uncomfortable for me. Well, that and the three incredibly unruly little boys who ran amok while the ranger tried to control them and their mother ignored them. Wait. That's not quite right. She would say, "Boys! Don't do that." Then, she would turn her back on them and let them do whatever they wanted. I felt sorry for the ranger who was trying to protect the many artifacts in easy reach throughout the house.

When we had finished the tour of the huge main house, we walked through a two-room house where slaves once lived. Twenty people lived in a house better suited to four. It was dark and cramped, and we were glad when we walked back into the beautiful sunshine.

When we got back in the car, Dawn turned the air-conditioning on high, then said, "I think that's enough plantation culture for me."

I agreed.

We set out to see what the back roads of South Carolina had to offer. The answer was a lot of small towns and 45-mph roads, which suited us fine. We stopped for lunch in a wide spot in the road called Johnston, South Carolina.

It was the kind of small-town café that caters almost

exclusively to locals and rarely sees a stranger walk through the door. We caused a bit of a turning of heads and a few murmurs just by being strangers.

One thing Dawn had been commenting on was that she hadn't heard much in the way of the famous Southern drawl. That was about to change.

A pretty young waitress brought us ice water and menus, then looked at Dawn and said, "Do you want anything else to drink?" Dawn just stared at her, as though she might be speaking a foreign language.

"I'm sorry, what?"

The young girl smiled broadly and said, "Do you want anything to drink other than water?" I understood her, but as I mentioned, I had lived in the South on several occasions. This girl's drawl was so broad and pronounced that Dawn couldn't make out what she was saying.

I tried not to smile while I ordered for both of us, serving as interpreter for Dawn for the rest of the meal. Dawn kept focusing on what the waitress was saying, but all the extra, drawn-out syllables and y'alls were just too much for her.

I paid our bill and thanked the young girl. On the way to the car, I asked Dawn, "Still feeling like you're not getting enough Southern accents?"

"I need to be careful what I wish for."

We drove north, switching roads so often I could barely keep up on the atlas. In late afternoon, we crossed over into North Carolina. The first thing we saw was what I can only assume was a piece of roadside art. There was a white toilet, lid up, sitting beneath a sign that read: *NO TRESPASSING*.

Because I knew you wouldn't believe me

I've never been good at following orders, or signs, so, risking a load of birdshot over my head, I asked Dawn to pull over. I hopped out and ran back to the potty. I had to know if it was functioning or just for display.

There was a bit of rainwater collected in the bottom, but, aside from that and a few empty beer cans, it was thankfully empty. And now you know.

Day Thirty-Four

We'd had thirty consecutive days with temperatures at least into the upper eighties, and we were ready for cool weather. Each night, I lay across our motel bed, opened the atlas and looked longingly at Maine, Vermont, Upstate New York, or the Upper Peninsula of Michigan. By the time we got there, I was sure, it would finally be cooler.

This was mostly a day for driving. We were tempted to drive out to the Atlantic coast again, but since we were in the middle of North Carolina, it would have added another day or two to the trip to get over there. I had promised Dawn I would have her home in time to decorate our new house for Halloween. So, it was a matter of making choices, every day.

To take a trip where tough choices and prioritizing weren't needed would probably have demanded four or five months. Maybe when we were twenty we could have done that, but we're too old to spend that many consecutive days on the road. We missed our dogs and cat, not to mention the comfortable bed awaiting us at home.

This day, then, rather than scoot to the coast, we drove straight up through North Carolina and Virginia. Our one tourist stop was in Richmond, Virginia, where we investigated the Edgar Allan Poe Museum. Poe is most closely associated with Baltimore, but he spent his formative years in Richmond, and when you are as famous and accomplished as Poe was, cities end up fighting over your legacy.

I've been a big Edgar Allan Poe fan since I was very young. One day in junior high, I was home sick with the flu. At least I think it was the flu. It might have been one of those "I didn't do my map of South America that was due today" illnesses. In any case, I was desperate for something to read and grabbed a book off the coffee table. It had "The *Murders in the Rue Morgue"* in it. I was hooked. I haven't read everything Poe wrote, but a good chunk of his works, including, of course, "*The Raven,*" "*The Telltale Heart,*" and "The *Pit and the Pendulum.*" I also saw *The Oblong Box,* based on his story, at the drive-in in Baker City, Oregon, in 1970, and it scared the heck out of me, if that counts.

One of the cool things about the museum is that it's centered in a house built in 1740, the oldest standing house in Richmond. It's called, fittingly, the Old Stone House, and for its age, it's holding up pretty well. The Old Stone House and surrounding buildings contain a rich array of Poe memorabilia, including rare first editions, Poe's writing chair, a lock of his hair, and his childhood bed. Everything is clearly presented, so it's possible to get a good feel for Poe's life even if you don't know much about him going in.

One oddity is that, because of the age of the building, the rooms arranged into a museum aren't very big but all have closing doors, like bedrooms. So you end up touring these very small rooms in close quarters with strangers. A slightly surreal experience.

Poe's greatest works are macabre, of course, but the museum offers a sense of how justified his morbid nature was. He was effectively orphaned at a young age—his father abandoned the family, and his mother died when he was two years old. His foster mother, who was kind to him, died when he was still a young man, but he didn't learn of her death until he returned for a visit. His brother died of alcoholism at a young age. His first wife died of tuberculosis in her early thirties. If ever a writer had a pool of horror to draw on, it was Poe. Out of death and tragedy, he created genius.

The Poe museum is in an old area of Richmond, and the surrounding environs were not welcoming. Once we finished our tour, we were happy to get into the Silver Bullet and head north to historic Fredericksburg for the night. I do have to note, though, that when you are driving through this particular corridor of the United States, almost every town deserves the title *historic.*

Day Thirty-Five

I've mentioned how seat-of-the-pants my planning has been on this trip, right? This day was the perfect example. Sitting in our hotel room in the morning, I worked out three great stops for us. Then, we got to the first one and I didn't want to leave. So, everything else was pushed to the next day.

Today, we drove to Harpers Ferry, West Virginia, which was endlessly fascinating to me. First, about that name: My instinct is to write it as Harper's Ferry, with the apostrophe. That shows ownership (the ferry at one time belonged to Harper, so it was Harper's ferry) and it was the correct way to spell it for many years. Of late, however, the town itself has dropped the apostrophe and proclaimed itself to be simply Harpers Ferry. If Prince could decide, once upon a time, to be known as an unpronounceable symbol, then Harpers Ferry can certainly shed its apostrophe.

Harpers Ferry has been part of my imagination since I was a young boy. Around age 10, I found an Illustrated Classics book that told the story of what happened there, and it has stuck in my mind ever since. I don't remember what slant that comic book took on the story—whether it presented John Brown as a sinner or a saint—but it has stayed with me for four decades plus.

Our first effort at finding the historic part of Harpers Ferry did not go well. We entered something like "Harpers Ferry Historical Site" into Google Maps, and it confidently gave us directions, which we followed. Eventually, it told us we had arrived at our destination. It didn't look right to me, but we went into the big building anyway. When we asked if this was where a tour of the Harpers Ferry historic site might start, a very understanding lady said, "Google Maps? Yeah, we've been trying to get them to change that for years now, but they never do."

The directions had led us to an administrative building for the park service, but nowhere close to the Harpers Ferry historic area. Luckily, this seems to happen pretty regularly, and the woman gave us good directions to get where we wanted to go. So, Shawn's Safety Tip of the Day is, *don't trust Google to help you find Harpers Ferry Historic District.*

Harpers Ferry is named after one Robert Harper who came through the area in 1747, saw what he believed to be an opportunity, and bought his way in. History is full of interesting footnotes, and here's one: Harper "bought" his property from a man named Peter Stephens. The problem was, Stephens didn't own the property; he was just a squatter with no legal right to sell it. They weren't as careful about title searches in the eighteenth century as we are today. When he discovered he had been bilked, Harper negotiated with the rightful owner, Lord Fairfax, and purchased the property a second time.

What Harper saw was the place where two rivers—the Potomac and the Shenandoah—came together. He began running a ferry between their banks. Thus, the name.

Another historical tidbit that ultimately played a large role in the uprising that would take place there: In 1784, a young man named George Washington spent time in the area, working as a surveyor for that same Lord Fairfax. He was impressed by the possibilities presented by the location—the confluence of two rivers and a convenient pass through the Blue Ridge Mountains. When Washington became our first president, he selected Harpers Ferry as the site of a national armory—a place to store armaments the young nation would need in case of war.

Before we get to the consequence of that decision, I want to tell you what the historical part of Harpers Ferry looks like. To get there, you can either hike a mile or two down from the visitors center or hop on one of the buses that run on a loop. We opted for the bus.

Locating a town at the confluence of two rivers was great

for trade and shipping; the downside was the strong possibility of, but of course there are downsides, too, such as flooding. Harpers Ferry has been flooded so often that the lower part of the town was mostly abandoned years ago, and the modern-day Harpers Ferry town sits on a hill high above. A 1936 flood brought waters up to just below second-story windows on some of the buildings.

The old town's architecture puts you in the mood for a historical drama. St. Peter's Roman Catholic Church looms over the town and properly prepares you for what is to come. There are no new buildings to take you out of the mood and, after just a few minutes of wandering through the town, you can start to feel as though you have stepped back in time a couple of centuries.

Follow the road all the way through town, and you come to the point where the rivers come together. It is a breathtaking vista, and you can see three states—Virginia, West Virginia, and Maryland—at the same time. You can also see that passage through the mountains that so entranced young Mr. Harper that he was willing to buy the same real estate twice.

The historic town probably wouldn't be so well remembered if not for John Brown, an abolitionist willing to go to extreme lengths to eliminate slavery.

To me, that presents a conundrum. Slavery was obviously a horrible wrong that needed to abolished. Is it worth any price to advance such a cause? To a slave living on a plantation, the answer would understandably be yes. But it does raise the question of whether the ends always justify the means.

John Brown's journey from abolitionist to what we would now call a terrorist began in the territory of Kansas, which was then seeking entry into the Union. There was a big question: would it be a slave state, or a free state? The issue was hotly debated, and the debate eventually turned to violence. Lawrence, Kansas, was burned by pro-slavery forces. In retaliation, John Brown and his followers killed five pro-slavery men in

Pottawatomie Creek, Kansas, in May of 1856.

Brown, now a wanted man, avoided capture for this crime for three years, until 1859. That's when he emerged from hiding and launched what became known as John Brown's Raid in Harpers Ferry. The choice of that town was no accident—his plan was to capture the armory located there, grab huge numbers of weapons, disburse them to slaves in the area, and encourage them to stage an armed uprising. His hope was that the uprising would spread through all the Southern states and force them to give up slavery.

The first part of his plan worked flawlessly. With a tiny force of only eighteen, he launched a surprise attack on the armory and took it over without a shot being fired. That boggles my mind a bit. With minimal force, he was able to capture one of the largest weapons armories in the United States. For an organization that was mass-producing weapons, they were lightly guarded. Once he held the armory, his plan was to send his small force out into the countryside, capture slave owners and their slaves, then bring them all back to the armory, hold the slave owners hostage, arm the slaves, and encourage insurrection.

The problem was it took too long to accomplish that second part of the plan. It took much longer for his forces to locate and kidnap local landowners than he had anticipated. While most of his force was out doing that, the men who worked at the armory showed up for work the next morning. They were met by armed men, who took them hostage.

As you can imagine, the good townsfolk of Harpers Ferry didn't take kindly to a stranger coming into town, forcibly taking over the armory and taking locals hostage. A gun battle ensued. Of course, communications weren't nearly as fast in that time, but eventually President James Buchanan was alerted, and he dispatched a company of Marines, led by Robert E. Lee and J.E.B. Stuart, to quash the uprising.

Brown took his hostages and meager remaining forces and

barricaded himself in what came to be known as John Brown's Fort to make a last stand. When the Marines arrived, Brown attempted to negotiate with Lee and Stuart, but they weren't having it. Brown was told that only his unconditional surrender would be acceptable. Brown further barricaded himself inside the building, but the Marines grabbed whatever was at hand to use as a battering ram and forced their way inside, one at a time.

Let's think about that scene for a moment. You've got an armed group of men holed up inside a building, feeling they've got nothing to lose. You are able to create a hole just big enough for one man at a time to get through. Would you want to be that first brave Marine to enter? Once the Marines breached the building the fight lasted only three minutes. After some intense hand-to-hand combat, John Brown's Raid was over.

John Brown was taken alive.

John Brown's Fort

That was October 17, 1859. In six weeks he was tried, found guilty of treason, and hanged. The wheels of justice moved a lot faster in the old days.

That's the story. Looking back on it through the prism of the present day, what does it all mean? John Brown stood on the right side of history in abolishing slavery. But he was also a fanatic willing to do whatever he needed to push his agenda forward. He murdered people, first in Kansas, then in Harpers Ferry. He accomplished a lot, becoming a lightning rod whose drastic action forced people to decide where they stood.

How does all this resonate in our world today, when terrorists are use similar methods to advance their goals? I have lots of questions and thoughts, but no answers. I will say that the idea that the end justifies the means is a slippery slope, one that can be used to justify many crimes, but carries little weight with me.

Skipping the rest of our day's adventures to spend more time in Harpers Ferry was an easy decision. It turned out to be one of the best stops in this whole Lap Around America. It got me thinking, and that's always a good thing.

As soon as we got on the bus to head back to the visitors center, it started to rain. Precipitation followed us all the way to Somerset, Pennsylvania, where we crashed for the night.

Day Thirty-Six

Google Maps got us lost once again. When we got seriously lost in Utah, ending up clear on the wrong end of the state from where we wanted to be, I think it was mostly operator error. But in Harpers Ferry, it was definitely a problem with the software. Same thing this day.

We left our hotel in Somerset early because we wanted to try to hit two major Pennsylvania landmarks the same day: the Flight 93 National Memorial and Gettysburg. I entered the main entrance to the memorial on the GPS and relaxed. Less than an hour later, Google announced that we had arrived, and we had—at an abandoned gate that looked like it might have been used as a temporary park entrance years ago.

I got my fold-out map of Pennsylvania out, discovered where we had gone wrong, and backtracked a few miles until we saw signs for the real entrance. Google Maps, you're working your way onto my naughty list.

Like so many of us, I watched the drama of Flight 93 unfold in real time. On the morning of Sept. 11, 2001, I had been on my way to a real estate seminar an hour from home. I had gotten ready to go in a quiet house, with no television or radio turned on. In my car, I tuned to a Seattle sports radio show. The first thing I heard the host say was, "If you're listening to us, why? Please tune in to a news channel for information about what is happening."

I switched to KIRO News Radio 710 just after the second tower had been hit. I turned the car around and went right back home. I knew everything had changed, and there would certainly be no real estate seminar that day.

When I heard the Pentagon had also been hit and that Flight 93 had crashed in a Pennsylvania field, my first thought was, "How many aircraft are in the air above the United States at this minute? How many potential weapons could impact other areas of the country?"

Later I was thankful there were only the four planes hijacked. Still, it is an event that echoes in the world's consciousness, more than a decade and a half later.

Before we reached the memorial, we pulled over to the side of the road and looked back at Shanksville, Pennsylvania, the tiny town Flight 93 had barely missed before crashing into the empty field. It was easy to picture the shock and chaos of that morning. A quiet hamlet, its peace suddenly and unexpectedly shattered by a huge aircraft flying low over their roofs.

The story of Flight 93 is tragic, of course, but also heroic. Flight 93 was supposed to have taken off at the same time as the other hijacked flights but had been delayed and took off approximately 40 minutes later. That gave the passengers time to learn what had happened to the other flights and formulate a plan.

Putting myself in their place, I can only imagine the pain of discovering the inevitable fate of this plane. They decided to put fear aside and do whatever was necessary to give themselves, and whatever target the hijackers had selected, a chance. No one knows for sure what target the terrorists had chosen, but it has been speculated they were aiming at either the White House or the Capitol Building in Washington, D.C.

The passengers rushed the hijackers. The plane crashed in the middle of an empty field, killing everyone on board but preventing what would surely have been many more casualties.

With that background, the Flight 93 National Memorial can't be anything but somber, and it is. I found it also tasteful, thoughtful, and extremely well done. Having hit a lot of national parks over the past five weeks, I was impressed with the work done everywhere by the National Park Service. I have yet to see a bad example. They do a wonderful job of straddling the line between protecting our history and making it accessible.

Inside the visitors center is a gift shop. We didn't linger there. It's hard for me to imagine many people wanting an orange Flight

93 sweatshirt, but they're for sale, so someone must.

Half a dozen long walls are filled with screens and memorabilia establishing a timeline for the events of 9/11, including television broadcasts of the day, mementos of the flight, pictures of the passengers and crew, and so on. From an observation deck, you can trace the flight of the plane to its landing spot, marked by a boulder.

Dawn and I walked down to the field itself. It is pastoral and, aside from the other people walking along it, perfectly quiet. It is a truly random place for a plane to fall from the sky.

Dawn turned to me and said, "Why?"

"Why, what?"

"Why did they do this? What did they hope to accomplish?"

"I don't know," I admitted. "I'm not at all sure about what they were hoping to accomplish. Strike back at the undefeatable enemy? Make a statement? I don't know. The sad thing is, I think I know what they actually *did* accomplish."

"What do you think?"

"I think they made us afraid. It feels like our whole country has changed since 9/11. We were the policeman of the world, often to our detriment. Ever since the towers fell, it feels like we are afraid. I hate to see us making decisions as a nation out of fear of the unknown, or the worst-case scenario."

"Hmmm." This is Dawn's catch-all phrase. It means, *I'm not sure you're right, but I'll think about it for a while.* I knew we would continue this conversation later.

We walked back up the hill and to our car. It was the middle of the week, but the memorial was busy. There were half a dozen school buses, huge tour groups, and stragglers like us. As sad and somber as the memorial is, it was gratifying to see so many people coming to pay their respects. Even the kids, not always noted for their broad perspectives, were quiet and respectful. It's the least we can do for those who chose to do the right thing.

When we left the Flight 93 memorial, we had a choice: I-70, or Highway 30. The interstate would have been faster, but by now I'm sure you know what we chose. We'd driven a lot of country roads on this trip, but I think my favorite was Highway 30 between Somerset and Gettysburg. Parts were so twisty that I said a little prayer of thanks that I never get carsick. It was an incredible way to spend a few hours.

Pennsylvania doesn't look like anything we're used to—not the houses, the small towns, the foliage, none of it. Seeing the old houses all decorated for fall, with the leaves beginning to change colors, put us in a happy place.

Which, I admit, was a good thing just then. Even after the Flight 93 site, Gettysburg is about as somber as a place can get. It's actually a lovely small town, as I'm sure it was prior to the Civil War battle of 1863, but let's face it, it's best known as the place where an awful lot of Americans died fighting one another. You may have noticed that we drove all the way through the South without reflecting on the Civil War. Truth is, I am not a big Civil War buff. I watched the Ken Burns documentary about it when it was on PBS, but that's about the extent of it. The previous day, we had driven right by the Battle of Antietam site without even stopping.

But Gettysburg is different. It wasn't just the bloodiest battle of the war but became a national touchstone for a nation torn apart. At least, it is to me. On my Facebook page, people are saying our nation has never been as divided as it is right now. When I read that, I think people have short memories. We might have deep factions of conservatives and liberals in our nation, but 30,000 people aren't dying on a battlefield like they did in Gettysburg.

One thing we hadn't realized before was *how huge* the whole Gettysburg battlefield area is. It's not confined to a single field, or connected fields, or a hill, or a forest. It's spread all over the entire town and surrounding countryside. When we first pulled up to the visitors center, we had no idea what to expect. It was already mid-afternoon, and so we were short on time. It would have made sense to get a hotel room and tackle Gettysburg the next day, but there was a problem. Every hotel, motel, and bed-and-breakfast was booked up solid. That meant we would have to drive down the road to sleep, and I hate to start our days by backtracking, so today was it for Gettysburg.

The visitors center is immense. And popular. The crowds gathered at the Flight 93 National Memorial were nothing compared with what we saw here. It was a Tuesday afternoon in late September, and it was packed. In fact, when we picked up a few things in the gift shop, I had to stand in line so long to buy them that Dawn had time to find two more things before I got to the cashier.

There's an array of things you can do at the memorial, including an excellent movie and presentation, a car tour, etc. Gettysburg National Military Park isn't cheap, though. It's free to get in, but if you want to go on the car tour, it's $65. The movie is $12, which is reasonable, but I sure didn't feel like driving thousands of miles to Gettysburg, then sitting in a theater to see it.

So, we chose to do the guided driving tour with an audio CD. If you have the time, I recommend it. They say you can see the whole thing in 90 minutes, which I guess you could do if you didn't ever slow down to look at anything. We wanted to drink things in, though. Dawn and I took about three and a half hours to do the 26-mile, 16-stop drive all over Gettysburg, listening to the audio cues.

As I say, I'm not a huge Civil War guy, but listening to the excellent narration brought the three days of the battle to life for us. It's enough to make me want to go home and watch the whole Ken Burns documentary again. During the tour, you get to park and overlook all the key locations: Round Top, Devil's Den, Culp's Hill, the Peach Orchard, and Cemetery Ridge, where Pickett made his charge.

If you, like me, aren't exactly a Civil War scholar, the short version of the whole conflict is that the Confederate forces, led by Robert E. Lee, were tired of playing defense and sought to take the fight to the north. They clashed with the Union forces, led by General George Meade, at various sites around Gettysburg over July

184

1 to July 3, 1863.

Both sides made strategic errors that I didn't begin to understand until I could see the battlefields spread out in front of me and understood where each army was positioned. In the end, it was Lee's decision to order his undermanned forces in a movement that became known as Pickett's Charge, which was bold, ballsy, and ultimately the turning point in the battle. His forces were rebuffed by the strong position of the Union forces and torn apart, and the whole Confederate force ended up retreating to Virginia.

The site of Pickett's Charge

It was a devastating loss for the rebels, but it certainly didn't end the war. That stretched on for almost two more years. From a historical standpoint, it was the bloodiest battle ever fought in the Western Hemisphere. That's according to the park service CD, by the way. I don't pretend to know these types of things.

One thing you will quickly learn is that Gettysburg is the land of a million statues and memorials. Every which way you turn, you will find statues memorializing the forces that fought from various states. If you like military statues, Gettysburg will be a little slice of heaven for you.

When we got to the end of our audio tour, the sun was below the horizon, the sky was burnt orange, and we were looking out on the area where Major General George Pickett led his charge. We felt the enormity of the history and the sacrifices made by brave men and women on both sides of the battle.

This was one of the most emotional days of our trip. Flight 93 and Gettysburg, broken by a lovely three-hour drive through pristine villages and farms. We were asleep less than an hour after we reached our motel in Hanover, Pennsylvania.

Day Thirty-Seven

The first thing I did every morning on this trip was a little search of the town we'd stayed in overnight. It was cool when we got lucky and found something nearby we wanted to see. My search in Hanover revealed that the Gettysburg Electric Map, which offered a visual orientation to the battle at the Gettysburg visitors center for years until it was deemed too old-fashioned and mothballed, was still on display here. Scott Roland, a local man, bought it at a government auction in 2012 for $14,000. That's either a lot of money for a piece of outdated equipment, or a steal of a deal on a historic artifact, depending on your viewpoint.

It took Roland four years of working on the display and rewiring it to get it up to speed. If he was willing to spend four years of his nights and weekends on the project, I thought the least we could do was swing by and look at it while we were in town.

We found the building where the Electric Map was displayed, walked into the lobby and found a locked door and a dark room beyond. There had been no mention of odd hours on the website I'd been reading, and there were no hours at all listed on the door. I marched up a set of stairs to the left of the door to see if I could get more information.

Turns out there was a retro video arcade upstairs where patrons paid by the hour to play classic arcade games—something I would have been interested in if we weren't driving around the country. The gentleman who ran the arcade said, "Trying to see the Gettysburg map?"

"Yes. Do you know what time they open?"

"I'm not sure they're going to be open today. I've got the guy's phone number, so I'll give him a call."

Two minutes later, he was back, shaking his head. "He won't be here at all today. Maybe Saturday." As in, three days away. Hanover was a nice little town, but I didn't see staying there three days just so we could gawk at an old light-up map of the Gettysburg battlefield.

✓ I thanked the man for his time, and we headed back for Highway 30. Important safety tip: If you want to see the Gettysburg Electric Map, you would be wise to call ahead.

We finally figured out what made the small towns feel so different to us as we drove Highway 30: the houses that sit smack up against the road wherever the highway cuts through town. If one wanted to, one could spit on a porch while driving by. We don't see that in Washington, where there's always a distance between the front door and the highway. That's probably a legacy of the time lag between town and highway construction in Pennsylvania, but it made everything feel strangely intimate as we puttered through one small town after another. Time and again, we pulled off the road to look at an ancient barn or house.

There's something about this barn…

After a few hours, we crossed the Delaware River into New Jersey. Neither of us had been to New Jersey before, so we didn't know what to expect. I didn't know much about the state, aside from its proximity to New York City. Today, I learned that western New Jersey is filled with small farm towns, rolling hills, and lots of trees, and is perfectly lovely. Not at all what you would associate with something like *The Sopranos*. I was also pretty pumped that we managed to drive quite a distance through New Jersey without having to pay a single toll.

As we drove down one winding road, autumn leaves already beginning to shake loose and fall, we saw a small stand next to a house with a simple sign that read: *Pickles*. Who can resist that? Not us. We stopped and knocked at the door, but no one answered. The stand had two jars of pickles for five dollars apiece. I stuck a ten-dollar bill under a rock and happily added the pickles to The Magical Mystery Bag. Life is always better with pickles.

We drove through New Jersey and, just before dark stopped for the night in the hamlet of Central Valley, New York.

Day Thirty-Eight

As we drove northeast out of Central Valley, we were forced onto the freeway for a while. We hit several toll booths in short order, and we learned something: Tolls were more expensive in Florida, but the toll takers there were human beings and occasionally smiled. I'm almost sure there was no human DNA in the toll takers in New York who grunted and growled at us today as we went through. Welcome to New York!

As we reached western Connecticut, the scenery was lovely. The leaves were starting to turn and we saw color everywhere. We began to hope for great leaf-peeping ahead in New Hampshire, Maine, and Vermont.

By late morning, we made it to Hartford, Connecticut, which we learned was the wealthiest city of America at one point in the late 19th century. It's not any more, but it is still a well-laid-out, gorgeous city, with a plethora of historic buildings. We were there to see just one, though: the Mark Twain House. Or the Samuel Clemens residence, I suppose, if you want to be really accurate.

So far, we've seen Hemingway's house, which was impressive, the Edgar Allen Poe Museum in Richmond, which was pretty good, and now we've added Mark Twain's house. While I like Hemingway and Poe's writing, Mark Twain was my earliest favorite author. I've always loved his short works best—"The Stranger," "The Man Who Corrupted Hadleyburg," "The Million Pound Bank Note," and so on. I think I've read everything he's ever written, including his travelogues. In addition, he spoke out in favor of equal rights for all, which wasn't a popular position in the late 19th century.

It's easy to think how Mark Twain became wealthy. After all, he was among the most popular authors of his time, known worldwide. It wasn't writing that paid for the magnificent house, though, as he'd published only one minor book when it was built.

He managed that by marrying well. His wife, Olivia, was an heiress, and they used her inheritance to build the massive, 11,000-square-foot home. Many a parent has told his son, "It is just as easy to marry a rich girl as a poor one." Apparently, Samuel Clemens paid attention.

The Mark Twain House

The house was built in American High Gothic style. I'm no architectural expert, but I can tell you one thing that means: It was dark. Inside, it took my eyes several minutes to adjust to the darkness caused by curtained windows, dark wood, and limited lighting.

One thing I'd noticed about many of the older houses we toured on this trip was that they are made up of lots of small rooms. I'm sure this had something to do with keeping them warm. In the Mark Twain house, there were lots of large rooms—it really is an elegant house. But it wasn't merely a showplace; it had obviously been lived in and used by a family.

The house is laid out as much as possible as it was when Clemens, his wife, and children lived there. It's easy to see that he doted on his children. The great sadness of his life was that he outlived three of the four, as well as his wife.

On just about any other day, the Mark Twain House would be the fanciest place we would see, but today it wasn't even close. That's because we next drove to Newport, Rhode Island, where the uber-wealthy of the nineteenth century built their summer cottages. And by "cottages," I mean huge, sprawling mansions on immaculate grounds, many of which face the Atlantic Ocean.

I thought I would show Dawn how we would live if I ever became a bestselling author, so we visited The Breakers. Okay, that's not quite true. We did visit The Breakers, but neither Dawn nor I would ever have any interest in living in anything remotely like that.

The Breakers is impressive beyond words: massive, ornate, and like walking through a museum. Who would want to live like that? The answer, of course, is Cornelius Vanderbilt, who used The Breakers as a little summer getaway.

Yes, this is our little summer getaway

The Breakers has 70 rooms in its 125,000 square feet and is decorated in Gilded Age style. How many people would it take just to keep that dusted? When we visited Mark Twain's home earlier in the day, that home felt immense—but you could fit more than a dozen houses of that size in this one. Almost half a million people visit The Breakers each year. It is one of the rare historic homes that allows photography, so bring your camera if you ever visit. The third floor is not open to the public, as it is still occupied by Countess Sylvia Szapary, who has a life estate, which means she can live there for as long as she chooses.

I had to stop and think about that. What would it be like to live in a home the size of a Walmart Supercenter (albeit one decorated somewhat more opulently) and have more than a thousand people a day tramp through your lower floors? I can only imagine, and now I think I have yet another short story to write, but that is for another day.

As we were leaving, Dawn observed, "Babe, if you'll just buy me The Breakers, I'll never ask for anything again."

I took that under advisement, but for now, she will have to make do with a few postcards and a magnet I picked up for her at the gift shop.

By the time we left The Breakers, it was actually cooling off a bit. Temperatures had dropped down into the 70s, which was the closest thing to cool we had found since we hit Eastern Washington. We found a small motel called the Sea Whale, with a view of the water.

One of the things I had promised Dawn on the trip was her first whole lobster, and we made that happen in Newport. Me? I am not much of a seafood enthusiast, so I stuck with a delicious shepherd's pie. Luckily, the waitress recognized that we were not professional lobster eaters and gave Dawn a quick tutorial in how to attack it. She mastered it quickly.

Day Thirty-Nine

One thing about Rhode Island is that, no matter which direction you're going, it doesn't take long to drive out of the state. I think it takes longer to drive across Los Angeles than it does to drive across or up Rhode Island. The latter drive is a lot more pleasant, though.

We had our sights set on Massachusetts, and more specifically, Salem. I'm pretty sure everyone is familiar with the infamous Salem witch trials. We wanted to get a feel for the town where fear and hysteria overtook an entire population in the 1690s. In my blog, I referred to the witch trials as "example 1083-B of what happens when self-righteous people with a limited worldview are put in charge of everyone else." I'll stand by that statement.

My first exposure to Salem and the trials was way back in the mid-1960s. Long before I read about the historic event in books or in school, I saw an episode of *Bewitched* set in Salem. Sure enough, as we drove through the middle of town, we saw a statue of Elizabeth Montgomery in character as Sam from that television series. I'm pretty sure the current citizens of Salem would rather people remember the town through a sunny sixties sitcom than through the horrible reality of what occurred in the seventeenth century.

The Salem witch trials were certainly not the only instance of ordinary people being accused of supernatural crimes and put to death for it. In fact, a rash of these events occurred across New England. Mass hysteria is usually blamed for the outbreak of righteousness and poison that swept the upper east corner of our nation. I can't help but wonder how much of it was actually a settling old scores, rejections, bad business deals, and so on.

I always knew how terrible the whole enterprise was. But, once we got to the simple memorial for the victims of the hysteria, the reality came home. That memorial is simple and profound: Beside the cemetery called The Burying Point is a row of benches, each inscribed with the name of one of the victims.

The one that most affected me was the memorial bench of Giles Corey. Most of the other accused were hanged, but Corey refused to enter a plea. I understand where he was coming from, and think I would have done the same thing. Once you were accused, you were essentially dead, one way or another. When Corey refused to plea, the judges decided to use a technique called "pressing": The accused is laid in a pit, a board is laid across him or her, and heavy stones are laid on top of the board. When I say "heavy stones," I mean stones so big it took several men just to pick them up. Every time the sheriff asked him for a plea, Corey would say, "More weight!" After three days, and after once again saying, "More weight!" Corey died.

Giles Corey's Bench in Salem

Not that any of the accused had it easy, but imagine the incredible suffering he endured to not give in. Dawn says I am the most stubborn man she's ever met, but I don't think I could hold a candle to the bravery and unwillingness to bend that Giles Corey displayed.

People still leave small mementoes and flowers on various

195

benches, paying tribute to lives that would have been long forgotten if not for fate choosing them for a certain infamy.

We'd seen some old cemeteries on our trip, but I don't think we'd seen any graves as old as we did in The Burying Point. Some dated from the 1600s. Many of the stones had degraded to a point where they were no longer legible, but still they stood.

We did see a lot of graves belonging to a family named Hathorne, the clan of Nathaniel Hawthorne, who wrote *The House of Seven Gables.* His ancestors were part of the witch trials, so he added the "w" to his name to separate himself from that infamy. In fact, a relative, John Hathorne, was the only known judge who never repented his decision to kill people he believed to be witches. I understand the name change.

The house Hawthorne wrote about in his most famous book is also in Salem, so we took the tour. He never lived in the house that had once famously had seven gables, but his cousin Susannah Ingersoll did, and he often visited there. His cousin loved to tell him stories that involved the history of the house, so when he wrote the followup to his novel *The Scarlet Letter,* he chose to write a gothic novel set in the house.

If I had read and loved *The House of the Seven Gables*, I'm sure seeing the house would have had more impact on me. I had been assigned *The Scarlet Letter* in high school, though, and didn't particularly enjoy it, so I never returned to Hawthorne.

One interesting aside: When Hawthorne saw the house, it had been remodeled and only had three gables. He didn't like the ring of a book called *The House of Three Gables*, though, so he wrote about it as it had once looked.

We'd seen some old houses on our trip, but nothing as old as this one, which dates to 1668. As far as I have learned, it's the oldest surviving wooden private home still standing in America. It was at risk of being torn down in the early twentieth century, but a woman named Caroline Emmerton bought it, established a foundation, and restored the property.

The House of Seven Gables

Unfortunately, when they did the restoration, they made the original building adhere more to the novel by adding a secret passage, which we got to use. The secret passage was very narrow and twisting, like a shorter version of the passage we used to climb up inside the Statue of Liberty a few years ago. Personally, I would have preferred the house as it had been built, but tourism is an important factor in keeping it up.

We liked much of Salem, although I will admit Dawn enjoyed it more than I did. There was something about the memorial and the hangings and pressings that cast a pall over the town and the day for me. One thing we both hated was the traffic in Salem, with its narrow streets, hyper-aggressive drivers, and confusing intersections. At one point, Dawn had stopped to let an old woman with a walker cross in the crosswalk in front of her. The driver behind us laid on his horn the whole time. I guess he would have preferred us to just run the old girl over. In Salem, we walked wherever possible, and that was much more pleasant.

I had planned on taking another ghost/historical tour of

197

Salem as soon as it got dark. We'd loved the tour we took of New Orleans that way, and thought we'd probably learn a lot of history that isn't easily available in books.

Once we got to our motel and checked in, though, I felt terrible. I didn't know if I was coming down with a bug or the bad vibes of the historical events were weighing on me. Either way, I lay down on the bed to rest for a few minutes, and I was lights-out until morning.

Day Forty

We had a decision to make. The far northeast was beckoning to us. We had been dreaming of Vermont and Maine ever since we started the trip, and now we were tantalizingly close. But, just a bit behind us to the south lay Boston—one on the short list of cities where we had hoped to spend at least a few hours.

We knew that having just a few hours in Boston was laughable. It is one of the most historically rich cities in the country. We knew we couldn't get through a tenth of what we wanted to see in half a day, but if nothing else, we wanted to get the flavor of the city.

We immediately learned that Salem's traffic wasn't so bad after all. Boston's was much worse. Boston's road system seemed to specialize in three things—tunnels, side streets so narrow a car will barely fit, and bridges. We had somewhat negative encounters with all three and spent more time lost in Boston than we did anywhere else on the trip.

It was a gloomy, gray day with a spitting rain reminiscent of Washington. We almost felt at home. We only had time to hit a couple of sights, but both were excellent.

Our first stop was at Paul Revere House. This was much more modest than the other famous houses we'd toured thus far. Paul Revere was a silver mason and a business owner, but distinctly middle-class. He had sixteen children with his two wives, eleven of whom survived into adulthood. It's no wonder Revere worked so hard. We enjoyed having the opportunity to walk through his home and get a sense of what his eighteenth-century life was like, especially in a more modest home. Nothing will make you appreciate a home with central heat and air, cable television and Internet as much as walking through a dark, smoky house from that era.

The Paul Revere House

Later, we drove around Boston for a while. We found some tree-lined streets that were quiet and attractive, and a few neighborhoods where things looked a little rougher. Basically, like any other city.

Dawn loves the movie *Black Mass*, starring Johnny Depp as Whitey Bulger, so we contemplated looking up some of the locations from the film, but that would have been time-consuming and entailed us driving through more Boston traffic, which didn't seem like much fun.

So, we swung by the USS *Constitution* and walked through both it and its well-laid-out museum, which gives an excellent perspective on what life was like for the sailors on board the ship during the War of 1812. The biggest thing I learned while walking around the craft itself was that I'm glad not to have been a sailor in those days. It's hard to picture spending my days clambering up and down those slippery ladders or ropes. I think my life expectancy at sea would have been plus or minus one day.

One last word on Boston: That famous accent, where "r's"

are nowhere to be found, has never been my favorite accent. Okay, I'll be honest. I hate a Boston accent. It just rings harshly in my ear. Dawn, on the other hand, is thrilled by it. Everywhere we go, when people talk to us, I can see her mumbling to herself, repeating their accent, cementing it in her mind. Watching TV in the room at night, whenever she hears someone speak in that distinct accent, she repeats it back until she's got it. As we drove through the city itself, she would ask if I would like to "Pahk the cah." When something amused her, she called it a "pissah." I think I've changed my mind on this accent now. When Dawn does it, it's very fetching.

After being completely soaked in Boston, we turned north and drove through New Hampshire.

We knew we'd hit a lot more of that state on the way back through, so we drove right on through to Maine.

Aren't there certain states that just have a resonance for you, even if you've never been there before? If you grew up on the east coast, I can see states like Colorado or California, or even Washington, having that aura of attraction. For Dawn and me, Maine has that effect on us. It's been number one on our hit parade from the time we left home.

For one thing, the chance to see Maine in October, when the leaves are changing, was irresistible. Getting to Maine also meant we would officially be driving toward home every day from now on, and that was starting to sound pretty good, too.

We stopped for the night in Old Orchard, Maine, a picturesque little beach town. I'm sure it is hopping in the summer, but in the first week of October, you could set a bomb off in the middle of the main drag and not hurt anyone. Everywhere we looked, we saw signs that said "Closed for the Season," or "Thanks for a great year! See you next summer." It had a bit of the feeling of driving through an amusement park after it had closed. In fact, since we were in Maine, now, home to Stephen King, it specifically reminded me of his ghost story

Joyland, about mysterious happenings in an old amusement park.

We were staying in a little hotel right on the beach. The weather had definitely turned and it was cold out, but if we left the slider open, we could hear the ocean. We checked in just before it got dark but still scrambled down to the beach for a walk along the seashore. It was windy, rainy, and we got soaked. It almost felt like we were home.

Day Forty-One

The rundown little beach hotel we stayed at the previous night had laundry services, so we started the day with an empty "dirty clothes" suitcase, which always gave a little boost to our day. That got me thinking about how many more times we'd need to find a laundry before we got home. That, in turn, led to me punching our home address into Google Maps to see how far from home we were. The answer, by the way, was 3,281 miles. That distance normally might have seemed daunting, but since it was the closest we'd been to home in more than a month, it didn't seem so bad. Google also said that if we drove straight through, we could be home in just over 48 hours.

Instead, we would take our time and meander across the northern portion of the United States, using a couple more weeks to cover those miles. We'd also take a lot of side trips and continue to avoid freeways.

The first thing we wanted to see in Maine was a lighthouse. We have lighthouses just down the coast from where we live, but those are *Washington* lighthouses. We wanted to see a *Maine* lighthouse. There are so many different lighthouses to choose from on the Maine coast that we were a little overwhelmed, but eventually we chose the Portland Head Light. It was relatively close to us, and historic. In fact, it's the oldest lighthouse in the state, having sent out its welcoming beacon for the first time in 1791.

We drove to Portland Head expecting to be properly impressed by the lighthouse itself, but didn't anticipate the effect of the bay below it. When we first pulled into the parking lot and walked toward the bay, Dawn sucked in her breath, put her hand over her mouth, and said, "Oh." That was about all I had to say at the moment as well. It was wild, gray, and powerful.

We climbed a little promontory to look down on the bay and heard the most miraculous sound. The waves were rushing in over millions of pebbles rather than sand. When the violence of the water meets the rocks, it jostles them, and as it sucks back out to sea, it all makes a sound like nature's rattle. Dawn thought it sounded like that moment when, in felling a tree, the tree suddenly gives up and begins to go over. To me, it just sounded like heaven—as musical as anything I've ever heard in nature. If I could set a tent up on that little hill and listen to that melody all night, I would sleep like a baby.

Our musical bay

I have tinnitus, a continuous whining and ringing in my ears. It's been with me for so many years that it has become my constant companion. There was something about the water rustling the rocks that put it in exactly the right harmonic range to match and cover the ringing. For those few minutes, the ringing disappeared, which is kind of heavenly all on its own. We came to see the lighthouse, but having discovered the sound of the melodic rocks, we had a hard time leaving it.

There are actually two lighthouses in this location. Portland Head, the big brother, gets all the press, but there is also a small lighthouse that stands in the middle of the bay called Ram Island Ledge Light Station. Rough waves beat over this smaller lighthouse as we watched. I can only imagine what the view would be like from there in the bay, looking in toward the glorious light of Portland Head.

Eventually we hiked up to see the star of the show. The Portland Head lighthouse is so picturesque, so perfectly what we expected, that all our hopes of Maine lighthouses were immediately met. The body of the lighthouse is sparkling white, with the glassed-in lantern room above. There is a lighthouse keeper's cottage below, also white, with a steep-pitched red roof. The entire operation is automated today, but the lighthouse keeper's dwelling now serves as an excellent maritime museum.

Portland Head Lighthouse

Portland Head lighthouse was built at the direct order of George Washington, who asked the masons who built it to remember that our young country was still poor and to take every opportunity to use thrifty methods to build it. Somewhere over the centuries, it seems like our government has lost that attitude, much to our detriment.

Oh, one last interesting tidbit about the Portland Head light. Even though it was in operation on Christmas Eve 1886, the *Annie C. Maguire* ran aground right in front of it. That wreck remains a bit of a mystery, as it apparently happened in daylight with good visibility, upon a rock marked to this day with paint. She was wrecked so close to the shore that the lightkeeper, his family, and some other volunteers were able to help all hands safely to shore. (No word on whether the black box was ever recovered, or if blood alcohol content was checked on the captain.)

Our desire for the perfect Maine lighthouse sated, we turned north, looking for leaves to be peeped. This was pretty close to the moment when I realized that I was no longer a kid but officially an old man: I'd included "leaf-peeping" on my must-do items for a trip around America. Well, if you're ever going to do it, Maine and Vermont in October are the right time and place.

We had one small problem, though. Maine had suffered through a terrible drought this summer, which according to experts I consulted (a couple of old guys with awesome Maine accents in a small grocery store) caused the changing of the leaves to be pushed back by a few weeks. So, even though the first week of October is typically prime leaf-peeping season, it wasn't optimal this year. They did tell us that the color change started in the north and slowly made its way south, so the farther north in the state we went, the better it would be.

We didn't plan a specific route. We just got the atlas out and picked back road after back road that would take us north. There were times we were so lost we sincerely had no idea where we were. We had faith, though, that eventually we would either hit the Canadian border or find a town that actually appeared on a map.

We kept our eyes peeled for anything interesting and pulled off to see a small cemetery ringed by orange and red trees. The cemetery itself was unremarkable—too modern to be of much interest to us—

but things definitely got interesting after that.

We knew we were going to hit somewhere between 13,000 and 15,000 miles on this trip—around what an average driver might drive in a year, but we were going to have done it in two months. Statistically, that meant we had a decent chance of either being in an accident or having a close call.

It was to our advantage that Dawn would be our driver on 98 percent of those miles. I am not ashamed to admit that Dawn is a safer driver than I am. If we need to get through traffic in a big city, or get somewhere with a definite drop-dead time, then I'm your guy. For just about everything else, I recommend Dawn. Since those two described circumstances rarely applied during the trip, she was our driver. On this day, at this precise time, I truly believe that having Dawn behind the wheel saved our lives.

A small highway ran alongside the cemetery. As we left, I asked Dawn to stop for a second so that I could hop out and take one of probably 300 photos I took of trees that day. I snapped the shot, climbed into the passenger seat, and we were ready to head north.

Dawn pulled up to the edge of the road. The speed limit on the highway was 45 mph. There was a line of traffic heading south, but that was no impediment to us, as we were turning north. Dawn looked left, saw that it was absolutely clear and inched toward the northbound lane. At that moment, a silver pickup truck (F250, I think, but can't swear to it) came up on the southbound traffic at high speed. It pulled out to pass the traffic, an action that I'm sure looked fine to that driver as there was no one coming toward him from that direction. Except, half a second later, *we* would have been coming from that direction. He came so close to the front end of the Silver Bullet, it shook the whole car. It was easy to write the equation: Big pickup + high rate of speed, slamming into a mid-size car = horrifying accident and the two of us waking up on the other side of life's curtain.

Very nearly the last photo I ever took

If I had been driving, the accident almost certainly would have happened. I tend to anticipate when I drive. So, I would have checked left and, seeing it clear, would have already had our two front tires in the lane. Dawn is much more cautious. She checked left, and for some reason, checked again right, just as that silver blur rocketed by us, missing us by a foot or two at most. We didn't even have time to scream. We just looked at each other, knowing that we were fortunate to still be converting oxygen to carbon dioxide. I asked Dawn if she was alright, she said she was, and off we went, continuing our search for beautiful leaves. What else were we going to do? I will say that everything looked a little lovelier, the air smelled a bit fresher, and I appreciated life just a smidgen more for the rest of that day.

We tooled through the hills for another hour or so, then turned south again, for Bangor.

Day Forty-Two

Why Bangor? Because Derry, Maine, is a fictional place, and I couldn't visit there. If that's confusing to you, it's possible that you are not a Stephen King fan. I know lots of people who aren't Stephen King fans. *Too scary. It gives me nightmares.* I get it. But Stephen King is and has been my favorite writer for many decades now.

My appreciation for all things King started about as early as it could have, when I found a paperback copy of *Carrie*, King's first novel, sitting innocently on a desk in Mr. Grimes' English class in 1975. I was fifteen years old, and the story of the telekinetic Carrie and the high school hell she had to endure every day reverberated with me. I became a fan midway through the first chapter, and I've never jumped ship. In fact, I named the high school loser in my book *The Unusual Second Life of Thomas Weaver* Carrie, in homage to the master.

Derry, by the way, is the town in Maine that serves as the nexus of many of the horrors that came pouring out of King's mind. Sadly, as I say, it is fictional, so I couldn't include it on our itinerary. What I *could* include, though, was a visit to his home, which is probably Bangor's best-known tourist destination. It's even in Google Maps. You can just punch in "Stephen King's home," and it will take you right to it.

So, on a bright and beautiful autumn day, we rolled into Stephen King's neighborhood. Visiting his house and neighborhood only made me love him more. It's a pleasant, upscale neighborhood, with large houses and manicured lawns, some of which are behind fences, but it's not one of those snobby, elite neighborhoods where people look at you crossly just for driving through. It's nice, but it's not a community you might expect a guy who has sold 350 million books to live in.

I had dedicated my book *Rock 'n Roll Heaven* to him, and I wished I had thought to bring a copy along so that I could leave it at the gate, but all my copies were boxed up back in Seaview. Mr. King, if you ever happen to stumble upon these words, drop me a line. I'd love to send you a copy.

The house sits behind a black wrought-iron gate, which doesn't disappoint. The gate itself is shaped like wings, and there are two formidable bats standing guard on it. But, beyond that, the house is pretty accessible, which makes me happy for him. It would be a terrible life to be stuck behind gates, guards and roaming security on some kind of compound.

Dawn and I took turns standing in front of the gothic fence. In those photos, Dawn looks vaguely uncomfortable, as though she feels she is invading someone's private space. I, on the other hand, have my arms flung wide in a welcoming gesture and am smiling from ear to ear. That might tell you all you need to know about us.

Shawn, stalking Stephen King at his home

We left Bangor in time to arrive in Waterville, Maine, about lunchtime. Waterville wasn't really on our tourist radar, but two of my favorite people, Bob and Karen Lichtenwalter, had moved there, and I wanted to take the opportunity to see them. Since we live 3,000 miles apart, I don't often get the chance to say, "So, I'm in the neighborhood …"

I met Bob when I was the Managing Broker of a real estate office in Enumclaw. He had called me one Friday night, asking if he could talk to me the next day about possibly joining our office.

Since it was a Saturday, I was dressed down when I went into the office—sweatpants, a T-shirt, and Nikes. Bob walked in wearing slacks, a sports coat, and a tie. The disparity was so great we had to laugh, and we became friends on the spot. Bob scared me when he told me he had been an engineer before becoming a Realtor, because engineers are kind of famous within our field for not having a sense of humor. Not so with Bob. He was one of the driest, funniest guys I'd ever met.

Eventually, I got to know his wife, Karen, as well, and she is the perfect complement to Bob. When Karen spoke, I quickly learned that I should listen.

Bob, by the way, gave me the best piece of marital advice I ever got. He said that if he was ever tempted to disagree with Karen, he considered what they were talking about, then asked himself, "Bob, is that the hill you want to die on?" I've taken that to heart ever since.

After an entertaining lunch, we said goodbye to Bob and Karen and drove west. For the first time since we left, we were driving toward home. This trip had felt like the experience of a lifetime, and we were seeing and learning so many new things, but still, heading west was cause for a small celebration.

We spent the rest of the day taking our time, wandering through western Maine and eastern New Hampshire. We felt so at home there, it was almost as though we'd been there before, although neither of us have. I got the atlas out and that explained it, at least a bit. Maine, New Hampshire, Vermont, and New York are all on a pretty similar latitude to Washington state. It looks a lot like home to us.

We ended up staying at a terrible little Days Inn in Concord, New Hampshire. We had made every effort to not stay at chain hotels on the trip, but sometimes that was all that was available. From that point forward, we decided that if our choice is between staying in our car or staying in a Days Inn, we will vote for the Silver Bullet.

I am not going to go into specifics about what made this place horrible, but when I talked to the woman at the front desk, who also said she was the manager, she said, "Oh, I know. Isn't it awful?" Glad to see she has a handle on the situation.

Day Forty-Three

This day, we woke up in New Hampshire, went to bed in upstate New York, and spent the bulk of the day in Vermont. A busy day on the road.

Like Maine, Vermont brings a picture to mind—snow, hills, falling leaves, maple syrup. It was early enough in the year that we didn't get to see any snow, but everything else was what we'd hoped it would be.

I mean no offense to any of the other states we drove through on this trip, but I believe Vermont was the prettiest, most picturesque state so far. We adored Maine, but I have to admit that Vermont is something special. As we drove through Maine and New Hampshire, I heard the occasional complaint about Vermont: *Oh, those Vermonters. They think their poop don't stink. They think an awful lot of themselves over there.*

Now that we've driven through, I kind of get it. If I was a Vermonter, I might have my nose in the air just a bit, too. We drove through a dozen small towns, every one of them seemingly auditioning to play the role of "perfect village" in the next Hollywood blockbuster. We stayed off the beaten path and drove through a lot of places I'd never heard of, but every place we looked was immaculately maintained and beautiful.

✓ Our first goal was to nab some real Vermont maple syrup. I don't easily fall for advertising campaigns, and I am skeptical by nature, but before we left on the trip, someone told me, "If you don't think there's a difference between Vermont maple syrup and whatever else you've ever had, then you've never had the real stuff." That was good enough for me, and Dawn didn't take much convincing.

Fortunately, wherever you go in Vermont, people are quite happy to sell you some. Each town we came to had a little farmers market, or stand, or store of some kind that specialized in the sweet, sticky stuff. We pulled over to the first one we came to and picked up several little bottles as souvenirs for people back home, and one decent-sized bottle that we would keep for ourselves. As soon as we left that store, though, I could tell Dawn wasn't satisfied. Her maple itch was still flaring up.

I wasn't surprised when, without a word, she pulled over into the Corse Maple Farm in Whitingham. It was like a maple mall. I was afraid I would never get Dawn out of there. The lady behind the counter was knowledgeable about maple syrup in a way I didn't know you could be. She knew the history of the area, how to properly take care of your syrup (my suggestion to just put it in a cupboard and use it on pancakes marked me as unredeemable) and, of course, how to order more once our half-gallon ran out. How much is a half-gallon of 100 percent pure maple syrup, you might ask? $37.75. From the fanatical glow in the woman's eyes as she proselytized Dawn on the many benefits of maple syrup, I was sure it was worth it.

We escaped with several bags full of syrup, maple candy, and, of course, a magnet. Dawn's itch had now been sufficiently scratched.

We had just crossed the Vermont–New York state line when we saw the Big Moose Deli and Country Store. It's kind of hard to miss, really. There's a truck outside with a life-size moose, gorilla, and Uncle Sam. There's a crashed airplane protruding from the roof. There are garden gnomes blown up to fiendish size. In short, it's my kind of place. We hadn't had lunch yet, so we couldn't resist all this campy Americana.

The sandwiches we got there were great—big enough to serve as dinner as well—but the store was the highlight. It was like a rural version of Spencer's Gifts, with a million corny signs, jokes, and pieces of memorabilia. From the front, it looks small, but its tiny, packed aisles wend and wind through room after room. We left with more than our food, obviously.

We drove on through upstate New York, enjoying the rolling

hills, quiet roads and everything that distinguishes the rest of the state from those teeming millions down at the bottom. New York is like Washington state in so many ways, if we squinted our eyes a bit, it almost felt like we were in a part of western Washington we'd never been to before. It made us a little homesick.

We spent the night in the Finger Lakes region of New York. More specifically, we stayed in Skaneateles, New York. Let that one roll around on your tongue for a bit. For the life of me, I couldn't figure out how to pronounce that name. Was it pronounced like skein, with an "eteles" after it? Or a "ska" sound, like in the beginning of Schenectady?

When we checked in to the wonderful little Skaneateles Inn, I asked the lady behind the counter.

She smiled indulgently, then said it so fast I could hear it whiz as it went over my head.

"Again, please?"

An even more indulgent smile that showed she now realized that she was speaking to someone of lower than average intelligence. "Skinny atlas."

I blinked. "Skinny atlas?"

A nod.

So, Skaneateles is apparently pronounced "skinny atlas." I admit, I never would have gotten there.

Day Forty-Four

This morning, we left Skaneateles, which I will always remember as Skinny Atlas, and drove to Niagara Falls.

I need to tell you a quick story that will illustrate how Dawn has the patience of a saint to be married to me. Yesterday, as we were driving, we saw signs for Schenectady, New York. I have this habit of reading signs as we drive by them. When I said, "Schenectady," I kind of liked how it sounded. Say it yourself. "Schenectady." Satisfying, isn't it? Kind of like Walla Walla, Washington.

So, over the next hour or so, I found 112 different ways to work the name "Schenectady" into our conversation. For about the last 110 of those times, I could see Dawn's ire rising. Which, of course, is why I continued to say it. Dawn and I became friends when she was eleven and I was fifteen. This is one of the ways it still shows, four decades later.

Then, we passed a sign for the town of Tonawanda. When I said that was also a cool name, Dawn gave me the Level Five death glare that said, *Shawn, if you start saying "Schenectady" again, I will remove one of your testicles.* I've never been able to resist a challenge, and I relied on the fact that she was driving the car to keep me safe. So far, so good.

We had two big events to look forward to on this day. One was seeing my writer best friend, Terry Schott, and the other was seeing this place where water drops a long way very quickly.

Terry and I have been online friends for years. He is the author of the bestselling *Game is Life* series. We met in person for the first time at the Smarter Artist Summit back in March, but this would be the first time Dawn got to meet him. Because we're a high-brow sort of folk, we met at a pizza restaurant where there were pinups of naked girls in the bathroom. Okay, so it wasn't exactly the Algonquin Roundtable. It was perfect for us, and the pizza was terrific.

Dawn and Terry took to each other instantly. Terry is hilarious, and Dawn's super power is taking people who are hilarious down a peg or two. They were insulting each other like old friends before the pizza got cold.

At one point, Dawn held up her hand and said, "Wait a minute. Is one single thing you guys have said today actually true?"

I had to point out that when politicians don't speak the truth, it is a lie. When writers do that, it is just the beginning of a new story. We try to never let facts ruin the presentation of a good story.

We couldn't persuade Terry to come with us to Niagara Falls, so after we said goodbye to him, we drove straight there.

Here's the thing: I've been to the falls before. Back in the early eighties, I traveled with the Unlimited Hydroplane Circuit for three summers. One of those years, we had a race in upstate New York, so on an off-day, I drove to Niagara Falls. I walked up to the observation deck, saw the falls, shrugged, and drove back to Buffalo. In Buffalo, I saw *The Empire Strikes Back*, which impressed me a lot more than Niagara Falls. *Mea culpa.* I was a twenty-three-year-old kid, dumb as a box of rocks. Natural beauty didn't impress me much back then, I guess, but because of that, I wasn't sure how impressed I would be today.

Happily, thirty-three years have taught me a few things, including how to appreciate Niagara Falls. Dawn had no preconceived notions, so she was excited before we even got there. Once she saw it, her smile didn't falter for the rest of the visit.

We walked to the Observation Deck, and that was cool, but we didn't want to stop there. We wanted to get wet. So, we got on one of the Maid of the Mist boats, famous for getting millions of people up close and personal with the falls, not to mention soaking wet. They provide free plastic ponchos that theoretically keep you dry. Why did they make them hot pink? I have no idea, but it makes for a striking image—dozens of people with dripping-wet hair wearing shocking pink ponchos.

The Maid of the Mist ride isn't long—I think the whole thing lasted maybe 25 minutes, but it is so worth it. I can't imagine going to the falls and not taking a ride to really see the falls crashing down toward you. Yes, you will get soaked. No, the ponchos won't keep you dry—imagine wearing a poncho into a running shower, and you'll get the picture. Mostly, though, you will see the falls, both the American and Canadian side, from a viewpoint you will never forget.

Niagara Falls

After the boat ride, we wanted to linger, so we walked along the Niagara River, which is beautiful in its own right. Finally, we knew we had to leave, though we didn't want to. Visiting Niagara Falls was a tremendous experience. There are some historical landmarks (Mount Rushmore springs to mind for me) about which, once you see them, you think: *Yep. There it is. How about that*. Then you get back in your car and go on to the next stop. Niagara had a much bigger impact on us. If you ever get a chance to see the area, I strongly recommend it. It's very inexpensive. You can view the falls for free, and it's only $18 per person to ride the Maid of the Mist. We've paid more for a lot less elsewhere on this trip. It gets two thumbs up from Dawn and Shawn.

Here's a good *Lap Around America* piece of trivia: What were the three states that we would drive through two separate times? The answer: New York, New Hampshire, and Pennsylvania. We hit those three twice on our loop around the upper northeast.

We made it to a brand-new hotel in Erie, Pennsylvania, just as it was getting dark. We were noticing that we were running out of sunlight a lot sooner than when we left. After staying in a series of rundown, dilapidated (or worse) motels for the last week or so, it was nice to stay in a place that still had the equivalent of that "new car smell."

Plus, it had a pool and a laundry room. For us, this was heaven.

Day Forty-Five

Man, Cleveland gets a bad rap. It's been the butt of jokes for so long, I have to wonder if Clevelanders ever get defensive about it. Here's a story I recounted on my blog the day we passed through Cleveland:

In May of 1981, I was driving around Seattle, listening to the Seattle Mariners game on AM 710, KIRO. I don't remember much about that particular game, but I do recall this conversation between Dave Niehaus and Ken Wilson, the Mariners' play-by-play team:

Dave Niehaus: "Well, it's all done in Cleveland, and it's a perfect game for Len Barker of the Indians."

Ken Wilson: "I think there's been some sort of mistake, Dave."

DN: "Pretty sure it's right; it just came over the wire. Indians win, three to nothing, and Barker throws a perfect game."

KW: "We've both spent our share of time in Cleveland, and so we both know … nothing can be perfect in Cleveland."

Cue rim shot.

I remember wondering at the time what made Cleveland so bad. Thirty-five years after Len Barker's perfect game, I finally got a chance to see for myself, and I still don't know why everyone hates on Cleveland. I guess it might be because when manufacturing changed, Cleveland was a little bereft for a while. Also, the weather isn't the greatest. Their sports teams were awful for a long time. Oh, and the Cuyahoga River was so polluted, it caught on fire once.

But, those things are mostly in the past. Sure, the weather still isn't great, but business in Cleveland is booming again. Lebron James and the Cleveland Cavaliers won the NBA Championship in 2016, and the Cleveland Indians came within one game of winning the World Series. We won't mention the

Cleveland Browns, who are so terrible, they are likely to still be terrible no matter what year you are reading this.

We started our jam-packed tour of Cleveland with a tour of the Lake View Cemetery. We had seen cool cemeteries in Pioche, New Orleans, and Augusta, but Lake View was at the head of the class.

It is immense, covering more than 70 acres. It doesn't really have a cemetery feel, to be honest. In most sections, it feels like a park where people just happen to be buried. There are lakes, and trees, and manicured hills that are so peaceful, Dawn said, "If I didn't want to be cremated, I think I'd like to be buried here."

"Seriously, in Cleveland? We don't know anyone within 1,000 miles of Cleveland."

"I know. But look at that little lake. Close your eyes and just feel how peaceful it is here."

She was right, but I think we're both intent on eventually having our ashes scattered over the Pacific Ocean someday. Hopefully in the middle of a windstorm, so no one really knows where I go.

Lake View Cemetery isn't just about the beauty of its surroundings, though. Several famous people found their final resting place there. Eliot Ness, the famous G-man, is buried somewhere there, although we never found his grave. John D. Rockefeller and members of his immediate family have a lovely spot on top of a hill. U.S. president James Garfield, his wife, daughter, and son-in-law are entombed in their own castle on the grounds.

I had my heart set on finding two specific graves: those of Alan Freed and the Haserot family.

Alan Freed is special to me because he played such an integral role in the early days of rock 'n' roll. He wasn't a musician but rather a disc jockey who probably did more for the advancement of the new phenomenon of rock 'n' roll than any other. He came to fame at WJW in Cleveland, and it was there that he ran his famous *Moondoggers* show.

In my own book, *Rock 'n Roll Heaven*, as my protagonist Jimmy Velvet, Buddy Holly, and an angel named Pertime are walking down a street in the 1950s section of Rock 'n Roll Heaven, I paid tribute to Mr. Freed:

Their path moved away from the small-town business district housing Buddy's roller rink, toward a section of larger buildings. As they walked under an awning, Jimmy glanced through a large picture window and saw a man sitting at a 1950s radio board with half a dozen potentiometers, two turntables and a hanging microphone. Above the sidewalk, speakers broadcast what he was playing. The last few notes of The Fleetwoods' "Come Softly" faded out.

"This is Alan Freed, King of the Moondoggers, playing the songs that matter, the records that have stood the test of time and crossed over with me to Rock 'n Roll Heaven. These are the Moonglows, from Cleveland, Ohio, waaaay back in the ole US of A." He pushed a button and the record started to spin. The doo-wop intro of "Sincerely" played, with just a hint of scratchiness as the 45 turned.

"That's Alan Freed!"

"Yeah, it is," Buddy drawled. "You can't be surprised to see Alan in Rock 'n Roll Heaven. He doesn't have a regularly scheduled show, but he goes on the air whenever he wants."

Alan looked out the window and waved as he cued up the next record. By the time they were out of earshot, "Sincerely" had finished playing and segued directly into "Mr. Lee" by The Bobbettes.

I put that section in the book for several reasons. One, I thought Rock 'n' Roll Heaven needed a disc jockey, and two, I have always thought Alan Freed got a bum rap, not unlike his hometown of Cleveland, Ohio. Yes, he was found guilty of accepting payola for helping to turn records into hits. However, if every disc jockey that took payola in those days was taken off the air, there would have been a lot of dead air across America. From 2002 until 2014, Alan Freed's ashes resided in the Rock & Roll Hall of Fame. At that point, the Hall decided they didn't want him there anymore, which I find very tacky.

His family made him a marvelous tombstone, shaped like an old Rock-ola jukebox, and had his ashes interred in Lake View Cemetery. As final resting spots go, it's very cool.

Earlier, I mentioned being excited about finding the Haserot family graves. The family isn't famous, and their gravesite is definitely not in a prime spot in the cemetery. What makes their final resting place memorable is the statue they commissioned to sit above the graves: *Angel of Death Victorious*, sculpted by Herman Matzen in 1924.

As soon as I read about her, I knew I needed to see the statue, also commonly called *The Weeping Angel*, with my own eyes. That wasn't easy. A website said the statue was where Sections Two and Three in the cemetery meet. We found that spot, but there was no weeping angel in sight.

I approached a maintenance man I spotted sitting atop a lawnmower, smoking a cigarette and taking a break, and asked where I could find the statue. He kind of sneered at me and waved a hand in a vague direction. Very helpful. We set off hiking in the direction he waved, but couldn't find her. We walked up and down rolling hills in the climbing morning heat, to no avail. If I weren't so stubborn, we would have just gotten in the car and moved on.

I *am* exactly that stubborn, though, and refused to give up. Eventually, I saw that some graves are kind of shunted off to the side of the road that connects the different sections. I climbed up that hill, ducked through some low-hanging branches, and there she was, in all her glory.

The *Angel of Death Victorious* is said to be haunted. Strange noises and occurrences are rumored to happen around the gravesite. I cannot testify to any of that, as all was quiet on the haunting front when I was there. Even without other-worldly creaks, groans, and rattling of chains, the weeping angel was spellbinding.

The Angel of Death, Victorious

Larger than life-size, she sits peacefully, her magnificent wings stretched out on both sides and supported by a smooth stone structure. In her hands she has a large, upside-down torch, signifying the extinguishing of life. It is her face that draws attention, though. The statue is made of bronze, and years of exposure to the elements have caused black rivers of tears to stream down her face.

I lost track of time as I stood before her, mesmerized. If Dawn hadn't come and laid a hand on my shoulder and said, "Time to go, now," I think I might still be there, staring into those unseeing eyes, blackened with tears.

I think Dawn pulled me away because she wanted to see the castle where Garfield is buried. No. Not the cartoon cat, the president.

I'm interested in Garfield, although he is not well remembered today. He is one of four presidents to have been assassinated (along with Lincoln, McKinley, and Kennedy), and was president for only a few months before he was shot. He was well qualified for the job, and it would have been interesting to see what he might have done with his full term. Instead, an insane office-seeker named Charles Guiteau shot him twice at close range. Even though this was after the Lincoln assassination, U.S. presidents at that time still did not have any kind of guard when they were out in public. Can you imagine? Being out for a bite to eat and looking up to see the president of the United States sitting a few tables away?

Garfield lingered for eleven weeks after he was shot and died a horrible death. Even though he is not much talked about today, he has the grandest resting place of all U.S. presidents. It is literally built like the spire of a medieval castle. Picture the rook on a chess board, and you'll be close. Inside, there is a much larger-than-life statue of Garfield in a dramatic pose. Inside, you can climb clear to the top, where you will be rewarded with a tremendous view of downtown Cleveland, or descend to where the president and his family are entombed.

The man who ran the tiny little gift shop/information booth inside the castle was a big James Garfield fan, extolling his virtues and bemoaning that he was shot less than three months into his term of office. I never knew there were James Garfield fans, but now I do.

The burial and interment spots for the famous were all very cool, but they weren't what put Lake View Cemetery over the top for us. What touched our hearts was the statues scattered about that were meant to memorialize ordinary people.

We saw a bench with the figure of a happy, smiling man, playing guitar, looking like he was about to burst into song. There were also statues of beloved pets, and my favorite: a young girl, eternally sitting on a park bench reading a favorite book. On the back of it is a quote from Albert Camus: *In the depths of winter, I finally learned that within me there lay an invincible summer.* I can't imagine a happier resting spot than that.

Before we knew it, we had whiled away three hours in what I thought would be a quick stop at the cemetery. Some things just can't be rushed, though, and Lake View was just that for us.

Still. The Rock & Roll Hall of Fame loomed. If you've made it this far in the book, or if you've read any of my other books, you'll have noticed that I include musical references a lot. Specifically, musical references from the mid-fifties through the eighties. Music is my constant companion, and it leaks into pretty much everything I do.

You would think, then, that the Rock & Roll Hall of Fame would be high up on my must-visit list. But, really, it wasn't. To me the Hall has always been a little too corporate for my tastes. Rock 'n' roll, from the time it first jumped off the screen in *The Blackboard Jungle*, has been about anarchy, and free spirits, and creativity. The Rock & Roll Hall of Fame has always struck me as being as free-spirited as a box of Wheaties. Basically, I believe it is managed by the same empty suits that have run the entire recording industry into the ground over the past two decades.

All of that is about the board that runs the place, though. I was not going to drive right by it and not go in as some form of protest. I'm not big on biting off my nose to spite my face, and I was sure there were some amazing artifacts there.

The hall itself is pretty wonderful. First of all, it's huge. We spent two and a half hours there and didn't even scratch the surface, really. If you're impressed with rock 'n' roll memorabilia, you're going to be in heaven there.

Want to see Ringo Starr's Beatles drum kit? No problem. Handwritten lyrics from the greatest songwriters of the rock era? Yep. Greg Allman's Hammond organ? On site. There are sections of the hall devoted to different eras, styles, and performers, and it was all very cool.

Seeing all these legitimately legendary things from so many of my favorite artists helped me arrive at a truth for myself. For me, it's all about the music. Yes, seeing the lyrics to "In My Life" in John Lennon's own handwriting is cool, but that doesn't move me as much as hearing the song through nice headphones or a quality stereo.

Scattered all over the four floors of the hall are little theaters that play various films, and that attracted us. We sat and watched a tribute to Dick Clark and *American Bandstand*. It made me realize that if there were a cable station that played old episodes of *Bandstand* or *Top of the Pops* in their entirety, I would definitely watch it. Maybe throw in a few broadcasts of early MTV, commercials, inane veejay chatter and all, and I would be a fan.

We left and drove right through downtown Cleveland during what should have been rush hour, but traffic was smooth and easy. Dawn's blood pressure stayed at normal levels. We peeked into Progressive Field as we rolled by and saw that the Indians were getting ready for their first playoff game, part of a run that would see them fall one game short of a World Series title.

It was getting late in the day, but we had one more stop to make. Leaving the downtown area, we drove through a residential neighborhood of small, older houses. It was completely forgettable and nondescript until we turned a corner, and there it was: the house from *A Christmas Story*. I suppose there will be people who read this who have never seen the movie. I am sorry. You're missing out on many different levels of awesome.

We pulled in at the house next door, which is where the Bumpuses and their damn dogs lived in the movie. It really was like driving onto a film set. Dawn and I tried to estimate how many times we'd each seen *A Christmas Story,* but the math was too hard. Since TBS plays it for 24 hours straight on Christmas Day, we've seen parts of it hundreds of times, and the complete movie at least twenty-five times each.

Shawn Inmon

The *A Christmas Story* house

We walked around the front of the main house, and sure enough, there was a *major award*—the infamous leg lamp, right there in the front window. The man who bought the house is very serious about collecting memorabilia from the movie, and the word he passed on through the tour guide is that none of the original leg lamps from the movie still exist.

There is an *A Christmas Story* gift shop in a house across the street, and you can buy a guided tour of the house there as well, which of course we did. As often as we've both seen the movie, we still learned a lot on our tour.

One of the things we learned was the reason they shot the movie in Cleveland. The 1994 film is based on a memoir Jean Shepherd wrote called *In God We Trust*. Shepherd was born in Indiana, making that the logical place to shoot the film. However, it was made on a small budget, and the producers needed access to a large department store after hours to shoot the Santa Claus scene. Director Bob Clark, fresh off the success of directing *Porky's* (maybe I should emphasize *financial* success) sent scouts

228

to department stores all over the Midwest, looking for one that would give them the access they needed. They struck out dozens of times, until Higbee's Department Store in Cleveland agreed to participate. Just like that, Cleveland was chosen to stand in for Hammond, Indiana.

Another interesting side note is that the film originally was a bit raunchier, with a few cuss words sprinkled through the script. The owners of Higbee's insisted that everything be toned down several notches—they were a family department store and didn't want to be associated with anything that wasn't family-friendly. In the end, I think the clever way they depicted Darren McGavin's character's cussing worked out better than if they had gone with the original script. And if they hadn't made those changes, it's doubtful the movie would have become the perennial classic that it has.

It bothered Dawn to learn that during the January they shot the on-location scenes, it didn't snow in Cleveland at all. So, every bit of snow you see in the movie is manufactured rather than natural.

Our guide also revealed that while parts of the movie were made in Cleveland, others were shot on a soundstage in Hollywood. Here's how you can distinguish between them: Any of the interior house shots with the drapes closed were shot in Hollywood. Any scenes with the curtains open were shot in the house we toured in Cleveland. It made us want to watch the movie again, just so we could tell which was which.

We were staggered a bit by how small the house was inside. In the movie, everything felt spacious, but in reality, the kitchen and eating area, all one room, are tiny. The magic of Hollywood.

It seems the neighborhood got into the spirit of things. If you remember the scene where the deliveryman drops off the "major award," that wasn't an actor playing the deliveryman but a neighbor. At the end of shooting, he was given a replica of the leg lamp, which you can still see proudly displayed in his window as you drive by.

One last story about the film: Among the most memorable scenes is the one where the family goes to a Chinese restaurant on Christmas after the Bumpus dogs steal their turkey. Highlights of the scene are the Chinese carolers serenading the family and chopping the head violently off the duck. Here's what we learned: Bob Clark gave Melinda Dillon, who played Mother Parker, a fake script, so she didn't know what was coming. When the carolers started singing, her laughter was authentic. Likewise, her surprised gasp when the duck gets its head lopped off. Next time you watch the movie, keep your eyes on the boys in that scene. They can't take their eyes off Melinda Dillon, because everyone but her was in on the joke. Her reaction made the whole scene, and it's the only one in the movie they got in one take.

We were probably thrilled by the tour and seeing the house more than the average person because of our affinity for the movie, but if you're in Cleveland, we both strongly recommend catching the *A Christmas Story House.*

Between walking around Lake View Cemetery, the Rock & Roll Hall of Fame, and *A Christmas Story House*, we were worn out. We made it a few miles outside of Cleveland before we found a motel in the immortal Maumee, Ohio. Tomorrow, Michigan!

Day Forty-Six

Dawn and I got to know each other when we were just kids. Days like the previous day, spent dragging ourselves from pillar to post in Cleveland, had convinced me that we are no longer those kids. We were whipped. In response, we took it pretty easy on this day.

We woke up in the northernmost corner of Ohio, with our eyes set on Michigan. There were a couple of ways to tackle the state—go up the eastern portion, around Detroit, or head farther west and drive north toward what is called the Upper Peninsula, or U.P. I had a strong desire to see the U.P., so we got on Highway 223 and headed west.

I've heard stories about the U.P. all my life, about how it is so wild and different from the rest of Michigan that it should be its own state. When I was a radio deejay, I played songs by a band called Da Yoopers. A "Yooper" is someone who comes from the U.P., and I wanted to see what kind of an area could spawn a group as crazy as they were.

We drove through south-central Michigan via back roads, hitting small towns like Adrian, where Dawn had to suffer through my terrible Rocky Balboa imitation—*Yo, Adrian!*—Cement City, Litchfield, and Homer, where she had to suffer through my Homer Simpson imitation, which is slightly better. She is a patient woman.

We saw mile after mile of husked-out cornfields and farms by the dozens. Every time I hear Michigan mentioned in the news, it seems to be about Detroit, with houses selling for twelve dollars, or Flint, where it hasn't been safe to drink the water. Those problems are very real, but there's no sign of them in the central and western part of the state, which is where we drove today. This part of Michigan seems totally disconnected from those big-city problems.

I saw that Battle Creek, Michigan, wasn't too far ahead. I knew we had to stop there, as it represents another childhood memory. If you grew up in the sixties, it's likely you remember a phrase like "Send three box tops and a self-addressed envelope to Battle Creek, Michigan for ..." some worthless little toy. I'm surprised to note how many stops we've made based solely on my childhood memories.

Before we got to Battle Creek, our trip odometer clicked back to zero, meaning we had traveled 10,000 miles in forty-six days, or an average of 217 miles per day. Not too bad, especially when you consider we've stayed in one place for two days on several occasions.

We had an odd experience just before we got to Battle Creek. I was looking at the map, trying to decide what we would manage to see while we were in Michigan. I looked clear up into the U.P. and saw something called the Great Lakes Shipwreck Museum. I read Dawn the description I found on Google.

"It's at the very top of the U.P., though, so it's a good drive from here."

"So, what are we going to be doing if we're not driving there? Driving somewhere else?"

Another example of why I never win an argument with Dawn.

Now, here's the weird part: as I was reading to her what was on display at the Shipwreck Museum, I mentioned that the recovered bell of the Edmund Fitzgerald was there. Just as I did, what came on our satellite radio? Yes. Gordon Lightfoot's *The Wreck of the Edmund Fitzgerald.*

We both laughed, a little nervously. Dawn looked accusingly at me, as though I had set the whole thing up, but for once, I was innocent.

"That's just a little weird," Dawn said.

"So, I guess I'll be adding the Shipwreck Museum to our itinerary!"

We ate lunch at a cute little place in Battle Creek called Clara's on the River. By cute, I mean cute in a *my Grandma would love this* kind of way. I was surprised the menus weren't crocheted. Still, the food was good, and that's all we cared about.

We headed out of Battle Creek on yet another winding little country road. We had no other stops planned for the day, just plenty of driving. We were only a few miles outside of town, though, when a twenty-foot Gandalf, from *The Lord of the Rings*, caught my eye.

"That's something you don't see every day," I said to Dawn. "A twenty-foot-tall Gandalf."

She narrowed her eyes at me, but kept driving.

"Seriously."

Her raised eyebrows expressed her cynicism. I may have called "Wolf!" too often since we've been married. Eventually, though, I managed to get her to turn the car around.

What we found was the Leila Arboretum and the Battle Creek Fantasy Forest.

In 2002, Michigan was invaded by the emerald ash borer, a beetle that has killed 50 million ash trees across North America. There were once forty-four ash trees in the arboretum more than a century old, and all were killed by the emerald ash borer. Trying to make the best of an awful situation, the town turned a group of chainsaw artists loose on the trees and created the *Battle Creek Fantasy Forest.* The trees were carved into fantasy scenes— wizards in castles, battling dragons, Bigfoot, Groot from *Guardians of the Galaxy,* and the aforementioned Gandalf. It was sad the trees were lost, but once they were, it was a great idea to renew them as an attraction. We had no idea it was there, and if I hadn't glanced out the window at that exact moment, we would have missed it. It pays to stay on your toes!

We didn't make it quite as far north as we had hoped, but we were ready to be off the road by late afternoon. We stopped in

Big Rapids, which is about fifty miles north of Grand Rapids. Apparently, the rapids here are big, but not all that grand.

Since we'd had a good lunch, we resorted to The Magical Mystery Bag for dinner, which offered up only some bread, peanut butter and jelly, and ramen noodles. Might be time to stop at a store soon.

Day Forty-Seven

✔ This turned out to be one of our most memorable days on the road and ended with our worst motel experience ever.

We started the day pointing north toward the Upper Peninsula of Michigan. Before we got there, though, a name jumped off the map as I unfolded it: Cadillac, Michigan.

To most people, Cadillac is unremarkable. If you happen to be a KISS fan, it is a legendary location, and I wasn't about to miss an opportunity to see it.

Here's a very short history of KISS and me. On Halloween weekend 1976, I was sitting at home, watching the small black-and-white television in my bedroom. It only got one channel, but luckily for me, that channel happened to be the one broadcasting *The Paul Lynde Halloween Special.* The special musical guest on the show was KISS. By 1976, KISS had started to break big, but not big enough to have made much of a dent on my consciousness in the flyspeck town of Mossyrock, Washington.

That all changed the moment Paul Lynde introduced them and they launched into *Detroit Rock City.* My sixteen-year-old brain, already limited by the fact hormones were doing most of the thinking, essentially shut down. Mouth agape, I watched these four otherworldly creatures wearing spandex and kabuki makeup jumping around the stage like maniacs. As the last note of *Detroit Rock City* faded away, my mom stuck her head in my room and said, "Jerry's on the phone."

I ran into the kitchen, and as soon as I put the phone to my ear, my best friend was shouting, "Turn on the television!"

"I know, I know! I'm watching it."

We didn't have a lot to be excited about on television those days.

"Inmon, we've got to figure a way to *be* those guys."

My friend Jerry was always an out-of-the-box, big-picture

guy. Long story short, we spent the next two years as KISS II, wearing spandex and kabuki makeup, and jumping around various stages like idiots. We had a great time doing it.

Then, in 2010, a few people from our high school class asked us to bring KISS II out of mothballs for the school reunion. So, we did. Once again, we had a great time, although I am the first to admit we didn't jump quite as high as fifty-year-olds.

Now, here's why Cadillac, Michigan, shines so brightly in KISS lore. In 1974, the Cadillac High football team started the season 0-2. One of the assistant coaches got an idea to loosen the players up at practice and before games by playing KISS music. The team went on to win seven games in a row and a district championship.

Word of this reached KISS. They always had a good nose for publicity, and they volunteered to go to Cadillac for the 1975 homecoming game.

Picture the scene: into a western Michigan town of 10,000 people drops one of the biggest rock bands in the world. KISS met the mayor, the principal, the high school students, and the cheerleaders. They gave a full-blown KISS concert in the Cadillac High School gym. Yes, I would give anything to have been there to witness that. They had breakfast with everyone the next day. Then, being rock stars, they had a huge helicopter drop down in the middle of the football field and whisk them away, dropping thousands of leaflets that said, "Cadillac High – KISS Loves You!" They knew how to make both an entrance and a departure.

Those few days have now become the stuff of legend. In 2015, on the 40th anniversary of the event, the town of Cadillac erected an eight-foot memorial of the event—at the corner of the football field. How could I not go and see it?

On the day we arrived, the clouds were steel gray with black edges that looked threatening. The wind was howling, and rain came in at an angle. It had been 82 degrees the day before as we drove through southern Michigan. The temperature on the bank sign in Cadillac read 45 degrees. We were in weather shock. For the first time since we started the trip, we pulled our jackets out of the trunk of the Silver Bullet.

It took some driving around, but we soon found the monument in the corner of the football field. It has the KISS logo, and an article and picture from back in the day when KISS invaded Cadillac. Driving down the main drag of Cadillac, mentally connecting the present-day town with the videos I'd watched from forty years ago, I could tell that not much had changed there.

Shawn shivering by the Cadillac KISS Sign

"Pretty cool that the city fathers put the monument up, don't you think?"

Dawn looked at me. "Think about it. How old would those high schoolers from 1975 be now?"

Realization dawned on me. "Mid-fifties."

"Right. So, those pimple-faced high schoolers *are* the city fathers now."

My bride often arrives at the truth before I do.

We left Cadillac, intent on not stopping until we had crossed over into the U.P. We were both anxious to get there. We love places that seem to have their own cultural identity, and the U.P. definitely does. It even has its own language, of a sort, called Yooper English, or Yooperese, which incorporates the German and Scandinavian roots of many of its residents.

Michigan is a long state, top to bottom, so even starting from the middle it took us until afternoon to cross the Mackinac Bridge. It's an awe-inspiring sight, the longest suspension bridge in the Western Hemisphere. I didn't tell Dawn this, because she was driving and can get a little nervous about crossing long bridges, but in high winds (which we were experiencing) the bridge can move as much as 35 feet from side to side.

The Mackinac Bridge

The bridge across Lake Pontchartrain north of New Orleans was the longest bridge we would cross, but the Mackinac was the most impressive—and the scariest. As we approached, there was a flashing sign that read, "High wind warnings ahead," but I chose not to tell Dawn what that could mean. I didn't want to have to use power tools to pry her fingers loose from the steering wheel. As you cross you can see a Great Lake on either side—Michigan and Huron. I was born in an area with lots of lakes. I know now that our lakes are just puddles. *These* are lakes.

✓ As soon as we rolled off the northern end of the bridge, we were in the Upper Peninsula. The U.P. is sparsely populated. In fact, it covers just under a third of the land mass of Michigan but contains only about 3 percent of the population. And yet, as we discovered, it is quite the tourist destination, especially on weekends.

We'd both been lucky to have stayed pretty healthy to this point in the trip. I'd been sunburned in Florida, but it's not much of a headline when an Irish guy with a pale complexion gets sunburned. Dawn had an upset stomach a couple of days, and I didn't feel 100 percent one night in Salem, but considering the length of time we'd been traveling, we felt fortunate.

However, as we crossed into the U.P., I saw a lightning strike off to my right.

"That's weird. Did you see that lightning?"

Dawn looked at me a little strangely. "Not exactly the right conditions for lightning, is it?"

I looked around at the mostly clear skies. "No, not really."

Five minutes later, I saw another one, this time directly in front of us. "There! You had to have seen that one!"

Dawn just shook her head.

Then, the buzzing in my ears started. Like an invasion of locusts, drowning out everything. I knew. I've had migraines for about twenty years, but they've stopped coming as regularly as they once did. In fact, I'm down to one or two a year now. This was the day that lucky number came up.

As I've grown older, the migraines have also become less

severe. In my thirties, they would send me whimpering to a dark room for several days. Now, I can function through them, but it's like having a vice around my head, slowly, painfully, clamping down. My trip through the U.P. would be seen through the haze of that pain.

Headache and all, we pushed on up the U.P. Our destination was the Great Lakes Shipwreck Museum. Being a Pacific Northwesterner, I will admit to total ignorance about the Great Lakes. Here's something I learned recently: The amount of water contained in the five Great Lakes would cover the entire continental United States nine and a half feet deep. Also, even though I had played Gordon Lightfoot's "The Wreck of the Edmund Fitzgerald" several thousand times, I had no idea how many shipwrecks had occurred on those lakes. It's a lot, and the museum does a wonderful job of educating and memorializing them. The people who put the museum together were mindful of the sacrifices so many made in the name of moving cargo.

The most famous wreck, of course, is the aforementioned *Edmund Fitzgerald,* thanks to the song. At 730 feet, "Big Fitz," as the boat was nicknamed, was the largest boat on any of the Great Lakes. Forty-one years after the sinking, no one knows exactly what sank the ship on that stormy November night. There was a trailing ship that kept an eye on it through the storm, until its lights just winked out and the *Edmund Fitzgerald* sank to the bottom.

It was found very quickly—resting more than 500 feet below the surface. Discovering it was the extent of things until 1995, when a crew descended into the inky depths of Lake Superior and pulled up the bell, now on display in the museum. A video shows the bell being pulled to the surface. The coolest thing is that the team had a replacement bell engraved with the names of the twenty-nine men who perished that day and placed that one back with the wreck.

The *Edmund Fitzgerald* bell

In addition to the main museum, you can also tour the Whitefish Point Light tower and its keeper's house. I think of lighthouse keeper's quarters as being spartan, but this one is a cut above, with lots of wood-wrapped windows and doors that make for a cozy feeling. Dawn said that if they'd offer us the job, we'd move in there and watch the light for free. I like the way she thinks.

Dawn has made a point of putting her feet in the water in the Pacific, the Gulf of Mexico, and the Atlantic on this trip. She wanted to do the same with Lake Superior, but it was not to be. Where Lake Superior hits the coastline at the shipwreck museum, there were white, frothy breakers rushing in. Add in a howling wind and temperatures in the lower 40s, and there was no way she was kicking her shoes off and running into the surf.

After we left the museum, things got interesting. As I mentioned, the U.P. is thinly populated. About ten miles south of the museum is a small town called Paradise. We looked at the map and knew that if we wanted to find dinner, it would have to

241

be there. Being the off-season, only one place was open. Lots of tourists and a single place to eat meant a long wait for dinner. No problem. We met nice people in line, chatted until our table was ready, then ate and left.

By then, it was getting dark, and it turned out that all the hotels and motels in Paradise were booked. In fact, according to Hotels.com, Expedia, Trivago, and so on, every hotel and motel in the whole Upper Peninsula was booked. However, we knew that quite often, websites will show all rooms booked when there are still a few for walk-in customers, so we started driving. Every time we found a hotel or motel, we went in and were told that they had given their last room away thirty minutes before. That 30=minute wait for a table in Paradise came back to haunt us.

Finally, we arrived in a town called Newberry. It was dark, cold and windy. If there was no place to stay there, we were looking at a long drive through dark and twisting back roads to find the next town. Each place we stopped told us the same thing: no vacancy. Finally, we hit our last hope. If they were booked, we were going to have to either sleep in the Silver Bullet or make the long drive into the night.

The desk clerk told us the usual, "Just gave away our last room about twenty minutes ago." But then he dangled this: "Our *regular* hotel is all booked up, but we do have an *ancillary* building that has a vacancy."

I didn't like the way he put the emphasis on *regular* and *ancillary*. It gave me a bad feeling. But, so did the idea of driving through a national forest with no other town in sight.

I was blunt. "How bad is it?"

He was honest. "The hallway is gross, but the room is okay."

He was at least half right. The hallway was gross. The "ancillary" hotel appeared to be a halfway house for people working their way back into society. We met two nice men that had the shakes, smoking a cigarette. They had a three-legged dog with them. Dawn wanted to ask if their dog could stay in the room with us.

The desk clerk showed us the room, which was awful in a truly awful sort of way. The clerk shrugged and said, "This is the last room available in the entire Upper Peninsula tonight. Had a call from a guy at a hotel in Marquette, looking for a room because they had accidentally double-booked." That was very bad news. Marquette was the only other town of any size on our horizon, and it was close to two hours away.

We took the room. Luckily, the floor was covered in inexpensive laminate so there wasn't a smelly carpet to deal with. Still, there were lingering odors we couldn't quite place. Strange noises echoed around the building all night. Between the room and the migraine, neither of us slept much.

Day Forty-Eight

The upside to staying in an awful room in what is essentially a halfway house? We were both up and moving early, eager to put it all behind us. The downside? Dawn will never let me forget it.

We started our day backtracking about thirty miles. In the descending darkness the night before, we had passed a number of different waterfalls we wanted to check out, but we were hurrying, trying to find a room. That became the first item on our agenda today.

We visited both Upper and Lower Tahquamenon Falls. Less than a week ago, we saw Niagara Falls. None of what we saw today compares to Niagara, which is immense, both in height and drop. They are a huge tourist stop. The falls in the Upper Peninsula are much smaller, but equally charming, in their own way.

For either the Upper or Lower Falls, you have to hike quite a ways to get to them. The water of the Upper Falls is a rust-colored brown. This is caused by tannins that leach from cedar swamps, which the river drains. It looked like weak coffee going over the rocks. The falls itself isn't tall—maybe fifty feet—but it's the setting that makes it worth the hike. The water below the falls pools into placid lakes, surrounded by the vibrant and changing foliage. It was one of the most peaceful spots of the whole trip.

Upper Tahquamenon Falls

We stopped in the gift shop, of course, to pick up a coffee mug and a magnet, and I asked the woman who rang me up how to pronounce Tahquamenon.

"It's easy," she said.

I wanted to say, "It always is, when you know the answer," but I kept quiet.

"It's just like 'phenomenon."

I rolled that around in my head and it felt right. Now I have a blue-speckled coffee mug that reads *Tahquamenon Falls State Park*, so when people stop by for a cuppa, you know I'll be asking them to guess how to pronounce it.

The Lower Tahquamenon Falls are smaller still, but there are five of them, so they look a little like stair steps. Like the Upper Falls, they are surrounded by tranquil, natural beauty that makes it worth the hike.

The falls are a great way to spend an afternoon in Upper Michigan, especially on a sunny Sunday afternoon in mid-October, when all the colors of the rainbow were found in the foliage.

I mentioned earlier that the U.P. is a culture of its own, and it really is. It feels like the people who live there like it that way and take pride in it. If you're an outdoorsy type, I think you would be in heaven.

They also have a sense of humor. Earlier, I mentioned that I used to play a band called Da Yoopers, on the radio. As we were heading out of the U.P., we drove through Ishpeming, and saw something called *Da Yoopers Tourist Trap* on the side of the road.

In front of the Tourist Trap, was a pretty good sized gun. By that, I mean they have a rifle approximately the size of a mobile home. They claim it was even fired once.

Da Yoopers' gun packs a whallop

Inside, it was exactly as advertised: a tourist trap, with a million tchotchkes and useless souvenirs. I bought several.

As I was making my purchases, I asked the lady running the place if Da Yoopers still play and record music. She looked sad and said, "Well, the band is kind of a thing of the past." She lowered her voice, then added, "And, some of them are dead, too." I can see where that would put a bit of a crimp in band morale.

Too bad. I love Da Yoopers.

Also, we loved the U.P.

Day Forty-Nine

You knew it was inevitable, right? On a trip around America that has taken every possible detour in pursuit of Americana and roadside attractions, at some point you knew that we would come across the World's Largest Ball of Twine. When I woke up today, I knew I was going to see the ball of twine, but I never anticipated meeting JFK, who made it. No, not the former president. The *other* JFK.

We slept in an extra hour this morning, because we gained an hour when we reached the western extreme of Michigan. There's no better way to spend an hour, when you've been running non-stop for seven weeks, than sleeping, right?

When we left Ironwood, Michigan, I thought we were heading toward a spot in Wisconsin where John Dillinger had engaged in an epic shootout with the FBI before escaping on foot. That location is now a lodge/cafe, and there are still bullet holes in the wall. It's also where they shot a portion of the Johnny Depp movie *Public Enemy.* This is the kind of thing that is right up our alley – a little pop culture, and history, all blended together. As we pulled out of the parking lot, though, Mama Google warned me that the place didn't open until 5:00 PM. Since it was 10:00 AM, and the place was only an hour away, that plan went out the window. The John Dillinger shootout location will have to wait for another day.

So, we headed toward Duluth, Minnesota, figuring I would find something along the way that was interesting or unusual. That's where JFK and his ball of twine entered the picture. JFK is James Frank Kotera, and in a world where most people are drawn in shades of grey, he is drawn in vibrant full-color.

To meet Mr. Kotera is to know him, as he will hold nothing back. I glanced through his visitors log and saw that he gets several visitors every day, from all over the world. I believe he tells each and every one of them his story, and here it is, paraphrased from memory.

On April 3rd, 1975, he was in his bedroom when he felt the hand of God on his back. He had an interesting conversation with God that went something like this:

"James, this is the real God."

"The real God? Right here in my bedroom?"

"Right here in your bedroom. James, you need to quit your drinking and straighten out your life, or you will never be the famous JFK, the twine man."

Now if I had this conversation with God, I would have mentioned that there was already a pretty famous JFK, but Mr. Kotera is a better man than I. He listened to God and told me he has never had another drink since that morning.

For some reason, he waited to get started on his life's work, but on the 4th anniversary of his conversation with God, he started building his ball of twine. Thirty seven years later, he is still working on it. He told me he had already worked on it for several hours this very morning.

"Over and under, over and under, and it will never fall apart." He said in a sing-song voice that made me suspect he had said it perhaps a million times before.

I was tempted to say, "Wax on, wax off," but I already loved Mr. Kotera, so I didn't.

Have you seen the late-seventies movie *Being There*, starring Peter Sellers as Chance the Gardner, or perhaps read the novella of the same name by Jerzy Kosinski? If not, the basic plot is that Peter Sellers plays an exceedingly simple man who only talks about gardening and television. Everyone who encounters him hears the same simple homilies and respects his wisdom.

Mr. Kotera is the closest I have ever come to meeting a real Chance the Gardener. I've never met anyone who is so happy, so satisfied with their lot in life, so convinced they are doing exactly what they should be doing every day. I felt blessed to have met him, and will not forget him or the life lessons he effortlessly imparts. One of my lessons for the day is, a gift can spring up from the most unexpected places. JFK and his perspective was one of those gifts.

By the way, the sign in front of JFK's house says "Dump and

249

Twine Man" because he still works three days a week at the dump, which he also loves.

JFK keeps meticulous notes and measurements about his ball of twine. He measures and weighs each piece of string he adds to it. He told me that as of this morning, it weighs 22,200 lbs. Because of the way he has to build it, it's actually more of an "egg" of twine now, as opposed to a "ball." Mr. Kotera explained that is a function of the very heavy twine resting on the concrete blocks, There's no way for him to add more twine around the middle.

I said, "Unless you got a crane in here, lifted it up and set it on a new base."

He nodded. He was way ahead of me, as usual. "Yep. $8,000."

Enough said. It will continue to be the World's Biggest Egg of Twine until someone wants to kick in eight grand.

JFK's Egg of twine

I knew nothing could top the experience of finally realizing the ultimate roadtripper goal of finding The World's Largest Ball of Twine, but it was only noon, so we had to go on with our day. We stuck to the backroads. In some spots, the leaves were falling so fast, it felt like a psychedelic snow. Much of Wisconsin felt like we were driving through a postcard.

When we crossed over into Minnesota, it crossed another state off my "to visit" list, marking #49 out of 50. Only North Dakota has eluded me.

• Duluth was the first city we hit in Minnesota. I was tempted to go by the home that Robert Zimmerman was born in. Who? Oh, right. Bob Dylan. Most people associate him with Hibbing, Minnesota, but he was born and lived in Duluth the first six years of his life. We decided against making the trek across town, for a couple of reasons. One, I'm just not all that caught up in seeing the birthplaces of musical icons. We've all gotta be born somewhere, and unless they did something noteworthy there, aside from maybe being potty trained, it just doesn't matter much to me. Second, I have to make a small confession: although I love his songs, I've never loved Mr. Dylan as a recording artist. I listen to Dylan songs most every day, but typically they are sung by other artists.

What we couldn't pass up was the Aerial Lift Bridge. It was built in 1905, originally as a transporter bridge. If you are like me, you may have never heard of a transporter bridge. Picture a cable crossing a river, with cable cars on it, ferrying passengers from one side to the other. There were only two of them ever built in the USA, and this was one. In 1929, though, it was converted to the Aerial Lift Bridge, which is almost as rare. The Aerial Lift Bridge is different from every other drawbridge I've ever seen. Instead of opening in the middle to let a boat pass, the Aerial Lift Bridge raises and raises—135 feet in the air—until even a mammoth ship pass underneath.

There was a time when you could stand on the bridge deck as it rose up and down. An accident in the early 1980s claimed the life of a woman who was riding the bridge, and that put an end to that.

Duluth's aerial lift bridge

Of course, since it is a busy roadway, it isn't constantly going up and down like an elevator. There is a schedule, and it can be hours in between lifts. Happily, the bridge is a rock star in Duluth, and the Maritime Museum has a television screen that shows scheduled ships. When got to the Maritime Museum, we found that we had about an hour's wait until the *American Mariner* was scheduled to go through. The *American Mariner* is 715 feet long, which gave us a perfect comparison to the size of the *Edmund Fitzgerald,* which was 730 feet, stem to stern.

The weather had been downright chilly in the Upper Peninsula of Michigan, but here in Minnesota, the sun came out, a gentle breeze wafted off the water, and it was shirt sleeve weather once again. We strolled along the approach to the bridge, all the way out to the farthest point, where you can first spot the ships and watch their approach. We saw the *American Mariner* when it was still miles away, a small dot on the horizon.

"It looks so small," I said, proving I didn't learn the lesson of perspective at any point in my life.

Thirty minutes later, it wasn't small at all. It motored smoothly past us, under the bridge, and it was gone in a matter of moments. It was so cool to witness that I ran back inside the Maritime Museum to see when the next ship was due. There was a thousand footer coming through at 5:00 PM. As interesting and fun as it was to watch, we didn't think we could justify a four or five hour wait to see another one. Someday, though, we might come stay in Duluth and just watch the bridge go up and down.

Since we are in the northern Midwest, now, we've been seeing signs of Paul Bunyan in various locations. A number of places here in the North-Central part of the United States lay claim to the legend of Paul Bunyan. There are statues of him scattered all over several states. Different places claim to be "The birthplace of Paul Bunyan." It's a fun argument, because like all the best arguments, it can never be settled. As we drove past several dozen of the lakes that give Minnesota its nickname, we saw an impressive likeness in Akely. He is 25 feet tall, even when he is kneeling. No sign of Babe, his blue ox, though.

We talked about driving to Brainerd, because of the Paul Bunyan statue that was shown in the movie *Fargo*. We love *Fargo*. It's an all-time Top Ten movie for us. I can quote from it obsessively. However, in doing a little research, we found that none of the movie was shot in Brainerd, and that the famous Paul Bunyan statue was something the Coen brothers had constructed just for the movie. Since it would have been a two hour drive out of our way, no Brainerd for us. Still, there is a rumor of a wood chipper in Fargo, North Dakota. Now, *that* would be something we would drive to see.

Day Fifty

We've experienced so much on this trip, it's going to take months to digest it all. We've seen two oceans, a gulf and five Great Lakes; at least a dozen National Parks, 30 states, and more monuments and memorials than I can count. The thing I am noticing is, what sticks with me, are the stories. Stories about people.

Arches National Park was one of the most stunning things I've ever seen, but getting a better understanding of what transpired at Harper's Ferry is what echoes in my mind. The Florida Keys were among the most beautiful places I've ever been, but somehow meeting and getting to know JFK and his World's Largest Ball of Twine sticks with me.

Today, I learned about the story of Robert Asp, and Dawn and I both can't help but wonder, "How is he not more famous?" As desperate as Hollywood apparently is for movie ideas (I am basing that on the rash of failed sequels and remakes that have littered the box office scenery of late) I don't understand how someone hasn't gotten the bright idea to turn Asp's story into a movie. Probably just as well. They would probably cast Jessica Simpson in the lead and make it all about her.

Here's an abbreviated version of Robert Asp's story. In the early '70s, Mr. Asp worked as a guidance counselor, shaping young minds and providing career advice. In the summer of '71, he was helping a fellow teacher work on his house when an accident occurred. He was injured badly enough that he spent the rest of the summer in the hospital. While there, his brother brought him a pile of books on Viking history. Laid flat out on his back, a dream was born: he decided to build a perfect replica of a Viking ship, and sail it to Norway.

Me? I would probably binge watch all the episodes of *The Sopranos* again. Robert Asp decides on a lifetime project. He was no simple dreamer, though. He was a man of action. He intended to build the ship all himself, and to do it in two years. A ridiculous goal, of course. In the end, he didn't do things on his own. He had many helping hands, including his supportive family and local community. A town not far from where he lived bought an empty potato warehouse and leased it to him for $10 per year. Local school kids did bake sales to raise money. Everyone collected cans so they could be melted down and turned into the metal parts the boat needed.

Even with all the help, the two years stretched out. The year he started construction of the ship, Mr. Asp was diagnosed with leukemia. He continued building the boat, saying, "I'd rather work on it than sit around waiting to die." By 1980, it was almost complete, and he was able to captain the ship out onto Lake Michigan. That was as far as he got, though, as he finally lost his battle with leukemia on December 27th, 1980.

Before he died, his family told him, "You take it as far as you can, we'll take it the rest of the way."

You know what? They did.

In June of 1982, members of his family and other volunteers sailed the ship through the Great Lakes, across a series of locks and canals, out into the Atlantic Ocean and toward Norway. The trip wasn't perfect. They hit a storm that nearly did them in (are you listening, Hollywood? All your drama is built right in) but they made it to Norway in their father's hand built, seventy-six foot Viking sailing vessel.

That's the power of a dream. It starts in one person, but even if they fall, it can be picked up and carried by others.

Today, that Viking ship, the *Hjemkomst*, (which means homecoming in Norwegian,) sits as the star attraction at the Heritage-Hjemkomst Interpretive Center, in Moorhead, Minnesota.

Elsewhere in the center, there's another example of the same principle in action, if somewhat less dramatically carried out.

In 1997, a man named Gary Paulson got the idea to carve a stave church, a perfect copy of the Hopperstad Stave Church in Vik, Norway. Again, a pretty big project that begins in the mind of a single man.

We got a guided tour of the inside of the church, which was like taking a trip back in time, about a thousand years or so. On the tour, we learned that when the King of Norway converted to Catholicism, so did the rest of the country, at least on the surface. Later, when another King converted to Lutheranism, so did all his subjects. It's good to be king.

The outside of the church is dark and foreboding, and it doesn't look like any kind of architecture I've ever seen in America. It's an odd combination of Viking, with dragons, and Catholic, with crosses. The inside of the church is light and airy, with pine wood everywhere.

As we left the center, a very nice woman told us they were serving lutefisk in the cafeteria that day. I am an adventurous eater, but Dawn preferred food she could recognize, so off we went.

We crossed the North River, and just like that, I accomplished a lifetime goal. On the west side of the North River was North Dakota. On the fiftieth day of our trip, I was finally in North Dakota. I've now been to every state in the union. Dawn and I commented on that when we were in the car, but didn't think much more about it.

We went to the Visitor's Center in Fargo, though, and two very cool things happened.

First, we saw the real star of the movie Fargo. No, not Steve Buscemi or Frances McDormand, but the wood chipper that is featured in the unforgettable final minutes of the movie. Dawn got into the spirit of things by pretending to push a leg down into the chipper while wearing an authentic Fargo hat.

What Dawn often contemplates doing to me

We were happy enough with that, but just as we were leaving, we heard another man come in and say, "North Dakota is my 50th state!"

It was like he was the millionth customer at a supermarket, or something. They smiled and shook his hand, took his picture, gave him a certificate, and a commemorative T-shirt. I waited until the excitement had died down, then told them the same thing, and the celebration started all over again. I got my picture up on their website, and a t-shirt that says, "You saved the best for last!"

Apparently, North Dakota is the last state for a lot of people who attempt to hit them all, so they have a lot of fun with it. I get that, and applaud them for their sense of humor. Let's face it— North Dakota is a little bit out of the way.

If you're going to visit all fifty states, I recommend making North Dakota your last one, and doing it in Fargo.

We spent the rest of the day driving, doing some backtracking. One of the things Dawn really wanted to see what Walnut Grove,

Minnesota. She is a nut about the *Little House on the Prairie* books and television show. We had read about a Laura Ingalls Wilder Museum in Walnut Grove, which is where the series was set, so we drove a few hours south-southeast.

We didn't make it all the way to Walnut Grove before darkness overtook us, so we stopped for the night in Canby, Minnesota.

I think it must be bird-hunting season in Canby, because the door of the Canby Inn & Suites had a handwritten sign that read: *Hunters. Please do not clean your birds in the bathroom in your room. It makes a mess that our maids don't want to clean up.* We made a mental note that we would not clean any pheasant or grouse while we stayed there.

Day Fifty-One

We've hit a number of famous author's homes and museums on our trip. All of them—Hemingway, Twain, Poe, Stephen King – were for me. It was only fair that we balance the scales a little and visit one of Dawn's favorites as well.

Most days, we've planned something and in the end, it turned out so much better, so much *cooler* than what we had intended. The turtle rescue in the Florida Keys, and visiting Boot Hill in Pioche, Nevada spring to mind.

Our visit to Walnut Grove, Minnesota, was not that. Of course, Walnut Grove, circa 2016, looks nothing like Walnut Grove of the nineteenth century. We didn't expect that. The city fathers make a few nods to the source of their fame by naming streets, "Ingalls Ave," etc. There is also a cafe called Nellie's Cafe, but more on that later.

We found *The Laura Ingalls Wilder Museum* to be underwhelming. There is a very attractive, hand-painted sign out front, but everything kind of went downhill from there. When the highlight of your museum is the sign, that isn't, pardon the expression, a good sign. Sorry.

The museum itself has a number of buildings, but only one of them really has anything to do with Laura Ingalls Wilder. For a place called *The Laura Ingalls Wilder Museum and Information Center,* that's disappointing. The building that has the Laura Ingalls memorabilia had some nice pictures, of the real people who were played by Michael Landon, et al, in the television series. Just for the record, Pa Ingalls didn't look a thing like Michael Landon. I have a hunch that seventies hairstyle Michael Landon wore throughout the series might have gotten him run out of the real Walnut Grove in that era.

I watched *Little House* when I was a kid, so at that time, Karen Grassle, who played Ma Ingalls, looked like an old lady to me. I haven't seen an episode of the show in decades now, so I was surprised when I saw her picture in the museum and realized that she was young on the show, and attractive. How our own perspective changes the things we see.

Much of the museum was a timeline of Laura Ingalls and her family's lives. Unfortunately, a lot of it looked more like what you would expect to find at a kid's science fair, as opposed to a legitimate museum. A lot of things were just cutouts of photos or information, pasted onto what looked to me like poster board.

There are several other Laura Ingalls Wilder museums in South Dakota and Missouri, and I have a hunch they got all the cool stuff. My recommendation is, if you are driving directly through Walnut Grove, Minnesota, it's worth a stop. Dawn and I both agreed if we knew what it was yesterday, though, we wouldn't have backtracked to see it.

There were several other buildings in the museum, but they didn't have anything to do with *Little House.* It was a little like going to the *Baseball Hall of Fame,* then finding several buildings of information about soccer.

When we were done seeing the entire museum, it was noon, and the aforementioned *Nelly's Cafe* beckoned. It looked modest on the outside, but we never judge a book by its cover. When we went in, we found that the sad and worn exterior was the best kept part of the cafe. The walls were paneled like the interior of a mid-sixties trailer, and the carpet was old and blotched with stains. We tried to ignore that and did our best to finish our lunch, which was, at best, entirely forgettable. Our waitress highly recommended the homemade chili, which tasted remarkably like Hormel's canned chili to my palate.

We put Walnut Grove out of our mind, and turned west, toward home.

We crossed the state line into South Dakota, adding a new state to Dawn's scorecard. We broke one of our own rules, and gave up on the small highways for a time. In South Dakota, those highways are scarce, and I-90 is smooth, fast, and beautiful.

We debated whether to hit the Mitchell Corn Palace on the way by, but as we so often have on this trip, we thought, *When will we be back in Mitchell, South Dakota again?* So, we swung by the Corn Palace, which bills itself as *The World's Only Corn Palace.* I can't prove that claim wrong, although there used to be a number of crop palaces scattered around the Midwest. These days, I don't think there's a lot of competition for the crown.

Mitchell Corn Palace

Mitchell is proud of its corn. Their town mascot is Cornelius, an ear of corn. Their local radio station is KORN. You get the picture. The Corn Palace itself is a multipurpose venue that hosts all kind of entertainment – plays, concerts, etc. The exterior of the corn palace is changed every year, with a new theme. This year's theme is *Rock of Ages.* The Corn Palace uses actual ears of corn to build massive murals on the outside walls. This year, the theme dictated that there be corn-y pictures of Willy Nelson, and Elvis Presley.

We didn't spend too much time at the Corn Palace. Once you've taken in the murals, and peeked inside and looked at the history of corn, there's not much left to do. In short order, we were on the road again.

We stopped in Murdo, South Dakota, for the night. If we're going to eat dinner out, we always ask the desk clerk what they recommend. We've learned there must be two types of desk clerks: the type that tell you the truth, and the type that get a kickback of some sort.

Tonight, our front desk savant directed us toward a place called *Prairie Pizza*. I have to say, *Prairie Pizza* is a little weird.

How so, you ask, very reasonably? Here are a few of the ways: I asked for jalapenos on my half of our pizza, just like I always do. The owner looked at me slightly askew and said they didn't have any. "Oh, run out?" I asked. "Nope. They're not very popular around here." *Especially when you refuse to supply them,* I thought, but did not say.

Also, they only make pizzas in one size at *Prairie Pizza:* 15". You want a personal, or small pizza? *Take a hike, bub. We make fifteen inchers at Prairie Pizza.* I knew it was a bad sign when I saw the one of the owners eating a Subway sandwich when we came in.

Finally, and weirdest of all, when the pizza arrived, the owner told us the crust was a little different. It had sugar and cinnamon in it and on it. "That way you've got dessert and dinner all together," the owner said. Which is fine, as far as it goes, but I happen to like pizza crust, and having my dinner and my dessert separate.

That's just the kind of day it was on the road in Walnut Grove, Minnesota, and Murdo, South Dakota.

Day Fifty-Two

We've seen any number of oddities on this trip, but as we were pulling out of the parking lot of the motel, I saw one of the oddest. We stayed in a place called Range Country Lodging, in Murdo. It was a very nice place—clean room, friendly people, lots of animal heads on the wall to let you know you were in South Dakota. Aside from the referral to *Prairie Pizza,* we give it an A.

As we were leaving, though, I noticed something strange in the far corner of the parking lot. There were what looked like four pieces of modern art, with a logo across the top. Closer examination revealed them to be Tesla charging stations. This seemed incongruent, at best. As I mentioned, Range Country Lodging seemed to cater to hunters of all stripes. I saw a lot of pickup trucks in the parking lot, but not a single Tesla. Why in the world would they need not one or two, but *four* Tesla charging stations to service their motel? Perhaps an international Tesla Fan Club holds their annual convention in Murdo. I suppose it will remain one of life's little mysteries for me.

We spent a second day in South Dakota, which is likely more than many people will spend in their lifetime. If you've never driven across South Dakota, I will fill you in: the scenery has a definite rugged beauty, but it doesn't change a lot. Once you enter the badlands, it looks like one huge open space, broken up by plateaus and a few canyons. Impressive at first, but it does grow stale after a few hundred miles.

Our adventure today started at the *Badlands National Park.* Just before we got to the park entrance, we saw a little community of prairie dogs. You might remember when we found prairie dogs in Lubbock, Texas. Dawn is crazy over the little furballs, so when we saw more, of course we stopped. These were pretty tame. Tame enough, in fact, to eat trail mix right out of

Dawn's hand. Several people commented on our blog at the time that Dawn was lucky she didn't get nipped by the little guys, but she never even came close. I think she fed a whole tribe of them, until we ran out of trail mix.

Dawn and friend

Badlands is a huge park—379 square miles huge. It's also filled with natural beauty not to be found elsewhere in South Dakota. When we were talking to the Ranger at the entrance, I asked him why it was called, "badlands." He said it was because everyone but the Indians had a hard time getting across it. It made for treacherous going, both on foot and on horseback.

There is a long loop road that you can drive through the park, with many opportunities to stop and look at amazing vistas and rock formations, or go for a short hike. We did all of that.

We stopped at one lookout where the hills undulated like ocean waves. It was through those very hills and valleys, the Lakota Chief named Hehaka Gleska, or Spotted Elk, and sometimes referred to as "Bigfoot," led his people on the way to

264

Wounded Knee. There, of course, both he and many of his tribe would die, on December 29, 1890.

South Dakota Badlands

This trip has changed me in many ways – deepened my understanding of the geography of our country, showed me that everywhere, people are the same, and thrilled me with the diversity and beauty of our great nation. However, it has forever changed the way I look at the plight of the indigenous peoples of America. I will never again be able to look at the way our country was founded and expanded with anything other than sadness at what was taken away from all native Americans. Injustice, no matter how many centuries old, should not be forgotten.

Onward.

After we left Badlands National Park, we drove north to Wall, South Dakota. Why? Wall Drug, of course. If you've ever driven across South Dakota on I-90, you've seen signs for Wall Drug, promoting their "free ice water" and extolling the many virtues to be found there. Wall Drug started out as an actual drug

Yes, I have driven across S.D.

store in the 1930s, but it is now a tourist trap, with cheap souvenirs. Yes, we picked up several more magnets and a sticker, not to mention a little prairie dog statue. There are also lots of clever photo opportunities, like the chance to get your picture taken in front of a faux Mt. Rushmore, or riding a huge jackalope.

We had lunch at Wall Drug, which wasn't too bad, then headed south again, toward Mt. Rushmore.

I've been to Rushmore before, but Dawn hadn't, so it was a must-visit for us. We also planned to stop at the Borglum Museum in Keystone, a town that's close to Mt. Rushmore. However, it seems that the entire town of Keystone closes up shop and rolls up the sidewalks sometime in September. The museum and everything else that looked vaguely tourist-y was closed. That was too bad, because I really enjoyed my last visit there—it gave a lot of perspective and information on Gutzon Borglum, the man who carved Rushmore, and the how and why of the creation of the faces.

This turned out to be the only National Park where we had to pay to get in. When we rolled up to the entrance, we showed them our *America the Beautiful Pass*, and they said, "Very nice. Eleven dollars, please."

When we inquired why, they said, "Oh, it's free to get into the park, but it's eleven dollars to park." Nice way to work around the pass, National Park Service.

I can't help but wonder, if Mt. Rushmore was undertaken today, what four presidents would be on there? I'm sure Washington and Lincoln would still make the cut, but maybe not Jefferson. He's gotten a little bad publicity the last few decades, and probably not Teddy Roosevelt. I can't help but think it might be our 20th Century martyred President, John F. Kennedy, or perhaps a popular President, like Ronald Reagan. We'll never know, but like all the best questions, it leads to an interesting discussion.

Very large faces

The truth is, I've never been all that crazy about Mt. Rushmore. Not that I'm not patriotic, but it is a bit of a drive out of the way to get there, they charge you to park, and it is still a decent little hike up to the faces. Once I got there, I had that vague feeling of, *Yep. There they are all right. Just like in the movies.* It was hard for me to imagine sitting for several hours, staring at the faces, but I suppose some people do.

Dawn liked it much better than I did. The extra driving, the $11 for parking, the hike, didn't faze her at all. In fact, she said it was one of her favorite stops. Just goes to show you how two people can see the same thing and see different things.

Since we were in the area, we thought we should also swing by and see the Crazy Horse Monument. This is a monument, not just to Crazy Horse, but to all indigenous people. It was started in the 1940s, and, since they are doing it all with private funds, progress has been slow. I was curious as to how much work had been done in the seventeen years since I had checked on it. And the answer is, to my untrained eye, not much.

267

Crazy Horse's face is complete, and substantially larger than the faces on Rushmore, and his straight arm is well-begun, but my memory is that most of that was done in 1999. I am not 100% sure what's been happening over the last decade and a half. If it ever gets done, it will be spectacular—a stern chieftain pointing out at the lands his people once roamed. When it is completed, it will be the largest mountain carving in the world. If I'm going to live to see it, though, they're going to have to step on the gas.

Day Fifty-Three

Home is in sight, now. We only have three states—Wyoming, Montana, and Idaho—standing between us and Washington. That makes it a little tempting to skip an attraction, and put another hundred miles or so under our wheels instead. That was the case with Devils Tower, in the southeastern corner of Wyoming. I'd seen it before, and it struck me the way Rushmore did. A drive out of your way, then when you get there, you kind of stare up at it, and think, "There you are!" Then you get in your car and go on. However, I knew that Dawn loved Rushmore, so I thought there was a decent chance she would feel the same about Devils Tower.

When I had been to Devils Tower before, I had driven there from I-90. This time, we came at it from a different direction, sneaking up on it from the back roads. When we were still about ten miles away, I saw it peeking like a nervous bride over the hilltops.

Eventually, it came out in all its glory and I stopped a few miles away to get a different perspective than you get from driving straight at it from I-90.

If there's anything else like Devils Tower in America, I'm not aware of it. The Native Americans had stories about a landscape this unique, of course. My favorite was about two young boys who went walking, got turned around, and started walking away from their tribe instead of toward it. After four days of walking, they were lost and tired, but then a gigantic bear chased them. They prayed to the Creator, who took pity on them and lifted the ground under their feet so high that they were able to escape. The bear was so huge, though, that he could almost reach them. He jumped and clawed and climbed after them, leaving his claw marks everywhere on the tower. Thus, the striations the run vertically up and down the tower.

Devils Tower

I love stories like that. I also love that although geologists have theories about what caused Devils Tower, they're not completely sure. I think we are sure about too many things these days, and a little uncertainty is good for our human consciousness.

Around 4,000 people climb the 867 foot high tower every year. We watched someone climb it while we were there. Well, mostly we saw someone standing still resting, but they were about a quarter of the way up, and that's farther than I'll ever get.

Only one person has gotten up there without climbing, though—a man named George Hopkins. Mr. Hopkins was an expert parachute jumper who managed to land on top of the tower after jumping from an airplane. He had rope with him that he planned to use to climb down the tower, but it was lost in the jump, according to historians. So, he was stuck on top. He had an amazing view, but not much in the way of supplies. Eventually, an experienced climber named Jack Durrance made the climb and helped Hopkins climb down.

By the way, why did Hopkins attempt the stunt? A friend of his had bet him $50 he couldn't do it. Word is, the friend paid up.

It was early afternoon when we left Devils Tower, but we weren't feeling great. Almost two months on the road was taking its toll on us. The migraine that had started in Michigan had proven particularly resilient, and had traveled half a dozen states with us now. We are doing our best to eat well on the trip, but our reality is, we eat one meal a day in a small café or the like, and the other out of a bag. It's all starting to catch up with us.

So, we drove west a few hours, then found a motel in Buffalo, Wyoming, and crashed for the night.

Day Fifty-Four

We woke up today, aiming at Greybull, Wyoming. That is a sentence you won't often read, as most people have never heard of Greybull, let alone had any intention of ever going there. I wanted to stop in Greybull because I lived there for a year in 1984-85.

I was working as a manager at a department store in the Tri-Cities in eastern Washington in 1984, when I got a call from my very first boss in radio, asking me if I wanted to come and manage a radio station he just bought in Greybull.

Managing a radio station seemed a lot more appealing than overseeing the sales of Levi 501s, so I gave notice at the department store, packed up everything I owned, and moved to Greybull. I ran an AM/FM combo there for a little over a year, until I got homesick for Washington and moved back.

Greybull would be the 4th city we've hit on the trip that I lived in at some point. It was one I was most looking forward to, because I wanted to see what the little radio station I started looked like, thirty years later.

Before we got to Greybull, though, we drove through the Big Horn mountains. I'm not all that crazy about driving through much of Wyoming. Like South Dakota, or eastern Nevada, it can all start to look the same after a while. The Big Horn mountains are the exception. Prairies merge into deep green forests, which give way to deep blue lakes and snow-capped peaks. The drive from Buffalo to Greybull isn't famous, but it is beautiful.

We approached Greybull from the south, a direction I didn't often use when I lived there. So, I was surprised when my old radio station materialized on our right. I had hoped to go into the station and introduce myself and look around a bit. The building is still there, the call letters are still in evidence, but the there was no one there.

I went around back and peeked in the window into the room where I used to do my morning show. It was an intense feeling of déjà vu, as everything looked the same as when I had last walked out, thirty years earlier. Aside from the addition of a computer monitor, everything looked like I had just stepped out for a cup of coffee.

Behind the station is the broadcast antenna, which we called a "stick" in the business. Behind that is a small brown house. When I ran the station, the man who lived there stopped in to tell me that our stick was so close to his house that his coffeepot played our station. He wondered if I would quit playing that Kool and the Gang song that was driving him crazy. How could I say no?

A Google search revealed that the station is still on the air, but it broadcasts satellite programming all the time, now, and it broadcasts out of Cody, an hour or so away. As much as I wanted to, I couldn't go home again.

There was one other thing I wanted to accomplish in Greybull. While there, I became friends with a man named Jeff Probst. No, not the guy who hosts *Survivor,* although he may be related to him, for all I know. The Jeff Probst I knew ran a store called Probst Western Wear. It had been in business for decades before I got there, so I hoped that it was still open for business, and maybe I could say hello to Jeff.

I remembered exactly where the store was, because it was on the corner where the only stoplight in Greybull was. Yes, it was literally a one stoplight town. Dawn parked the car on the side of the store.

The front of the store looked exactly like I remembered it—with the exception of the sign over the door that read, "Thanks for 71 great years. Come in and say goodbye." I was a little late to say goodbye, as the store was completely empty inside. Time, and retail, waits for no man.

Dawn and I had lunch at a little Chinese restaurant that

hadn't been there when I lived in town, then headed off for Cody. Cody is as close as we could get to Yellowstone, and starting from there would give us the maximum amount of time to spend in the park the next day.

By the time we arrived in Cody, it was late afternoon, which left us just enough time to tour the *Buffalo Bill Center of the West*. Kind of a big title, but it lives up to it. The *Buffalo Bill Center* is actually five museums gathered under one roof. We spent about three hours there and got through maybe half of it.

Buffalo Bill Center of the West

Buffalo Bill Cody was an extraordinary salesman, but he had the bonafides to back it up, as well. His life was long, and fascinating, and his section of the museum does a great job of detailing it. Of all the museums we've seen on this trip, I would put this at the top of the list. If you ever pop out of Yellowstone on the eastern end and find yourself in Cody, it's absolutely worth a visit. It's $19 per person, but easily worth that. The pass is good for two days, and if you have the time, I think you could well spend that long looking at everything.

We found another rustic little motel on the Yellowstone side of Cody, holed up for the night, and prepared for our assault on Yellowstone tomorrow.

Day Fifty-Five

The drive from Cody to Yellowstone is spectacular. We saw a number of spreads that had to have hundreds, if not thousands, of acres. It would take a special person to make a living off the earth in such a remote place, but I would bet the people who do wouldn't trade it for anything.

We spent our entire in Yellowstone, and of course that wasn't nearly enough time. We could easily have spent another few days wandering around the park. It's high on our "return visit" list.

In a word, Yellowstone is spectacular. Geysers, wild animals roaming free, and scenery to make your heart soar. We learned that two-thirds of the world's geysers are located inside Yellowstone.

We were a little concerned when we rolled up the east entrance to the park. As we had gained altitude, the temperature had dropped into the low thirties, and snow was pelting our windshield. There was a sign outside the entrance that stated: "Chains or snow tires required."

Uh-oh. The advice of my friend Al Kunz, who told us to drive clockwise around the country, echoed in my mind.

We asked the ranger at the gate if the roads were really bad. She shrugged, said, "I'd just be careful."

We were careful.

We looked at the road conditions, and figured that the average safe speed on the roads was about 20 MPH. Since the loop around Yellowstone is 140 miles, that would be a long day of driving.

Just a few miles inside the park, though, we dropped down in elevation, the snowflakes stopped, the road cleared, and we had great conditions the rest of the day.

Here's a few fun facts about Yellowstone National Park.

It was the very first National Park, thus earning it the nickname of the "Granddaddy of National Parks." Yellowstone is huge— it covers over 3,700 square miles. Anyone who thinks they can cover it all adequately in a single day needs to reconsider. There are over 300 active geysers,(don't think Old Faithful is alone in letting off steam) and almost 300 waterfalls. Also, there is a lake, cleverly called Yellowstone Lake, that has over 100 miles of shoreline.

The day we saw Yellowstone Lake, the wind was whipping whitecaps everywhere, and waves were crashing into the shore like it was the Pacific Ocean. It did not look inviting.

Most people come to Yellowstone to see the geysers, and we were no exception. We parked in the Old Faithful parking lot, and were just coming around the corner as it blew its top,. So we spent 90 minutes in the visitor's center, looking at exhibits, watching a film, and of course, buying another magnet. We are definitely going to have the best-dressed refrigerator in Seaview, WA.

Some people believe that Old Faithful goes off every hour, but that has never been the case. In fact, it's not regular at all – it's just predictable, within reason. A Ranger takes a measurement of how long it explodes, then does a lot of that math that I never thought I would need in real life, and predicts when it will blow again. They post that time in the visitor's center. They do list the caveat that the projected time is plus or minus ten minutes. They were actually about twenty minutes off for the one we saw, but no one complained.

The eruption lasted several minutes, and it was impressive, but I can see how they have a hard time gauging exactly when it will erupt again. It's like when I'm cooking, and it tells me to time something after it reaches a hard boil. I am constantly questioning whether it has hit that point or not. I'm sure the rangers who measure the eruption run into the same self-doubt.

Aside from the geysers, the other thing every tourist wants to see is wild animals. Bears, moose, elk, wolves, and bison roam freely throughout the park. As we drove away from Old Faithful, we were afraid we weren't going to see anything wilder than a chipmunk. Yes, chipmunks are a ton of fun, but we have those at home and were hoping for a bit more from Yellowstone.

For us, at least, the western portion of the park was much better for wildlife. We were poking along at thirty miles per hour when we saw half a dozen cars pulled off to the side of the road up ahead. This is always a good sign that something is afoot.

We joined the line and saw a herd of about fifteen bison, just hanging out in the field. They seemed completely oblivious to the fact that they were the stars of the show. I thought Dawn was excited by seeing the prairie dogs. Multiply that by several dozen, and you're closing in on her reaction to the bison.

Today is our wedding anniversary, and since we are still on the road, I tried to sell Dawn on the idea that seeing the buffalo was her anniversary present. In the moment, it seemed to have worked.

Just a few miles further on, we saw a small herd of elk grazing in a field.

We thought that might be it for the day, but the highlight came a few miles before we exited the park. We noticed cars were slowing, but not stopping ahead of us. When we caught up to them, we saw there was a herd of buffalo walking on the shoulder of the road. We passed one that had to be the old bull of the herd. He was massive, and he gave us a bit of the old fish-eye as we passed him. He was maybe five feet away.

I don't think he trusts us

We left the park and turned north, toward Montana. Since it was our anniversary, I picked a better class of hotel in Bozeman, which was a contrast from the dozens of squat little roadside motels we've stayed on during the trip.

Day Fifty-Six

When I was a small boy, I used to help my father on our farm after he got off work. One of our chores was to go out in the field and collect the horses that had been grazing all day. They were often a little reticent to move at first, but when they saw that open barn door and remembered that their oats waited them just inside, they would move from a walk to a trot, to a gallop.

The story is the same for Dawn and I today, but we were the ones heading for the barn door. We woke up in Bozeman and realized that Washington was less than a day's drive away. So, on Day Fifty-six, that's what we did—we drove.

This was the moment we gave up the pretense that we were on a trip and ran for home. Dawn has been homesick for weeks, and with the change in the weather, I admit I was ready to nestle in to our little seaside cottage and hunker down for the winter.

There are places we were interested in seeing in Montana. For instance, I used to live in Hardin, Montana, which is right next to the Custer Battlefield, where the Battle of the Little Bighorn was fought. It's a fascinating place, but we would have had to backtrack half a day to see it.

Instead, we drove all the way through western Montana, across the top of Idaho, and across eastern Washington. We drove right by the Petrified Forest we had seen on Day One of the trip, That felt like a symbolic completion of our Lap Around America.

Day Fifty-Seven

Realistically, we could have made it all the way home yesterday, but that would have gotten us home late in the day, and without our pets. While we have been traipsing around the country, our friends and family have been watching them.

So, we woke up early in Ellensburg, ready to pick up the pets and get home.

We stopped at our daughter Samy's house in Tacoma to pick up our little white kitty, who we call Georgie Girl. Being so perfectly a cat, she failed to notice that we had been gone for two months. We love her anyway.

Our next stop was at our friend Jeff's in Rochester. Jeff stepped up and took care of our two old Chocolate Labs, Hershey and Sadie. The dogs more than made up for Georgie's lack of appreciation. We thought they both might die of happiness at seeing us after so long. Seeing how much they missed us, we promised them we would never leave them for that long again.

Our turtle, who we call Kumar, is with our daughter Connie, but we decided to wait a couple of days before we retrieved him.

We turned the Silver Bullet westward one last time. Two hours later, we were home. Or, at least what was kind of home. We had never spent so much as a night in that house, and there were boxes stacked to the ceiling everywhere.

The most important things were there, though. My love, Dawn Adele, our fur-faced babies, and our comfortable bed. After eight weeks, 13,689 miles, a few sunburns, and a thousand indelible memories, we were home.

Afterword - March, 2017

I am sitting in my office in that same little cottage we returned to last October. The sun is shining, and Dawn and I are just about to go for a walk on the beach. Hershey, Sadie, Georgie and Kumar are all healthy, as are we. I spend most of my days sitting in this same spot, writing my stories and books. Life is good.

One year ago, I was a real estate broker, managing a few dozen other brokers. I was more stressed out, but life was good then, too, albeit more hectic. These days, Dawn and I don't do one darned thing we don't want to do.

If I could do it all over again, would we? Would we quit jobs we liked, throw our clothes in a suitcase and set out to drive around America? Would we give up the certainty of a life in the workaday world in exchange for time, freedom, and an uncertain financial future?

Yes. In a heartbeat. My only regret is that we didn't do it sooner.

Our lap around America taught us and showed us so much. The breadth of beauty in our nation is almost unimaginable until you see it all first-hand. The character of the people, living in cities, small towns, on farms and in seaside villages, is inspiring. I came back from this trip with a notebook full of ideas to write about, and those all traced from the people we met in our travels.

Our nation has been one of conflict since the first Europeans arrived centuries ago. I recently read an opinion that our nation has never been more deeply divided. I would send that person to Gettysburg, to witness the price so many paid, and ask them if they still thought that. Our nation has been divided before. I am old enough to remember the sixties, which saw the killing of two Kennedys, and Dr. Martin Luther King. I witnessed the protests against the Vietnam War, which nearly tore our country apart. And yet, we survived. I have no doubt we will solve this divide as well, and we will be stronger for it.

For you, my friend and reader, I want to thank you for taking this trip with us. It was life changing for Dawn and me. My fondest wish would be that some part of our story might inspire you to explore something in our great country that you have never seen.

Shawn Inmon
Seaview Washington
March, 2017

3.04 P.M. / Wednesday

"I enjoyed the journey. What a great country America is.

Acknowledgments

No book is written in a vacuum, and this is certainly no exception. I had a lot of help, both on the "real life" and the publishing front.

Dawn and I have four pets, and if we couldn't have found trusted people to care for them while we were gone, the trip never would have gotten off the ground. So, special thanks to our daughters Samy and Connie, and our old friend Jeff, for taking such good care of Georgie, Hershey, Sadie, and Kumar.

I worked with a new editor on this book, which is a nerve wracking thing. Trusting someone new with the words I've written isn't easy. I am fortunate to have found Doreen Martens, as she has been the best steward for my words that I can imagine. She often made me laugh with her comments, and her ability to untangle what I tried to say, and produce something that makes sense, is unparalleled. This was our first time working together, but will not be the last.

My cover artist, Linda Boulanger, on the other hand, is used to dealing with me and my idiosyncrasies, and yet she keeps coming back for more. I don't know which I appreciate more, Linda's creativity, or her stubborn unwillingness to rest until everything is perfect. She came up with the idea for this cover of the long road leading off into the map, and it represents the book perfectly. She also formatted the book for me, whereby she takes a Word document and makes it look like a book.

Finally, I owe a debt of gratitude to Debra Galvan, my sharp-eyed proofreader. No matter how many drafts a book goes through, some errors slip through to the end. Debra is my final defense against these typos and other mistakes, and she does a fabulous job.

More than anything, I would like to thank Dawn, my long-suffering wife who has to listen to all my bad jokes and my insufferably cheerful attitude first thing in the morning. Without Dawn Adele's unflagging support, this trip, this book, and my whole writing career would never have materialized.

As always, my most important thank you is reserved for you, my reader. You are the reason I work every day to be a better writer, and to think of new and better stories.

Also by Shawn Inmon

Feels Like the First Time
A true love story of loss and redemption, set in the '70s.

Both Sides Now
The flip side of *Feels Like the First Time,* told from Dawn's perspective.

Rock 'n Roll Heaven
Jimmy Velvet dies, but wakes up in the presence of the greatest icons in rock 'n roll history.

Second Chance Love
Steve and Elizabeth were best friends and undeclared lovers, until fate separated them. Twenty years later, they have a second chance, if they are strong enough to take it.

The Unusual Second Life of Thomas Weaver
What if you could do it all again? Thomas Weaver dies, but awakens in his teenage body and bedroom, all memories intact. it.

Life is Short
A collection of 13 short stories that reinforce the idea that life is, indeed, short.